Small is Dangerous

Small is Dangerous

Micro States in a Macro World

Report of a Study Group of
The David Davies Memorial Institute of International
Studies, edited by Sheila Harden

St Martin's Press, New York

All rights reserved. For information, write:
St. Martin's Press, Inc., 175 Fifth Avenue, New York, NY 10010
Printed in Great Britain
First published in the United States of America in 1985

ISBN 0-312-72981-2

Library of Congress Cataloging in Publication Data

Main entry under title:
Small is dangerous.
    Includes index.
    1. States, Small. I. Harden, Sheila. II. Title.
JX1318.S6 1985   327.1'1   85-2309
ISBN 0-312-72981-2

Typeset by Folio Photosetting, Bristol
Printed by SRP Ltd, Exeter

Contents

Foreword

In early 1984, the David Davies Memorial Institute of International Studies decided to undertake a study of the security problems of micro-states and invited me to chair the study group which has produced this report. The need for such a study was amply demonstrated by two events in the early 1980s – the Falklands War in 1982 and the Grenada crisis in 1983. Both showed not only the particular vulnerability of very small territories to external attack and internal destabilization, but also that events in such a country could have repercussions far beyond its borders.

These very small states are mostly legacies of the European colonial empires. Little attention has been paid to the problems generated by their small human and economic resource bases; problems not only for the states themselves but also for the international community. Whilst we have concentrated on the security problems of micro-states, we have also found it necessary to take a much broader look at the issues. Thus, whilst Chapter 1 contains an overview of the subject, Chapter 2 discusses the role of the various international and regional organisations with a real or potential security role and also considers the impact on micro-states of the defence policies of the United Kingdom and France, as two former colonial powers, and those of the United States and the Soviet Union. Chapter 3 sets out the legal framework, concentrating on those aspects of particular relevance to micro-states, including intervention. The recruitment and training of defence and police forces forms the focus of Chapter 4, with detailed consideration of the task of policing the Exclusive Economic Zone. The first part of Chapter 5 is concerned with measures which can be taken to avert crises. It opens with a discussion of the factors contributing to political stability, stressing the importance of economic considerations. Methods of strengthening the UN security system, and of giving it greater anticipatory and preventive powers, are then outlined. The second part of the chapter deals with the situation once hostilities have occurred. Attention is paid to the question of intervention and when this might be justified, politically as well as legally. The chapter ends with a discussion of peacekeeping.

In Chapter 6 we suggest a number of steps that could and should be taken, by the micro-states themselves and by the international community, both to increase the political and economic stability of these states and to improve their security forces. We have also drawn up a Draft Declaration on Micro-States for discussion and adoption by the General Assembly of the United Nations. We believe that such a measure is a necessary first step in bringing about a greater understanding and recognition of these problems.

The study group decided that the yardstick for qualification as a micro-state should be a population of one million or less. This is a widely used definition and enabled us to concentrate particularly on the groupings of island states in the Caribbean and the Pacific. The problems of the states in these regions are discussed in detail in Annexes B and C, while Annex A considers the states of Southern Africa and their attempts to escape from the economic and military dominance of South Africa.

Method of Work

At the outset, the group decided that individual contributions to the study would not be signed. Instead, the members of the group, through discussion and constant revision of individual papers would produce a text which all could agree upon. This book is thus a study to which each member contributed special expertise but for which we are jointly responsible.

I would like to thank Miss Esmé Allen of the David Davies Memorial Institute for her constant retyping of draft papers. We are also very grateful to a number of officials in Whitehall and elsewhere for their contributions and comments, in particular Dr Neville Linton of the Commonwealth Secretariat.

Peter Blaker
25 March 1985

The members of the study group are:

The Rt Hon Sir Peter Blaker, KCMG, MP (Chairman)
Mr Donald Anderson, MP
Mr Hugh Hanning
Professor Rosalyn Higgins
Mr David Jessop
Mr Patrick Keatley
Dr Peter Lyon
Lord Mayhew
Dr Malcolm Shaw
Professor Jack Spence
Professor Donald Cameron Watt

The staff of the David Davies Memorial Institute are:

Miss Sheila Harden (Director)
Dr Geoffrey Edwards
Ms Mary Unwin

1 The Scope of the Problem

The Falkland Islands in 1982 and Grenada in 1983 are just two recent examples of crises in peripheral areas which have had much wider repercussions. In the last century incidents in both Fashoda and Agadir, for instance, caused breaches between allies and led governments in London to engage in unforeseen and costly operations beyond Britain's shores.

The Falklands and Grenada are also, however, examples of a quite new phenomenon. The breaking up of the colonial empires has led to the emergence of a large number of very small states. Most of these micro-states have too few financial resources to enable them, ever, to be self-sufficient and a number of them are the subject of irredentist claims. In addition, many of these states – in the Caribbean, the Indian Ocean and the Pacific – because of their strategic positions can easily become pawns in the game of international power politics. Consequently, a new and significant strain has been placed on the international system. There is also an urgency to the problem now which did not arise in more stately times. While the danger of escalation can be exaggerated in the era of the jet, the missile and instant telecommunications, there can be no guarantee that a crisis in one of the world's micro-states will be containable, either locally or regionally. The threat to our stability is mutual, whether we be citizens of the small territory at the centre of the crisis or of a larger nation which finds itself drawn in.

This study, then, will have quite as much value for leaders in the Third World as it will for those in developed nations. The intensive examination of the lessons to be drawn from the Grenada crisis, which got under way in many world capitals in 1983, is now occupying some of the shrewdest minds at the United Nations. Individual governments, such as Britain, have set their own teams to work. In addition, the 49 member states of the Commonwealth, following the New Delhi summit, have put in hand a survey and assessment process. All these studies, including this one, must seek to identify and attempt to find solutions to the root causes of crises in micro-states; not just the external factors involving great power politics, but also the internal factors of poverty, thin resources, inadequate education and poor prospects.

It should be stressed here that the problems facing micro-states are not unique. Their particular difficulties arise from their greater vulnerability and lower capacity to respond to crises. By the very nature of their size, they are particularly susceptible to both natural and man-made disasters. A coup in an island only thirty miles wide will have a far greater chance of success than one in a larger area where it might be contained; and one hurricane can destroy the economy of a small state dependent on a single crop.

The political prescription which emerges from the following pages will not be a palatable one; yet the medicine is, we feel, one that must be taken if the disease is not to recur both in this century and the next. The cure involves hard work by political leaders in many countries. It will require them to 'think long' and to sell new ideas to their electorates. It will need an investment of money and trained manpower in places – such as Grenada – that voters know about only hazily at best. It will need courage and a touch of political inspiration.

These qualities came to the fore when an inter-party group of MPs in London, acting independently of the government of the day, sought to investigate the Grenada crisis while the residual American forces were still on the island. These were the members of the House of Commons Foreign Affairs Committee, under the chairmanship of Sir Anthony Kershaw, who exercised their right to call before them the leading figures involved at the British end, starting with the Foreign Secretary. The group travelled to the Caribbean, where they had the co-operation of the Governor-General of Grenada, Sir Paul Scoon, as well as the prime ministers of neighbouring island states. Their resulting reports make valuable reading for those concerned to identify the diplomatic and logistical factors which led to gross strains on the Anglo-American alliance. The heart of the matter is set out in one paragraph of the Committee's second report, of March 1984, in these words:

> As the world has so often learned in the past, and at such great cost, wars break out and alliances fall apart, not so often as the result of deliberate decisions by the major powers, but as the result of the

inability of the great power system, and the alliances which support it, to cope with the problems of small countries in faraway parts of the globe.[1]

The echoes of Neville Chamberlain's famous and disastrous words about Czechoslovakia in that statement are, of course, deliberate. In the jet age we have learned, at some cost, that these trip wires on the political battlefield are not all that far away. They may, indeed, be under our very feet as we bustle about on our day-to-day duties, our gaze fixed on what we conceive to be the high profile problems in the central arena of policy-making.

It may be as well to remind ourselves of how crises in small states can abruptly impose themselves on the diaries of prime ministers and cabinets. Anguilla is a Caribbean island with few resources, some 6,000 people, and a traditional antagonism towards its nearest English-speaking neighbour, St Kitts, seventy-two miles away. As part of the process of shedding the remaining vestiges of Empire, Britain began a tidying-up operation in the late 1960s, grouping island dependencies into convenient clumps ready for launching into nationhood. Anguilla, it was decided, would continue, as in colonial times, under the administration of St. Kitts, after the granting of sovereign status, and would be ruled from there in perpetuity.

The Anguillans, who are highly literate and keen radio listeners, were aware of Ian Smith's act of defiance in Rhodesia. They simply proclaimed a Unilateral Declaration of Independence. They attacked the police station, seized its stock of arms and ammunition, and sent the constables home by launch to St. Kitts. The world paid no attention. The Anguillans had calculated, rightly, that the Wilson administration in London, having decided against military measures to quell rebellion by whites in Southern Africa, would not wish to use such measures against non-whites in another colonial territory. That would have caused severe embarrassment for Britain at the United Nations, where Third World delegations were calling for military intervention, under Chapter VII of the Charter, to crush Ian Smith's forces.

The Foreign Secretary of the day, Michael Stewart, had orders from his prime minister to turn a Wilsonian blind eye to the rebellion in the West Indies. This strategy failed when it was learned that the Anguillans had enlisted sympathetic assistance from the delegations of black countries at the United Nations and were planning to bring the issue before the General Assembly, linking it bluntly with British

inaction in Rhodesia. By the time London gave the reluctant signal
for a military operation involving the paratroops and a seaborne
landing, the Foreign Secretary found himself with a political crisis in
the House of Commons, Anguilla spread across the front pages of the
newspapers and Britain suffering a major embarrassment at the
United Nations. It was, and remains, a diplomatic disaster, and
Anguilla seems destined to remain on the books in Whitehall as a
British dependency in perpetuity. When discussing the crisis, an
exasperated Foreign Secretary reported that, over a period of some
six weeks, his working hours had been consumed by Anguilla to the
extent of 40 to 50 per cent. Greater world problems, starting with
nuclear missiles and East–West relations, had to take second
place.

   Clearly the world's micro-states, whether enjoying technical
sovereignty or still classed as dependencies, have the capacity to
cause macro-political havoc at the UN and in major world capitals.
The Falklands crisis of 1982, and the Grenada debacle a year later,
have served to underline the point that the great powers seem
chronically prone to underestimate these problems. Perhaps the very
fact that they look like storms in teacups, when they first appear in the
in-tray of a busy foreign minister, explains why such crises are
ignored in the first instance, with the loss of valuable time. In what
inevitably turns out to be a not-too-well-disguised scramble of
improvisation, these same powers try to grapple with a problem that
might have been averted. They are forced to do this under pressure
from angry public opinion and sharp inquiry by press and
broadcasting organisations.

   It comes as no surprise that the ultimate political harvest of these
micro-state crises should take the form of friction and recrimination
between major allies, as with Grenada and the Falklands. This leads
to the departure of ministers from office and the imposition of strains
on the western alliance, serving only to weaken the joint stance of the
industrial democracies. At the same time, their relations with the
Third World come under parallel strain.

   It was inevitable that when the prime ministers and presidents of
the four dozen member states of the Commonwealth held their next
summit meeting after the Grenada crisis, in New Delhi in November
1983, they were under strong compulsion to come to grips with the
problem in a practical way. No less than twenty-seven of these states
come into the category of territories with a population of less than a
million, and the Grenada affair had imposed severe strains on the

relations between Commonwealth nations in the Caribbean. Some approved the American military intervention, some were strongly opposed and some, by an attempt to be non-aligned, incurred the wrath of both groups.

The skill of the then Indian Prime Minister, Mrs Gandhi, as chairman at the gathering, backed by the diplomacy of the Commonwealth Secretary-General, Shridath Ramphal, led to a felicitous outcome in New Delhi and ended by hastening the process of reconciliation between West Indian neighbours. But it had been sheer coincidence that one of the biennial summits came when it did, and the heads of government recognised their good fortune. Matters were unlikely to be so fortuitously arranged again; the wiser course was to see how to avoid a next time.

To this end, a group was assembled under the auspices of the Commonwealth Secretariat to study the issues. In his address to the opening meeting Mr Ramphal referred to the familiar phrase, coined by the British development economist, Kurt Schumacher, about how 'small is beautiful'. The small states that find themselves in the post-colonial era with no metropolitan power to guarantee their security or fund their infrastructure find that beauty, in the form of beaches and palm trees, must be turned into tourist dollars. But, as Mr Ramphal said, these states know that small is also weak and fragile, vulnerable and relatively powerless; they operate in a world where the weak are not rewarded for the beauty of their smallness, but are ignored, imposed upon and generally discounted. As Mr Ramphal went on to say:

> Sometimes it seems as if small states were like small boats, pushed out into a turbulent sea, free in one sense to traverse it; but, without oars or provisions, without compass or sails, free also to perish. Or, perhaps, to be rescued and taken on board a larger vessel.
>
> The truth probably is that the world community has not yet thought its way through the phenomenon of very small states in the world that is emerging in the end years of the twentieth century ... Can the world proceed any longer on the old assumptions that underpinned the concept of the nation state? Must the right to sovereignty and territorial integrity depend exclusively on the capacity of a state, however small, to defend itself, to assert its nationhood by superior arms? Must its survival be contingent on its capacity to repel predators? ... Or is it not, indeed, a premise of independence under the Charter that the

international community has obligations to help to sustain those whom it has helped to bring to freedom – and to do so not only by resolutions after the event, but by the machinery of collective security and the will to use it?[2]

There speaks the authentic voice of the small states, rendered articulate by one whose working life has taken him to most of the world's larger states as well. Those of us involved in the production of this book are in the reverse position; we live and work in one of the larger states, but our public and professional duties have taken us time and again to the small ones.

In our discussions, a collective view developed that this kind of study, to be practical and useful, must be specific. There must be specific lists of the problems; specific examples; and specific recommendations for action by governments. In seeking more guidance as to the scope of the problem, as seen from the point of view of the small states themselves, we were particularly interested in the words of the President of one of the smallest, the Republic of Maldives. President Maumoon Abdul Gayoom was invited to London by the Royal Commonwealth Society, to be the keynote speaker at its annual conference in June 1984. A lawyer by training he presides over an unsophisticated community of some 150,000 people. They live, as he candidly explained to the conference, on '1,200 coral islands spread over 90,000 square kilometres of open seas'.[3] It is an equatorial territory, extending some 500 miles from north to south, where the highest point of land is only nineteen feet above sea level and where there are no streams, energy resources or mineral deposits. The navies of the superpowers treat Maldivian waters as if they were part of the high seas. The Soviet Union's Indian Ocean fleet of some thirty vessels has established regular anchorages in the zone, marked by permanent buoys, where the water is only a few dozen fathoms deep in places. But a Soviet request for naval facilities at Gan Island, a British base in colonial times, has been politely rebuffed.

In his London speech, President Gayoom wryly quoted the old African proverb: 'When two elephants fight, it is the grass that suffers'. Although he heads a conservative administration in his own archipelago, President Gayoom expressed sympathy for the socialist administration in Grenada which was toppled by American military action:

It was only when the administration of the late Maurice Bishop was perceived to be conducting its affairs in a manner deemed incompatible with the vision of the Caribbean region held by the West, that it became subject to foreign military intimidation ... The invasion was essentially based upon the dangerous precept that if one state does not particularly like the social and political climate prevailing in another, it can carry out a military adventure. The British Prime Minister was correct, and well justified, when she condemned the invasion of Grenada in similar terms. She upheld a high and enduring principle – that of territorial integrity.[4]

The Maldivian leader defends his position by the logic of non-alignment; the right of his government, and those of other small states, to exist, free from external interference. In particular he referred to the 'hi-jackers' – subversive groups using dubious financial sources and hired mercenaries to try to take over small countries:

> In the past decade there have been attempts at alien subversion in the independent Commonwealth nations of the Bahamas, on Abaco Island, in Vanuatu and the Seychelles... And the kingdom of Lesotho has suffered the gross injustice of military incursions into its territory of a particularly brutal nature by the armed forces of South Africa.

But it is the vulnerability on the economic front of the Maldives and other micro-states that is the chief concern of President Gayoom. He sees a new deal between the economic 'Davids and Goliaths' as central to the whole search for a long-term solution to the security of micro-states. The prolonged recession has played havoc with these fragile economies.

> The Maldives has not, in company with so many others, been immune from the devastating effects of the recession; they have adversely affected our economy and, therefore, our ability to institute and carry out programmes of national development. In this respect, the widely held notion that many have of the island states as being remote and isolated ... is, in all terms practical, a fiction. While we could be so described in geographical terms, it is quite simply no longer true when related to the speed with which the effects of the conditions of the world beyond reach us.

It is significant that these words come from a leader who, quite deliberately, led his country back into an association with Britain that had been broken at the end of colonial rule in the 1960s. After fourteen years of going it alone, President Gayoom and his colleagues in government decided that their small state should follow the earlier examples of India, Sri Lanka and Bangladesh, and join the Commonwealth. He sees this, rightly, as a decision which does not impinge on his country's membership in the non-aligned movement but one by which there is an unquantifiable gain in the sense of a diplomatic shield that should make the Maldivian archipelago somewhat less vulnerable. This still leaves the economic factor in national stability to be solved:

> If more Grenadas are to be avoided, the very best manner in which the long-term security of the Commonwealth's small states can be obtained is to introduce, without delay, economic and trading reforms in the international market place which will, in turn, introduce economic justice and equity ...

President Gayoom emphasised the point again later when he declared:

> economic development ... is the front line of battle ... Remove the threat and the debilitating effects of poverty, and the first – the most important – battle will be won, and quite possibly the war. It will never be enough, or indeed good enough, for the small states of the Commonwealth to be just well defended bastions of poverty.

In our judgment, having heeded the words of the leaders of micro-states themselves, there would seem to be a common interest between the micro-states and the Western industrial democracies in which both sides have a practical role to play. The micro-states would do well to provide the right sort of economic environment that could attract investment, even if, initially, as in the Gambia, this only means hotels and tourism. The Western countries, some of them the former administering powers of colonial times, could do a great deal by lifting protectionist measures so as to help the small states reduce their dependence on aid handouts and increase their economic viability. This does, however, require a deliberate re-shaping of public opinion on the domestic political front.

Attached to this study is a list of the world's micro-states. We have
defined such territories as those with a population of less than one
million, the accepted yardstick now used at the United Nations and
the one which has since been taken by the Commonwealth
Consultative Group. In this category we have listed thirty-eight
independent sovereign territories of which twenty-seven are members of the Commonwealth. In addition, we recognise that those
territories which are still colonies, dependencies, or departments of
metropolitan powers must also be considered, since one of these, the
Falkland Islands, has been, and remains, a major political problem
for Britain. France has encountered different, but acute, difficulties,
with two of her island dependencies – Mayotte in the Indian Ocean
and New Caledonia in the Pacific. The vigorous resistance of the
settlers to a transfer of power caused costly and time-consuming
problems for successive French governments in the case of Mayotte
and is presenting a particularly intractable problem in New
Caledonia. In addition, the freewheeling French mercenaries who
caused such havoc in French and Belgian colonial territories in Africa
in the 1960s have not given up their penchant for intervention, as
shown by an audacious attempted coup in the Comoros in the 1980s.
So in this study we also list the thirty-six remaining dependencies
around the world, of which sixteen may be classified as British or
Commonwealth. These dependencies may, perhaps, be less hazar-
dous to world peace, for the metropolitan powers have demonstrated
their willingness to use their military forces to defend them.

Surveying the picture in geographical terms, it may be that the
Pacific area remains particularly vulnerable to conflict. Annex C
takes the reader through the region in detail. The Minority Rights
Group in London has performed a useful service by commissioning
a detailed report on one of these emerging states under the title:
'Micronesia: The Problem of Palau'.[5] This concerns the 16,000
people of a group of eight islands, part of the UN Trust Territory of
the Pacific Islands which has a population of some 133,000. The
United States has been the administering power since 1947 and is now
proposing a 'Compact of Free Association'. Considerable economic
benefits are promised, but the price is high in diplomatic terms.
Palau would be required to delete the anti-nuclear provisions in its
present constitution to allow the introduction of American nuclear
weapons, the establishment of a jungle warfare training centre, and
the provision of dumping facilities for nuclear waste. The proposed
amendments have been put to a referendum in Palau three times,

and rejected on each occasion, but the pressures are said to be building up. High Chief Ibedul Gibbons appeared before the UN Trusteeship Council in 1983 to register his people's anxieties about a number of projects that were being forcefully pressed upon his administration.

Of more immediate concern, in military terms, are the claims and counter-claims being pressed over the Spratly island group in the South China Sea. Interest in these hitherto worthless islands has been stimulated by reports of off-shore oil and mineral resources. Altogether there are about a hundred atolls, reefs and islands in the Spratly group, and China, while so far making no move to occupy any of them, claims the whole.

Vietnam has fortified four of the islands, including the main one, Spratly, which covers some six acres. The Philippines gazetted a claim to seven of the islands in 1978 and began fortification in earnest. They gave this group a new name, the Kalayaan Islands which, ironically, means 'freedom'. In 1982 Taiwan announced a three-year programme for developing the island of Itu Aba, allocated the budget for a migration programme, and began the construction of harbour facilities for eighty fishing vessels to be based on Itu Aba and the neighbouring Prata group. The Malaysian Navy moved into the zone in 1980, putting a marker buoy on Commodore Reef and issuing an official map to assert its claim.

Taiwan has established a garrison of 500 soldiers on its part of the Spratlys, together with fifteen amphibious landing craft, fourteen anti-aircraft guns, and lighter weapons. Vietnam has built a 550-yard runway for light military aircraft, and has moved in twenty-three main artillery pieces and large numbers of anti-aircraft guns. The strategic significance of the Spratlys was demonstrated by Japan in the Second World War, which used the islands as the base for the naval and air operations that led to the capture of the Philippines, Indonesia and Malaya. The situation is now complicated by the arrival of boat people fleeing from Vietnam as well as by settlers from the Philippines. With Vietnam already committed to giving the Soviet Navy full use of base facilities at Cam Ranh Bay, the spectre arises of potential Soviet naval operations in the Spratlys. All these moves are taking place in an archipelago that is roughly 200 miles in diameter. The islands held by the military forces of Vietnam and Taiwan are within artillery range of each other.

Quite apart from these manoeuvrings by the major powers in the Pacific area, the micro-states of the region are facing a new form of subversion. It would appear that they are now regarded as fair game by international corporations which go to some lengths to conceal their identity. These should not be confused with the well-known multinational corporations which deal openly with governments on issues such as oil drilling and mining rights. These shadowy corporations tend to operate from registered offices in Hawaii or on the mainland of the United States, mostly in California or Nevada. One of these, the Phoenix Foundation, had its cover blown at the time when Britain and France were ending their joint colonial rule in the condominium of the New Hebrides. A breakaway movement seized power by force of arms in one of the component islands, Espirito Santo. A curious rococo figure, Jimmy Stephens, emerged as the leader. Although Mr Stephens was at first regarded as some kind of practical joke, it soon became apparent that he intended to hold his island by force, proclaiming it a separate republic in a move reminiscent of the Tshombe regime in Katanga at the time of Congo independence. Some of his finance came from the Phoenix Foundation, whose directors had been quietly visiting the island before the ending of colonial rule, and had also entertained Mr Stephens on trips to the United States.

For political reasons, France was reluctant to take military action against a movement to which some, at least, of the French speakers were sympathetic, but was persuaded to join Britain in sending troops to seize the only town on the rebel island, and to stick to the agreed date for independence. Separate military action by Britain would have been of doubtful legality under the condominium and potentially disastrous for Anglo-French relations. The situation was resolved after independence with Commonwealth help when Australia, at the request of the Prime Minister of Vanuatu (as it was now called), Mr Walter Lini, sent transport planes, and Papua New Guinea provided troops to complete the operation. This episode had many curious features unique to a condominium but illustrated the vulnerability of small states to adventurers, local or foreign, the need for strong police forces well trained to forestall or deal with such attempted coups, and the interdependence of small states and their neighbours, large or small.

The *coups d'état* which brought down the Gairy regime in Grenada and the Sultan's regime in Zanzibar, and the example of Vanuatu, all demonstrate the devastating potential of well-planned military subversion within a micro-state. As one analyst has suggested, a variety of wild guesses can be made about the number of troops required to control a micro-state. If one makes an analogy with an American city of some 30,000, for example, which has a police force of about thirty people, the number of Cuban or other troops which might be necessary to control Grenada would be about a hundred. If one took the example of the Soviet Union, the ratio of controller-to-controlled might be estimated at one per 2,000, suggesting the need of a garrison for fifty men for Grenada.[6] Bernard Coard may not have had many more when he brought down his erstwhile colleague, Maurice Bishop.

In light of the above, and hand in hand with a policy of fostering prosperity in these micro-states by more active policies than have been pursued hitherto, the western democracies might also regard military and police training as a practical form of aid. There is a strong argument to be made that, in order to gain the efficiency of scale, the concept of regional police force training should be introduced. Forces that have trained together could, in a crisis, work harmoniously together.

The concept of Exclusive Economic Zones, arising from the Law of the Sea Conference, means that small island states now have formidable problems of patrolling sea lanes and fishing grounds. Britain has provided patrol vessels for the Bahamas because of landing by unidentified – possibly Cuban – teams on the 'out-islands'. This kind of aid, again on a regional basis, might be developed; so also could the technical training of personnel from small states, or groups of states, as in the Caribbean, in information and intelligence work. Finally, the metropolitan powers might assist in a practical way by providing experts to draw up contingency plans for individual micro-states or groups of them. These should comprise lists of equipment needed, route-planning for logistical supply, and blueprints for the additional experts who would be needed quickly in a crisis.

All this argues the case for earmarking, or sponsorship, by medium-sized powers willing to take on the duties of fraternal aid to particular micro-states on a permanent basis. A foretaste of this came in the Commonwealth Committee on Belize, which is pledged to consult as a matter of urgency in case of external threat, with Britain and Canada both committed to do so, together with Caribbean partners. But apart from military and diplomatic measures, it becomes apparent that the best guarantee against subversion of micro-states, from without or within, is the firm establishment of democracy and its buttressing by economic development.

There are half a dozen 'Factors of Vulnerability' which we have charted in the crises of recent times in the world's micro-states. They may be threatened by great power rivalries, or by territorial claims from more powerful neighbours. They may, as in Aden, be wanted for their strategic value. They possess rich resources, usually oil or other minerals, which are yet to be exploited. They may be the reluctant hosts of political refugees or 'freedom fighters' from neighbouring states with stronger military forces, as in Southern Africa and Papua New Guinea. But, perhaps most of all, internal factors should receive first priority. Poverty and unemployment among the inhabitants, poorly-trained and too few police and armed forces, corruption and suppression of democracy, as in the Gairy regime which preceded the coup which brought Maurice Bishop to power in Grenada, are primary factors and as such must be dealt with.

As with all potential aggression, deterrence must be visible and effective. This will require some hard political decisions by the larger powers to help finance that deterrence. Thomas Jefferson's far-sighted advice about eternal vigilance is as true now as it was two centuries ago. And it applies as much, if not more, to those who live in the macro-states as to those whose homes are in the small ones.

Notes

1. House of Commons, *Second Report from the Foreign Affairs Committee; Grenada*, HMSO, March 1984.
2. *Small is Beautiful but Vulnerable*, speech by Mr Shridath Ramphal at Marlborough House, Commonwealth Secretariat, 18 July, 1984.
3. Royal Commonwealth Society, *The Small States and the Commonwealth: Report of the Annual Conference 1984*, RCS, 1984, p. 8.
4. Royal Commonwealth Society, ibid., pp. 2–3.
5. Clark and Rolf, *Micronesia: The Problem of Palau*, Minority Rights Group Report No. 63, 1984.
6. See George H. Quester, 'Trouble in the Islands: Defending the Micro-States', *International Security*, Fall 1983, Vol. 8, No. 2, p. 164.

2 Micro-States and the International System

The problems posed by the vulnerability of micro-states call for some hard thinking not only by the small states themselves but also by the international community as a whole. The environment in which the micro-states operate is criss-crossed and shaped by a multitude of organisations, at the global, regional and sub-regional level. These organisations have either a clear security or defence purpose, or at least offer a forum in which disputes and disagreements can be argued out. This chapter gives a brief indication of the organisations concerned and, since the problems of micro-states have been on the international agenda for much of this century, begins with the League of Nations.

Although membership of such bodies can be important in the search for greater security, a number of independent micro-states also rely on bilateral security arrangements. The dismantling of the large overseas colonial empires of the West European powers has left a variety of new relationships in its wake, some again with a strong element of support and assistance. In addition, the interdependence of large and small nations is demonstrated by the involvement of micro-states in the major powers' search for bases and allies as a result of global East–West confrontation. We therefore necessarily look at the approaches adopted by the United Kingdom, France, the United States and the Soviet Union towards the security issues provoked by micro-states.

Micro-States at the Global Level

Micro-States and the League of Nations

Today, of the seven micro-states of Western Europe, four of them – Andorra, Monaco, San Marino and Liechtenstein[1] – are so small that their sovereignty is symbolic rather than substantive. They are each vestigial buffer states, politically quiescent and therefore relatively untroubled with acute internal security problems. They make no pretence to deal themselves with any external threat to their security; these are not immediate or apparent anyway. Indeed, today their external security is bound up with, and subordinated to, their circumvallating power (s).

Following the establishment of the League of Nations, five of the European micro-states applied for membership. Luxembourg was admitted in December 1920; but the application of Liechtenstein was rejected. The League had considered Liechtenstein's application on the basis of five questions formulated by the first Assembly. It concluded that 'by reason of her limited area, small population and her geographical position, she has chosen to depute to others some of the attributes of sovereignty'. Furthermore, it was noted that 'Liechtenstein has no army'.[2] Monaco withdrew its application; San Marino failed to respond to the Secretary-General's request for further information; and no action was taken regarding Iceland.

Subsequently, a sub-committee of the League's Assembly prepared a report on the 'Position of Small States'. Three alternatives to full membership were proposed for consideration:

(1) small states might be 'associated' with the League and given the right of full participation, but without a vote; or
(2) they might be 'represented' by some member of the League; or
(3) they might enjoy 'limited participation', with the exercise of a member's privileges limited to cases where their own interests were involved.

None of these was adopted as the Report was shelved without further consideration.

Micro-States and the United Nations

Membership of the United Nations has come to be regarded as particularly important for micro-states: it is seen by many as an expression of their international legitimacy; it also provides them with ready access to the services of the United Nations and its specialised agencies. Moreover, representation in the United Nations offers small states a much more cost-effective method of maintaining extensive relations with the outside world than bilateral diplomacy, which is often too costly both in financial and human terms for micro-states to contemplate. (The United Nations' location in New York is also helpful since it enables the Permanent Representative of a micro-state to the United Nations to be jointly accredited as Ambassador to Washington.) Indeed, the very fact that small states can nowadays participate in the activities of international organisations of various kinds advertises and underlines the basic and persisting conditions of international politics: the formal equality of sovereign states (regardless of size and resources) and their substantive inequalities.

The United Nations, unlike the League of Nations, began its life in 1945 with one micro-state – Luxembourg – among its founding members. The United Nations admitted one further micro-state, Iceland, in the first year but, unlike its predecessor, the new organisation did not classify and consider in specific terms a category for small states. It is unlikely that the drafters of the Charter at San Francisco, or the participants in the early sessions of the United Nations (and its specialised organs), imagined that within forty years the membership would have increased to 159 and that almost a quarter of these would have populations of less than one million.

It is often forgotten that the original membership of the United Nations was confined to the victorious allies and their supporters; the principle of universality, although implicit in the Charter, was rarely advanced in the early years. The drafters of the Charter were more concerned about the threat of future wars than the authors of the League of Nations' Covenant and placed greater emphasis on strategic considerations.

The admission of Iceland to the United Nations in 1946 illustrates this attitude. Iceland possessed neither an army nor a navy and had a population of only 132,750 at that time, and yet no one seems to have considered that the admission of so small a state might constitute an undesirable precedent. Its membership of the United Nations was accepted primarily as a recognition of its great strategic importance and value to the United States and its allies in 'The Battle of the Atlantic' during the Second World War. United States' forces were later stationed in Iceland as the Iceland Defence Force under the North Atlantic Treaty.

The years 1955 and 1960 constituted major watersheds in the membership of the United Nations and therefore in its political composition and character. The original membership of fifty-one had increased to sixty by 1950 and remained at sixty until December 1955. The admission of sixteen new members, almost simultaneously, in December 1955, as a result of the so-called 'horse-trading deal' between the Western Allies and the Soviet Union, brought an end to the stalemate. The new admissions immediately increased the total membership to seventy-six. Thereafter there was increasing reference to universality of membership as a desirable goal.

The year 1960 witnessed a further significant change. Eighteen new members were admitted during the 15th Session of the General Assembly, mostly from Africa, but including Cyprus. More importantly, during the same Session, Resolution 1514 (often subsequently referred to as the Anti-Colonialists' Charter) was carried by an overwhelming majority. This contributed greatly to the demolition of the hitherto established criteria for statehood. The Resolution (entitled 'A Declaration on the Granting of Independence to Colonial Countries and Peoples') affirmed, *inter alia*, that 'inadequacy of political, economic, social or educational preparedness should never serve as a pretext for delaying independence'.

For the first time, newly independent states constituted a substantial numerical majority in the United Nations and in other associated international organisations. From then on, the dynamics of decolonisation achieved a new momentum. By the early 1970s formal independence had been acquired by a large number of erstwhile dependencies, including many whose substantive claims and qualifications for statehood would not have been regarded seriously by the governments of most other independent states only a decade earlier.[3]

Alternatives to UN Membership

The question of the extent to which the United Nations (and its associated bodies) could accept micro-states as members without seriously undermining its own operational capability and efficiency did nevertheless receive attention in the 1960s. This was, however, decidedly half-hearted. Prompted by the admission in 1965 of the Maldives and The Gambia, U Thant, then Secretary-General of the United Nations, suggested that perhaps the time had come to re-examine the criteria for the admission of new members and to introduce some form of associate membership. Two years later, at the instigation of the United States, the Security Council resuscitated its Standing Committee on Admissions, which had been inactive since

1949, in the hope that the qualifications for statehood of prospective candidates would be scrutinised more carefully. However, although the Committee has continued to meet whenever a new request for membership comes up for consideration in the Security Council, in practice it merely rubber-stamps the request.

In 1969 the Security Council established a Committee of Experts to study the question. The Committee examined proposals from the United Kingdom and the United States and issued an interim report summarising these, but then ceased to operate. The United Kingdom proposal was that, when applying for membership, a very small state would voluntarily renounce the right to vote and to be a candidate for election; in return its financial contribution would be assessed at only a nominal level. The United States proposal was, essentially, for a form of associate membership that would exclude the right to vote or hold office in the General Assembly and would involve no financial obligations. The state in question would, however, enjoy 'appropriate rights' in the Security Council and the Economic and Social Council.[4] The British suggestion was simpler and did not require an amendment to the UN Charter (this is notoriously difficult to achieve since it is subject to the veto and almost invariably opposed by the Permanent Members). However, the UN Legal Counsel, in an advisory opinion, noted that the proposal might be hard to reconcile with the principle of sovereign equality in article 2 (1) of the Charter covering rights and obligations and with article 18 (1) which declares that each member of the General Assembly shall have one vote. He proposed instead a form of 'association' with the United Nations. This would have required the principal deliberative organs to lay down conditions, on the basis of Charter provisions, rules of procedure and practice, under which associate states might participate.[5] It would also have required the Security Council and the General Assembly to reach decisions on the nature of such status and its implications, something that never appeared a practical proposition.

Other possibilities for dealing with the problem have been suggested, including representation at the United Nations by another member state, limited participation and various forms of associate membership. All suffer from the same drawback of not being easily reconciled with the relevant provisions of the Charter. The possibility of joint membership has also been discussed, whereby several micro-states would combine their resources to cover all UN operations, but the difficulty of Charter amendment still applies. It also raises the very practical problem of whether sufficient identity of interest would exist for the concept to be feasible. The experience of the colonial powers, particularly the United Kingdom, in promoting federal ideas indicates that, at least in the early days of independence, states are subject to centrifugal rather than centripetal pressures.

Observer status is another option, but one which lacks appeal. In the past, observer status has been mostly accorded to states prevented by the veto from becoming full members: Japan (until 1956), the two Germanies (until 1973), the two Koreas (up to the present day), North and South Vietnam (until 1977). The exceptions are Switzerland, which has chosen not to join, and Monaco and the Holy See which have no ambitions to play a more active part in the organisation. Observer status has no formal legal basis and observers can take no part in UN proceedings. It, therefore, has little to recommend it. It should however be noted that a number of other international organisations do permit something less than full membership status and this option has been taken up by some small states.[6]

Since the micro-states themselves are loath to be treated as second-class citizens and see genuine advantage in full membership, none of these proposals are likely to be acceptable. It would, in any case, be difficult to justify closing the stable door after so many micro-states have slipped through. Moreover, Third World countries can now muster the two-thirds majority required in the General Assembly on 'important questions', which include budgetary questions (article 18 (2) of the UN Charter). So a few more members will not affect voting results. It is significant that, despite the resuscitation of the Admissions Committee, not a single candidate has yet been debarred from membership of the United Nations on grounds of size and/or viability, although a number have been debarred on political grounds.

There are two points of particular significance here. Firstly, many of the contemporary micro-states have arrived at their current sovereign status not because this had long been envisaged, but rather because several alternatives to independence were tried, found wanting and proved impermanent. For instance, in a number of Caribbean cases, neither continuance as a colony, nor membership of a West Indian or Caribbean-wide federation, nor even 'associated status' proved to be sustainable alternatives to independence. This frustrating record of fruitless searches for 'alternatives to independence' should be borne in mind before hasty and dismissive judgements are passed on the appropriateness and viability of micro-states as ostensibly independent units. Moreover, having achieved sovereign status, many micro-states have been reluctant to enter agreements which would appear to modify or dilute it, even though it is possible that their economic and political security might be better served by closer co-operation or even integration. Secondly, alternatives such as federations or the realignment of boundaries have often been seen as more likely to open up conflicts than to solve difficulties arising from a state's smallness. It may seem remarkable that administrative lines, drawn long ago to delineate the frontiers between rival colonial powers or for purposes of administrative convenience within these empires, have been so largely accepted by newly independent states as their international boundaries. But as Professor Ian Brownlie points out in his exhaustive study of African boundaries:[7]

> If the colonial alignments were discarded, alternative alignments would have to be agreed upon. Such a process of redefinition could create confusion and threats to the peace. Even if the principles on which revision was to be based were agreed upon, there would be considerable difficulty in applying the principles to the ethnic and tribal complexities of African societies.

He also noted that:

> Customary international law, which is based upon the consistent practice of states, has always contained the principle that a change of sovereignty does not affect the status of those international boundaries which do not cease to be international as an inevitable consequence of the change.

For Africa, the Cairo Resolution, adopted by the Organisation of African Unity (OAU) Assembly of Heads of State and Government in 1964, noted that the 'borders of African States, on the day of their independence, constitute a tangible reality' and, having referred to border problems as constituting 'a grave and permanent factor of dissension', ended with a pledge 'to respect the borders existing on the achievement of their national independence'. While the dangers of balkanisation are probably most acute in Africa, the principle of respecting former colonial borders has been almost universally accepted by Third World countries. Hence the emphasis in this study on the need to deal with the present world territorial status quo.

Micro-States and the UN Security System
Membership of the United Nations does not simply confer a degree
of legitimacy on its member states or offer possible material benefits.
Its primary purpose is 'to maintain international peace and security',
(chapter I, article 1). The security system outlined in the Charter was
based on the assumption that the five permanent members of the
Security Council (China, France, the Soviet Union, the United
Kingdom and the United States) would be primarily responsible for
keeping the peace and that a Military Staff Committee consisting of
the Chiefs of Staff of these states (or their representatives) would be
established to 'advise and assist the Security Council on all questions
relating to the Security Council's military requirements for the
maintenance of international peace and security, the employment
and command of forces placed at its disposal, the regulation of
armaments, and possible disarmament' (article 47 (1)). The Military
Staff Committee would be 'responsible under the Security Council
for the strategic direction of any armed forces placed at the disposal
of the Security Council' (article 47 (3)).

Although the system envisaged that the pacific settlement of
disputes (chapter VI) and action with respect to threats to the peace,
breaches of the peace and acts of aggression (chapter VII, articles 39–
51) should be primarily the concern of the Security Council, article 51
recognised 'the inherent right of individual or collective self-defence'
and chapter VIII recognised a complementary, or ancillary role for
'regional arrangements or agencies' in the maintenance of international peace and security. As the Cold War conflict between the
Soviet Union and the West deepened and intensified, the comprehensive system envisaged in article 47 of the UN Charter became in
effect still-born,[8] and great power alliances and regional security
arrangements took the place of the proposed concert of the major
powers. In Europe, NATO and the Warsaw Pact; in the Americas, the
Rio Pact; in the Middle East, the Baghdad Pact and CENTO; in
South East Asia, SEATO, and the Manila Pact; and in the South
Pacific, ANZUS – all came into being.

However, the majority of newly independent countries proved
reluctant to take sides in the Cold War, taking the view that
membership of the rival power-blocs not only undermined their
recent emancipation from colonial status, but also risked implicating
them in a future East–West conflict. They favoured instead a policy of
'peaceful co-existence' and non-alignment. The Afro-Asian Conference in Bandung in 1955 (attended by delegations from twenty-

nine Asian and African countries, mostly newly independent) was the first major forum where such views were crystallised.[9] The ten principles adopted by the Conference emphasised such issues as respect for the sovereignty and territorial integrity of all nations, and non-intervention and non-interference in the internal affairs of another country. Despite the participation of some states which belonged to regional defence pacts at that time (Iraq, Pakistan, Philippines, Thailand and Turkey), the principles adopted included 'abstention from the use of arrangements of collective defence to serve the particular interests of any of the big powers' (principle 6 (a)). The Bandung Conference inspired the philosophy of neutralism and non-alignment, which by the late 1960s was to become the professed policy of a large and increasing majority of Third World states, and was to develop into an organised movement.

The Non-Aligned Movement

The Non-Aligned Movement (NAM) has become the most significant contemporary Third World organisation and now comprises just over a hundred members. It proceeds primarily by means of summit conferences held at three-year intervals, with the host country of the previous Heads of State and Government Meeting providing the Chairman until the next summit. The Co-ordination Bureau, established in 1973, has its headquarters in Belgrade. The Movement also calls other meetings and conferences at different levels.

Twenty-five micro-states are members of the Non-Aligned Movement (Bahamas, Bahrain, Barbados, Belize, Botswana, Cape Verde, Comoros, Cyprus, Djibouti, Equatorial Guinea, The Gambia, Grenada, Guinea-Bissau, Guyana, Maldives, Malta, Mauritius, Oman, Qatar, St Lucia, São Tomé and Príncipe, Seychelles, Suriname, Swaziland and Vanuatu). Since the Non-Aligned Movement is based on the neutralist principle that the best form of security for individual states is to avoid participating in any form of defence agreement, it has understandably given little consideration to the security requirements of states. Membership of the Non-Aligned Movement can, however, be of service to micro-states subject to external threats to their independence. Both Guyana and Belize have benefited from Non-Aligned (and Commonwealth) support for their right to self-determination and the repudiation of irredentist claims. In the case of Belize, for instance, the Fifth Non-Aligned Summit in 1976 issued a declaration in the following terms:

> The Conference welcomed the participation of Belize whose aspirations for independence continue to be frustrated by territorial claims. It expressed its unconditional support for the inalienable right of the people of Belize to self-determination, independence and territorial integrity. In urging the strict implementation of United Nations General Assembly Resolution 3432 (XXX), the Conference called upon the parties concerned to pursue the negotiations in conformity with the principles laid down therein.

The backing of the Non-Aligned Movement has almost certainly contributed to the security of these two micro-states.

The Commonwealth

The Commonwealth is a unique post-imperial international association which, since 1965, has been vested with its own Secretariat and headquarters in London. Although the Commonwealth has evolved from the former British Empire, it is not a British-run club. Nor is it a military alliance; many of its members also belong to the Non-Aligned Movement. Of the Commonwealth's present forty-nine members, twenty-seven have populations of under one million; fourteen have populations of less than 200,000; and seven have populations of less than 100,000. The Commonwealth micro-states are mostly to be found in three areas: ten in the Caribbean, four in Southern Africa or off the east African coast, and eight in the Pacific.

In view of the large and rapidly growing number of micro-states, the Commonwealth has devoted considerable attention to their special problems. The security needs of micro-states were first discussed by Commonwealth Heads of Government in 1969 in the light of the problems facing Guyana. During the 1970s, attention was focused more acutely on the economic problems of these states, with a number of papers prepared at regional meetings and by the Commonwealth Secretariat and discussed at the Heads of Government meeting in Lusaka in 1979. Since it took place so soon after the action of the United States in Grenada, the New Delhi Heads of Government meeting of 1983 was particularly concerned with security issues, and this was reflected both in the Conference's final communiqué which called for a further study on micro-states, and in the Goa Declaration. The latter states:

> We are particularly concerned at the vulnerability of small states to external attack and interference in their affairs. These countries are members of the international community which must respect their independence and, at the very least, has a moral obligation to provide effectively for their territorial integrity. We have separately agreed on an urgent study of the issues. Additionally, however, we will play our part in helping the international community to make an appropriate response to the UN Secretary-General's call for a strengthening of collective security in keeping with the Charter.[10]

The Commonwealth as such has so far played only a limited military role. A number of its members have provided joint security forces on occasions, most notably in the Commonwealth Monitoring Force which, together with the Commonwealth Observer Group, oversaw Zimbabwe's transition to independence. In 1982, a small (thirty-six member) team drawn from eight Commonwealth countries was also sent to Uganda with the aim of assisting in the creation of a Uganda national army. Individually, several Commonwealth states have provided troops to a fellow Commonwealth country for training purposes or in civil support roles, including not only the United Kingdom, Canada, Australia and New Zealand, but also Tanzania, Papua New Guinea and Fiji.

However, while the Commonwealth has been much concerned about the problem of Cyprus since it became independent and a member in 1960, it has proved ineffective in its support for the Cypriot government following the Turkish invasion of 1974. On the other hand, in other cases, Commonwealth diplomatic support has been influential. The Commonwealth Ministerial Committee on Belize, for example, acted as a persuasive pressure group in mobilising support in the United Nations and among the Non-Aligned Movement for the right of Belize to independence and in exposing Guatemalan irredentism.

The Commonwealth not only provides a forum for discussion on political and economic issues, but has also established a number of development funds, operated by the Secretariat, and other technical services, such as the Commonwealth Legal Advisory Service, which have been widely commended. The Commonwealth Fund for Technical Cooperation (CFTC), with its small in-house consultancy unit the Technical Assistance Group (TAG), has been especially successful. The expertise of TAG's consultants covers a wide range of issues and sectors: the delimitation and negotiation of maritime boundaries; advice on public investment, economic management and statistical services; oil exploration and oil development strategies; and tax and royalty levels for various minerals. It works increasingly in collaboration with other agencies, and has indeed provided a model for other programmes. It has proved especially attractive to, and useful for, many of the Commonwealth's micro-states, most of whom have sought its services in one sector or another. The CFTC is funded largely by Britain (some 30 per cent), Canada and Australia, although all Commonwealth members contribute. It has grown considerably over the past fifteen years: from £400,000 in 1971 to an estimated £26 million in 1985/6. In view of the value attached to it, consideration should be given to its further enlargement.

Micro-States and Regional Organisations

The number, and perhaps the importance, of regional and sub-regional organisations is growing. Before independence, separatist tendencies were strong in many dependent territories; hence the failure of British proposals for federations in Africa and the Caribbean. Usually the small weak territories feared domination by their stronger neighbours while the more prosperous territories feared that the poorer ones would be a burden on their exchequers. In the Pacific, the Gilbert and Ellice Islands were divided into two states (Kiribati and Tuvalu). Banaba (Ocean Island), an island in the Kiribati group, also wished to separate but was prevented from doing so. The Trust Territory of the Pacific Islands, in a series of referendums, rejected a federal solution, opting instead to divide into four separate states after termination of the Trusteeship Agreement, although the Trusteeship Council has consistently pointed out the economic and other disadvantages of this course. Separatist problems in Antigua and St Kitts postponed the granting of independence to these two territories.

However, with the achievement of independence, separatist tendencies have usually subsided, to be replaced in several instances with a renewed interest in regional co-operation. Although centrifugal pressures remain, there has been growing discussion of the possible benefits of co-operation, in affording contacts, providing access to technical advice and assistance and offering the possibilities of common services which would be in the general interest. Security factors have not been absent in these considerations. There are four areas in the contemporary world with clusters of small states. These are: in and around the Caribbean; in and around Africa; in the Gulf; and in the Pacific. Three areas, the Caribbean, Southern Africa and the Pacific are discussed in greater detail in the Annexes. Here we give an outline of the various regional organisations in each of these areas in which the micro-states are, to a greater or lesser extent, involved.

The Caribbean and the Organisation of American States (OAS)

Although the Caribbean was the first region to be colonised by Europeans, it has, ironically, become almost the last major area to be de-colonised. Britain, France, the Netherlands and the United States all retain possessions in the area. The United States maintains bases in several countries including Cuba. Among the Commonwealth Caribbean states, although federation had been earlier rejected, several moves have been made towards closer co-operation. The free trade area, CARIFTA, gave way to the Caribbean Community, CARICOM, in 1973. While CARICOM is essentially economic in its concerns, the intention was to go further; not only were the Heads of Government Conferences responsible ultimately for determining the organisation's policy, including policy towards other international organisations, but a Foreign Affairs Committee was established with the aim of achieving a measure of co-ordination of foreign policy.

The subsequent development of CARICOM has disappointed many of the hopes of its founders. Increasing political and ideological divisions have exacerbated economic tensions and problems in and among the members. For some non-Commonwealth Caribbean states, however, such problems have not been enough to counteract a belief in the possible benefits of membership. Both Haiti and Suriname applied for membership and now have observer status. CARICOM's difficulties in achieving closer integration were a major factor in the decision to launch the Organisation of East Caribbean States (OECS) in June 1981, which *inter alia* provides for multilateral security co-operation among its seven member states. Security issues were also increasingly discussed within the wider CARICOM framework. At the Heads of Government summit, after a seven-year break, in Jamaica in 1982, talks were held on the possible options for a treaty for mutual assistance. Those discussions appear somewhat academic in view of events in Grenada; analysis of them and of the possibilities of a Regional Security Service is contained in Annex B.

One of the options discussed by the CARICOM leaders was accession to the Inter-American Treaty of Reciprocal Assistance (otherwise known as the Rio Treaty). Few Caribbean states have individually acceded to it; the Bahamas is one of the few. Moreover, while the states of the Caribbean have normally become members of the wider Organisation of American States (OAS) on gaining their independence, Belize and Guyana have been unable to do so because of objections by Guatemala and Venezuela respectively.

The OAS, defined as a regional organisation of the United Nations for the maintenance of peace and security, was established under the Charter signed in Bogota in 1948. It now has thirty-one members. The OAS Charter and the Rio Treaty call for both the defence of the Western hemisphere against external attack and the defence of internal security. Under article 2 of the Rio Treaty, all parties undertake to submit controversies arising between them to peaceful settlement. The Charter also incorporates the principle of prior resort to the Inter-American system before taking a dispute to the United Nations. Under article 15 of the OAS Charter, member states undertake not to interfere directly or indirectly in the internal affairs of any other member state.

The record of the OAS in settling disputes has been mixed. On a number of occasions it has brought parties to a dispute to the negotiating table, has won agreement to a ceasefire and has established a committee to observe or monitor that ceasefire. This occurred, for example, in 1969 when El Salvador and Honduras signed a ceasefire. On other occasions the OAS has not been involved. Ecuador and Peru, for example, ended their border dispute in 1981 with the help of the Four-Power Guarantee Mediation Group (Argentina, Brazil, Chile and the United States), which was set up in 1941. The OAS, as such, remained neutral. Following the United States' intervention in the Dominican Republic in April 1965, the OAS somewhat reluctantly agreed to send the OAS Secretary-General to help negotiate a ceasefire and set up an Inter-American Peace Force (IAPF) to replace the American force. (American troops were by far the strongest contingent.) OAS (and UN) Missions also supervised the elections held in June 1966 after which the IAPF was withdrawn.

It has been held by a number of commentators that the dominating role of the United States in the OAS system has been a weakness as well as a strength.[11] There is no veto in the Organisation, but in peace-keeping efforts, as in many others, it is believed that unless the United States is committed, the chances of success are limited (although, on the other hand, a number of resolutions passed with strong American support have had little effect; namely, respect for human rights in a number of Latin American countries). To many of its critics, the American commitment to OAS action has merely served as a cover for unilateral action. In some instances, the United States has been able to influence the outcome of OAS decisions by playing on both its economic strength and others' weaknesses, not least their indebtedness. In other cases it has been able to rely on the many conflicting territorial claims between Latin American countries. Both factors were present during the Falkland Islands conflict when Argentinian demands for OAS condemnation of British actions (Argentina had invoked the Rio Treaty) were significantly modified. On issues of importance there has seldom been any confrontation between the United States and Latin American countries.

None the less, there have been discussions about new groupings which would exclude the United States because of its dominant role. The frequency of such discussions has varied, depending on the degree of concern over the extent to which the continent is being drawn into more direct East–West rivalries. The growing military involvement of the United States in the conflict in Central America was a major factor in the creation of the Contadora Group in 1983 comprising Colombia, Mexico, Panama and Venezuela. The Group, despite intermittent American hostility, has sought to end the conflict through the withdrawal of all foreign forces from the region and a settlement on a regional, i.e. Central American, basis. While the Group has been successful in winning support from inside and outside the region, including support from the members of the European Community, peace has remained elusive.

Africa

The most comprehensive contemporary African organisation is the Organisation of African Unity (OAU), established in May 1963 with thirty-two members. There are now fifty members, ten of which are micro-states. It is a relatively loose association of states designed to promote unity and solidarity in Africa on the basis of the principles of sovereignty, non-interference in internal affairs of member states, respect for territorial integrity, peaceful settlement of disputes, the condemnation of political subversion and a dedication to the emancipation of dependent territories and international non-alignment. Decisions of the OAU are not binding on members; they are recommendations only.

Within the continent, only Egypt and South Africa have indigenous arms industries of any size. But given that the continent exhibits much the same gross inequalities of power and capability as does the international system at large, a few countries – notably Libya, Algeria and Egypt in north Africa, Nigeria in West Africa and, most emphatically of all, South Africa in Southern Africa – play leading, and at times dominating, sub-regional roles.

For the OAU itself, such fundamental difficulties are compounded by a number of procedural problems. The Commission of Mediation, Conciliation and Arbitration which was designed to handle all disputes among OAU members was stillborn 'partly because of its cumbersome legalistic structure and the desire of the Heads of State to keep their own thumbs on the highly political process of conflict resolution and dispute settlement'.[12] Yet, meetings of either the Council of Ministers or of Heads of State to investigate disputes have proved difficult (and expensive) and the role of the Secretary-General has remained constrained and limited. There has been of necessity, therefore, a greater reliance on *ad hoc* measures but even these have had little success.

It is a paradox that although the UN Charter (article 52 (2)) lays down that members should make every effort to achieve a pacific settlement of local disputes at a regional level 'before referring them to the Security Council', in practice regional organisations are often the least fitted to settle such cases, usually because their members set store by their relations with both parties to the dispute and are therefore reluctant to take sides. Although OAU members committed themselves to the principle of taking disputes to the OAU first, the OAU has often proved impotent for this reason. Its attempt to mediate in the Ogaden in 1977, for instance, resulted simply in a reaffirmation of the inviolability of colonial boundaries. The failure of the OAU to act effectively in the Shaba, Western Sahara and Chad crises are further examples.

In the case of Shaba, the OAU was obliged to stand by not just once but twice when Western powers, led by France, intervened. On the second occasion, in 1978, the OAU was ignored as the French and Americans organised and supported a 'pan-African force' to police the province and so take over from French and Belgian troops.[13] In the case of the Western Sahara, it was only in 1978 that the OAU agreed to set up an *ad hoc* committee to investigate the matter, some two years after the Polisario had set up a government-in-exile, which had been recognised by seven OAU members. The Secretary-General of the OAU himself gave recognition to the government-in-exile in 1982 and thereby caused eighteen member states to walk out of the OAU Ministerial meeting of that year. As one commentator put it 'by an ugly irony the OAU, instead of helping to solve the Western Sahara conflict has been incapacitated by it'.[14] The Western Saharan government was finally seated in 1984 with only Morocco withdrawing from the Organisation as a result.

The OAU has actually introduced a peace-keeping force on only one occasion, in Chad in 1982. The brevity of its existence is in marked contrast to the durability of the problems of Chad which began in 1968 and which still continue today. The move to introduce the force was taken after the collapse of an agreement reached by the National Conference on Reconciliation held in Lagos at the instigation of the OAU. The force, however, had no clear mandate and in the absence of a ceasefire was obliged to stand aside while fighting continued on the ground and the very much wider international repercussions of the conflict were played out. The Chad example is also revealing at a more practical level, not least in showing the financial weakness of the OAU. In 1982, overall contributions to the Organisation, amounting to $4 million, were paid, all or in part, by ten members. In the same year, the OAU Council of Ministers agreed to a budget of $22m. There were, in consequence, problems in financing the OAU's basic services, apart from the costs of a peace-keeping force. In addition, the three states which actually sent forces, Nigeria, Senegal and Zaire, were confronted with a number of logistical problems. Their forces were geared almost exclusively to internal use and there were therefore problems in relation to communications, in addition to those of command structure and those caused by differences in equipment and capability. Such difficulties suggest that even when the OAU has been sufficiently united to enable it to take action, it still faces problems of effectiveness.

Many states in Africa, large as well as small, have therefore sought security arrangements either with particular external powers, most notably with France, or in sub-regional agreements. Purely bilateral arrangements between African states have been rare. The example of Gambia and Senegal is one. Indeed, the two countries are also in the process of creating a confederation. The defence support extended by Tanzania to the Seychelles is another. A number of moves to establish regional economic organisations have also involved a regional security dimension; in the example of the Southern African Development and Co-ordination Conference (SADCC) both interests were clearly involved from the beginning (see Annex A).

In West Africa, the Economic Community of West African States (ECOWAS) was set up in 1975. In 1981 a Protocol on Mutual Assistance on Defence Matters was signed by twelve, later thirteen, of its sixteen members. The Protocol is significant for a number of reasons. Firstly, it was agreed despite suspicions that it would become dominated by Nigeria. Nigeria's position had been a factor in the earlier creation of the Communauté Economique de l'Afrique de L'Ouest (CEAO) by Senegal and the other Francophone countries in 1974. (In fact, CEAO continues to exist, sometimes uneasily, within the broader framework of ECOWAS.) Secondly, several states which signed the Protocol, such as Togo and Ghana, Senegal and Guinea-Bissau, had had border disputes or had accused each other of political interference. The Protocol had been preceded in 1978 by a Non-Aggression Pact among the sixteen ECOWAS states which contributed to a reduction of tension and so eased the way of the Defence Protocol. Thirdly, and largely at the suggestion of Senegal, the Defence Protocol was agreed by a majority of ECOWAS members rather than by the more usual unanimous vote. Two micro-states, Cape Verde and Guinea-Bissau, were among the few who refused to sign the pact; both have left-wing Marxist governments. (Mali was the other non-signatory.)

The Protocol calls for the setting up of a joint Defence Commission comprising Defence Ministers and their Chiefs of Staff and a Defence Council of Heads of Government. The project envisaged a joint force of units assigned from national armies, rather than a standing army, to act as an intervention or peace-keeping force. The purpose of the force is to counter aggression from any non-member state and to contribute to a mediatory effort in any conflict between member states. Unless there is external involvement in an internal conflict, other member states agreed to take no action.[15] However, both the Non-Aggression and the Defence Protocols join another nine protocols signed since 1978 that have yet to be ratified by the required seven member states.

The Arab World

All the Arab states except Egypt (some twenty in number), plus the Palestine Liberation Organisation, are members of the Arab League founded in 1945. Egypt's membership was suspended in 1979 following President Sadat's signing of the Camp David Accord. The League stretches from Mauritania in the West to the Gulf peninsula and includes the micro-states of Bahrain, Djibouti, Qatar and Oman. A number of defence-related committees and groupings have been established under the 1950 Treaty of Joint Defence and Cooperation which complements the League Charter. There is a Joint Defence Council of Foreign and Defence Ministers and a Permanent Military Committee of army general staffs. In 1964 a United Arab Command was established, primarily to attempt to co-ordinate Arab military policies in the Arab–Israeli conflict.

The League has contributed to the settlement of disputes on a number of occasions. Under the 1950 Treaty it is authorized to act in resolving disputes between member states and between members and non-members. Its attempts at conciliation have been reinforced several times by a collective peacekeeping force. In 1961, for example, a League force (largely composed of Saudi Arabian troops) took over from the British in deterring Iraq from attacking Kuwait. In 1976 an Arab Deterrent Force, under the League's auspices, was temporarily introduced into the complexities of the situation in the Lebanon. The Force was very largely made up of Syrian troops which remained in the country.

However, given the importance of oil and the continuation of intense local rivalries, there has been considerable skirmishing and client-seeking by outside powers. For almost a century, until the early 1970s, Britain was the principal military power in the Gulf. Despite its withdrawal from East of Suez, it still has bilateral understandings with a number of Gulf States, and continues to supply military assistance and military advisers. Increasingly, however, the area has become the object of the rival interests of the superpowers, both of which have sought and gained access to bases and facilities – the United States, for example, in Oman, and the Soviet Union in the Peoples Democratic Republic of Yemen.

It was against this background, and the rising force of Islamic

fundamentalism, that the Gulf Co-operation Council was established in 1981 by Bahrain, Kuwait, Qatar, Oman, Saudi Arabia and
the United Arab Emirates (UAE). The Council's purposes are
economic, political and military, for although defence co-operation
was not included within the original constitution, the summit
meeting which ratified it agreed to its introduction. The Council and
its members have either jointly or individually sought to use their
influence in the settlement of both the major disputes afflicting the
area. The Council (and the Arab League) supported the Fahd Plan in
the Arab–Israeli dispute, and the council has offered its good offices
in attempting to bring an end to the Iraq–Iran War.

The degree of defence co-operation among the member states of
the Council has varied. Although they have not been able to agree on
the creation of a joint Defence Council, they have held a number of
joint military exercises. The threat to shipping and oil supplies
arising from the Iraq–Iran War has posed particular problems and
has resulted in more intensive consultation and co-operation.

The Indian Ocean and the Pacific

While security issues have been discussed by the states of the Indian
Ocean, and most notably the question of establishing the area as a
nuclear-free zone, there are few organisations within the region
which have a security dimension. In the Indian Ocean, for example,
discussions between the Comoros, Madagascar, Mauritius and the
Seychelles have been limited to possible co-operation on economic,
social and cultural matters. However, further east, the Association of
South East Asian Nations (ASEAN) does have a security role.

ASEAN was established in 1967 by Indonesia, Malaysia, the
Philippines, Singapore and Thailand. Brunei became the sixth
member in 1984. (Papua-New Guinea has observer status.) Although,
under the original Bangkok Declaration, economic co-operation was
regarded as the primary objective, regional peace and security were,
and remain, of crucial significance. Indeed, the establishment of
ASEAN involved Malaysia's recognition by Indonesia after the
period of 'confrontation'. Moreover, in view of the war in Vietnam
and Cambodia, the growing deployment of naval units in the Pacific
and the Indian Ocean by the Soviet Union, and the uncertainties of
Chinese policies, security issues have frequently been to the fore
in ASEAN summit meetings. In 1971, for example, ASEAN leaders

called for the neutralisation of the area and its designation as a Zone of Peace.

Vietnam above all, notably its invasion of Cambodia and the massive flight of refugees from both countries, has continued to pose security as well as humanitarian problems for ASEAN. Following the Soviet acquisition of base facilities at Cam Ranh Bay in Vietnam, which extended Soviet capabilities in the region, the ASEAN members in 1976 signed a Treaty of Amity and Co-operation. Once again, although considerable attention was paid to economic issues, its 'prime purpose ... is political, stressing the co-ordination of policies so as to resist subversion, resolve disputes among the members and present a united front to the world'.[16]

While extending co-operation among themselves, all ASEAN member states except Indonesia have maintained close defence links with outside powers. The Philippines and Thailand have remained members of the Manila Pact, allying them to the United Kingdom and the United States as well as to Australia and New Zealand – the South East Asia Treaty Organisation, created by the Manila Pact, was not dismantled until 1977. Malaysia and Singapore are members of the Five Power Treaty Pact, and hence also allied to the United Kingdom, Australia and New Zealand. Finally, Brunei has also maintained an agreement with the United Kingdom which includes the continuation of a base for a Gurkha battalion.

The micro-states of the Pacific are individually incapable either of defending themselves from threats on the smallest scale, or of protecting their marine resources. They have, however, taken various steps to concert on a regional basis, primarily through the South Pacific Commission and the South Pacific Forum (see Annex C). The former is a non-political body chiefly concerned with training and aid programmes in the development and cultural fields. Its membership includes France, the United Kingdom and the United States as well as the countries and territories of the South Pacific (the micro-states, Australia and New Zealand).

Although the Pacific Commission is not directly concerned with political and strategic questions, indirectly it performs two useful security functions. Firstly, it lessens the isolation of these widely dispersed archipelagos in the South Pacific, forging both personal links between leading citizens and links in communications which lessen their vulnerability to attack; secondly, by helping to reduce the social and economic problems with which micro-states contend, it also reduces potential grounds for political instability.

The South Pacific Forum, on the other hand, is primarily a political organisation, comprising the Heads of Government of independent and self-governing states of the South Pacific Region; i.e. including Australia and New Zealand, but excluding the United States, the United Kingdom and France. It meets at least annually, more often if necessary, at Heads of Government level and issues a Communiqué at the end of the meeting which indicates the preoccupations of the participants. The 1984 Communiqué indicated two main security concerns: the situation in New Caledonia and nuclear problems affecting the region.

In addition to regional safeguards, the security of micro-states in the Pacific is underwritten by bilateral arrangements, and, although this is not always welcomed, by a strong American defence capability, the ANZUS Treaty and the American–Japanese alliance. (See Annex C.)

Bilateral Relations

Since nearly all micro-states are former territories of European empires, the links, especially any defence links, which remain with the metropolitan power are of particular interest. In addition, the global defence and strategic interests of the two superpowers have serious implications for the security of micro-states. This chapter therefore concludes with a brief over-view of relations established by the United Kingdom, France, the United States and the Soviet Union.

United Kingdom

The United Kingdom has been faced with the security problems of micro-states on numerous occasions; the twenty-seven micro-states of the Commonwealth were, after all, formerly British colonies. Britain's remaining colonies, while few in number, have continued to demand attention and occasionally military intervention, the conflict in the Falklands in 1982 being the most significant in terms of scale and cost. In addition to the garrison that remains on the Falklands, Britain also maintains forces in the colonies of Gibraltar and Hong Kong, as well as in Cyprus, Belize and Brunei. The two sovereign bases in Cyprus are significant not only in terms of NATO and European security, but also for peacekeeping operations both in

Cyprus itself and in the Lebanon. The small British force in Gibraltar is maintained primarily in the context of the Spanish territorial claim. Some 1,800 troops are maintained in Belize to deter Guatemala from following up its territorial claims with force. A Gurkha battalion continues to be deployed in support of Brunei. The Commonwealth framework has influenced British policy in many ways. The very success of the evolution of the Commonwealth from the British Empire contributed to Britain's estimation of itself as a global power second only to the United States in its continuing responsibilities. While that attitude gradually declined in the 1960s and 1970s in the face of Britain's own problems of economic adjustment, its legacy was clear in arrangements such as those of the Five Power Treaty. British troops were finally withdrawn from Malaysia in 1976 when Australia and New Zealand took on a larger share of the 'police' role. Moreover, while the ties binding Commonwealth countries together may have loosened, they have been conspicuous in persistently recalling Britain's attention to the remaining problems of Empire, most notably in Southern Africa. In the case of Zimbabwe, however, it was significant for both the United Kingdom and the Commonwealth that although British troops made up the bulk of the force, and were retained to weld regular and guerrilla forces into a single army, it was a Commonwealth Monitoring Force which oversaw the establishment of full independence. In Uganda, too, British help was given as part of a Commonwealth team to assist Ugandan forces after the overthrow of Idi Amin.

Britain's formal and less formal defence commitments extend beyond the Commonwealth. Despite the 1967 decision to withdraw from East of Suez, Britain remains, for example, a signatory of the Manila Pact. In the Gulf, too, Britain retains important links. Indeed its position was such that in 1978 its assistance was sought to quell internal disturbances in the United Arab Emirates. A number of states in the area continue to have arrangements with the United Kingdom and there are British forces on loan in both Kuwait and Oman. Visits to Gulf States, by the Queen in 1979 and Mrs Thatcher in 1981, were designed in part to reaffirm Britain's continued commitments as well as, in the Prime Minister's case, to open up further trading opportunities. The overall policy adopted by Mrs Thatcher's Government towards security in the Third World was most clearly summed up in the *1984 Statement on the Defence Estimates*. British efforts were to concentrate on three levels:

the provision of military assistance and training to countries of importance to Western interests which request our help; periodic deployment of British forces, including the deployment of naval task force groups and exercises ... and maintenance of a capability to intervene, either to protect our national interests or, with our allies, and in response to a request for help, those of the West as a whole.[17]

In all, the United Kingdom has agreements covering military training advice and assistance with some thirty countries, including eleven micro-states. Naval forces take part in exercises in the Indian and Pacific Oceans and two frigates have been on more permanent patrol in the Indian Ocean. One guardship has been maintained in the Caribbean. The capacity to intervene if necessary has also been expanded with the creation of a small military force for use in emergencies. Its role has been viewed very much as a contribution to a larger force made up of units from other allies and partners. Mrs Thatcher, for example, welcomed the American proposal for a Rapid Deployment Force with the words:

I made it clear that if such a force was created, the United Kingdom would be ready to contribute to it in the same way as, in conjunction with the United States and France, we had already stationed naval units in the Gulf in response to the situation in the Iran–Iraq War.[18]

Apart from its action over the Falkland Islands, which as a dependent territory was a direct British responsibility, the British Government has placed the emphasis on joint action. The consequences of unilateral action have increasingly been regarded as unacceptably costly in both economic and political terms. There has, therefore, been a tendency, accelerated by the 1967 East of Suez decision, to reduce purely British commitments, particularly where these were no longer relevant to British strategic interests in a post-imperial world. In some instances, responsibilities have been passed to the United States, as in the provision of Diego Garcia as a base. In others, commitments have been retained reluctantly on almost an *ad hoc* basis. On Belize, for example, British troops are to remain for an 'appropriate period' because of the threat posed by the irredentist claims of Guatemala. In this, as in several other instances, Britain has chosen to act in close consultation with the Commonwealth.

In general, the concept of burden sharing is considered more attractive.

Such an approach inevitably places a considerable premium on the like-mindedness of those with whom the burden is to be shared, most notably with the United States. Despite a residual 'special relationship', relations between Britain and the United States have periodically been strained over Third World issues. It has, for example, been suggested that 'The minimum lesson of post-war history is that neither Europe nor America will automatically accept the other's view of issues beyond Europe.'.[19] Grenada is one example where strong differences existed between Britain and many of its Commonwealth and European partners on the one hand, and the United States on the other, over the latter's armed intervention in Grenada's internal affairs. Such differences have often been caused by divergent views over the causes of conflict in the Third World and the extent and significance of Soviet involvement. Whereas American administrations have tended to view the Soviet Union as responsible for, or at least involved in, most Third World disputes, the United Kingdom has not. As Sir Geoffrey Howe, the British Foreign Secretary, put it in an article in the influential journal, *Foreign Affairs*:

> The world threat posed by the Soviet Union, its allies and its clients has become clearer than ever. So has the complexity of the sources of instability; the variety of local factors involved and the difficulties of calculating the best Western response in each instance.[20]

There have, in addition, been differences over the resources to be devoted in dealing with such conflicts. This issue has been a frequent cause of dissension, with American critics averring that Europe was shirking its defence responsibilities (although there has been an alternative theme which complains that Europe exploits its responsibilities in order to win commercial advantages). In the same *Foreign Affairs* article, Sir Geoffrey Howe took considerable pains to rebut such charges and to point out what Europe had already done, and what Europe had to offer in terms of 'capacity – and will – for rapid military intervention, whether as a component of internal peace-keeping or in response to more specific needs and requests'.[21]

France

It was suggested earlier that many states in Africa have looked for bilateral guarantees of their security in addition to, or in the absence of, regional defence arrangements. This has been particularly the case with the former French dependencies, which, to a much greater extent than the former British territories, have signed bilateral defence agreements with their former imperial ruler. These agreements are of two kinds: those providing for military aid and assistance which now number twenty-five, and those which provide for French intervention if the local government so requests and the French government agrees. There is, in these latter agreements, no automaticity in the French reaction; so the formal terms of such agreements are not necessarily a good guide to what will actually happen, although as one commentator concluded, 'in reality these agreements were signed when the decision to intervene had already been made'.[22] There are now eight such defence agreements, two of which are with micro-states, the Comoros (1973, renewed 1978) and Djibouti (since 1977). There are also reports of an 'understanding' rather than an agreement between France and the Seychelles.

France currently maintains some 16,500 of its military personnel overseas on security duties and four inter-service overseas commands: (i) Antilles–Guyana, (ii) South Indian Ocean, (iii) New Caledonia and (iv) Polynesia, and two naval commands, one in the Indian Ocean and the other in the Pacific. Their primary purpose is to provide security and support for France's remaining overseas territories. However, they are also available, and have indeed been used, as an adjunct to French diplomacy. The scale of the French presence in Djibouti (with over 3,250 men with mixed facilities) may be larger than elsewhere (in Western or Central Africa for example) but that is because it has a significant Middle East role as well as an African one. In addition, France has created and continues to develop a *Force d'Action Rapide* which is designed to play a role overseas as well as in Europe.

The willingness of French governments to intervene, especially in Africa – in Chad, in the Central African Republic or Zaire – has not always been accepted uncritically, either in France or elsewhere. French ministers, themselves, have sometimes regretted the inability of African governments to resolve their own disputes without relying on French guarantees of assistance.[23] Successive governments, including that of M. Mitterrand, have disclaimed the role of Africa's policeman although it has been suggested that when one considers President Mitterrand's trips to Africa, the obvious concern to reassure the French-speaking states and the omnipresence of the theme of security, one cannot help wondering whether the categorical assertion of the socialist government that, 'There will be no more new Kolwezis' will always be compatible with the renewed commitments to contribute to the security of the African states.[24]

After all, as one former (Gaullist) minister put it:

It is not possible that a few gunmen be left free to capture at any time any Presidential palace, and it is precisely because such a menace was foreseen that the new African States have concluded with France agreements to protect themselves against such risks.[25]

None the less it has been a characteristic of French interventions that they have occurred in an *ad hoc* way, largely outside the purview of traditional diplomatic channels and at the behest and direct authorisation of the French President, although within the legal framework of a defence agreement. It has also been the case that most interventions have been small-scale and of short duration. They have therefore been relatively inexpensive for France in financial terms, yet (the problems of Chad notwithstanding) they have achieved considerable dividends in terms of the local state's sense of security and, indeed, for French interests.

The strategic interests involved in French policy were well summed up by President Giscard d'Estaing when, in answer to critics, he declared:

Africa is a continent from where, traditionally, a certain number of raw materials come, and with which we have very close links, and Africa, even if remote for many Frenchmen, is the continent neighbouring ours. So that a change in the political situation in Africa, a general situation of insecurity and subversion in Africa, would have consequences for France and Europe.[26]

Economically, therefore, France has sought to retain as close relations as possible with its former colonies. Nearly all are members of the Franc zone. Bilateral ties have also been reinforced by multilateral ones, most notably those through association with the

European Community, first under the Yaoundé and later the Lomé Conventions.

There are also wider, less material links within the French *communauté*. Many of the older African leaders such as former President Senghor of Senegal or President Houphouet-Boigny of the Ivory Coast were prominent in French politics before independence. There remain a wide variety of cultural ties, which predispose the former colonies to look to France for continued support and France to intervene in their support. But another factor has also been involved: a sense of ambition which one observer summed up as follows:

> That ambition is a mixture of idealism and cynicism, of sense of duty and outright exploitation of the weaknesses of others, and corresponds to a desperate and somewhat successful attempt to refuse to adapt and yet to adapt at the same time, to the international system after 1945 and France's newly reduced international status.[27]

United States

A considerable degree of continuity in American policy has been re-established by the Reagan Administration after the period of uncertainty following the United States' withdrawal from Vietnam. Under the Nixon Doctrine, which was largely adhered to by President Carter, it was recognised that the impact of OPEC and the economic challenge of Japan and others had led to a diffusion of power in the international system. In these circumstances not all Third World conflicts were seen as necessarily involving American or the West's interests; many of the smaller disputes that broke out could be dealt with adequately by larger local powers such as Iran or Saudi Arabia. Revolution in Iran and the American hostages crisis, increased tension in the Gulf, and the Soviet invasion of Afghanistan, changed the situation radically. The Carter Doctrine on the use of military force in the Gulf was one response. The reassertion of American self-confidence and a resumed belief in America's global responsibilities under the Presidency of Mr Reagan are others.

To many in the Reagan Administration, *détente* is regarded as a fundamentally mistaken concept. So too were President Carter's efforts to 'reduce the centrality of strategic competition with Moscow in American foreign policy' in relation to Third World disputes.[28] As President Reagan himself declared when presenting his Caribbean Basin Initiative:

> if we do not act promptly and decisively in defence of freedom, new Cubas will arise from the ruins of today's conflicts. We will face more totalitarian regimes, more regimes tied militarily to the Soviet Union, more regimes exporting subversion . . .[29]

Given such a perception of the Soviet threat and the renewal of the domino theory, the need for stronger, more positive action has been a continuous theme of the Reagan Administration. In addition to the increases in the defence budget, there has been a re-affirmation of the utility of economic warfare and of force of arms, as well as frequent attempts to integrate defence policy more closely with foreign policy (although this has caused marked tension between the Secretaries of State and of Defence).

The return of East–West considerations to the predominant place in American thinking has had a number of important repercussions for many micro-states – as well as, of course, for its European allies and others. American action in Grenada is an obvious example (see Annex B). The United States has also shown itself willing to intervene militarily – both covertly and overtly – elsewhere in the region. In 1983 it stepped up its support for Belize, especially in terms of economic aid. This included funds specifically geared to internal security concerns and undertakings; some $10 million out of a total of $17.8 million of American bilateral economic aid came under the heading of Security Supporting Assistance in 1983.[30] For the countries of the Eastern Caribbean, some $20 million in 1982 and $35 million in 1983 also came under the Security Supporting Assistance heading (the respective totals for economic aid being $70 and $60 millions).

Events in the Middle East were particularly influential in the American re-assessment of its global role. The establishment of the Rapid Deployment Force (RDF) by President Carter and its development under President Reagan has had a number of important repercussions since, as the force has been built up, new bases and facilities have been required. Oman, to the concern of many of its Gulf partners, has become an important link in this new American strategy. In 1981, President Reagan pledged $200 million over three years to develop port and air facilities in return for the right to stockpile supplies for possible use by the RDF. Bahrain has also allowed its facilities to be used by the United States. The development of facilities in the Middle East complemented the already growing American presence in the Indian Ocean. The Soviet invasion of Afghanistan in some respects only reinforced an existing American anxiety caused by events in Southern Asia (notably the Indian–Pakistani War over Bangladesh) and especially by the expansion of the Soviet navy in the Indian Ocean. Of foremost importance to the United States has been the base at Diego Garcia, leased from the United Kingdom. Britain had detached Diego Garcia from a pre-independent Mauritius in 1965. It is still claimed by the Mauritians, who have the support of the rest of the OAU (and, predictably, that of the Soviet Union).[31] In the Pacific, too, the maintenance or acquisition of bases and facilities has grown in significance, with sometimes difficult negotiations over existing bases, as in the case of Palau, and problems over nuclear warships. (See Annex C.)

In Africa, the American position has been complicated by its policies towards South Africa, where strategic considerations have often appeared to override others, and over the issue of Namibia. The linkage between Namibian independence and the withdrawal of Cuban troops from Angola has alienated many, not only in Africa but also among America's fellow members of the Contact Group of Western States which are engaged in negotiating a settlement of the issue. However, from the outset, the Reagan Administration took an increasing interest in the relationship between military and development assistance. As the then Secretary of State, Alexander Haig, declared: 'Security and development assistance should be seen in the context of the international challenges that confront the United States'.[32] To this end, Third World votes at the United Nations were computerised in order to take them into account when considering aid requests.[33] The link between security and development issues in Africa was made even more clearly by Chester Crocker, who remarked:

> This does not mean that Washington should seek to create a new Pax Americana in the region, or that it should respond reflexively to each Soviet move. But the United States should shed its complex about arms sales, military training and political support for friendly governments facing severe security questions. Security

assistance should be directed towards strengthening the founda-
tions for stability and growth in Africa's more decent, durable and
(let's face it) helpful political systems.[34]

To a considerable extent this line of reasoning has been adopted
and implemented. The Presidential Directive of July 1981 declared:
'The United States views the transfer of conventional arms and other
defence articles as an essential element of its global defense posture
and an indispensable component of its foreign policy'.[35] Most of the
restrictions imposed by the Carter Administration on the sale of
armaments, including those relating to a state's human rights record,
were lifted. By 1984 the United States had clearly regained its position
ahead of the Soviet Union and France as the world's leading arms
supplier. Many micro-states have been able to benefit from this
willingness to extend military assistance and Security Supporting
Assistance (at the discretion of the American Secretary of State).
Botswana is one such recipient.

Some micro-states have successfully exploited their potential value
to the United States, or at least their loss to the Soviet Union. In
Africa, for example, Cape Verde and Guinea-Bissau have both
received military assistance in addition to economic and food aid,
even if the amounts are exceedingly small (less than $50,000 each in
military assistance in 1982 and 1983).[36]

Yet despite the emphasis on the strategic interest and the almost
Dulles-like rhetoric which sometimes supports it, there are also
certain constraints on American action, even in relation to micro-
states. The very extent of the Soviet Union's strength is both a
stimulus to, and a constraint on, American action. Philip Windsor
has suggested that both superpowers 'find themselves locked into a
kind of perpetual claim to a historical task historically justified in
terms of the present and the future, and in which the roles of both are
mutually reinforcing'.[37]

USSR

Soviet involvement in the Third World has grown steadily since the
mid-1950s. An important factor in this involvement has been the
Soviet Union's policy on arms transfers. In 1982 SIPRI suggested
that: 'Arms transfers play a far greater role than economic aid in
trade in this respect; it is the only area in which they [the Soviet

Union] have successfully rivalled the West'.[38] In 1984 Soviet arms exports were estimated by NATO to amount to some 40 per cent of its total exports to developing countries.[39] The Soviet Union has traditionally charged low prices and has offered favourable credit terms, sometimes even barter arrangements, although there have been increasing pressures for hard currency transactions. A number of micro-states have been among the 30 or so countries which, according to SIPRI, have received Soviet arms, including Botswana, Guyana and the Seychelles. However, the Soviet Union's position as the world's leading arms exporter was only a temporary one; it coincided with the imposition of restrictions on American exports introduced by the Carter Administration.

The Soviet Union has also provided logistical and other support, especially to Cuban forces in Africa, although, Afghanistan aside, it has rarely used its own troops in combat. It has, however, built up considerable capacity to intervene through the expansion of the Soviet Navy. Since the 1970s, the Navy has been present in the Atlantic, Indian and Pacific Oceans, the Caribbean and the Mediterranean. Such efforts to build up power and influence are in many ways predictable. The search for 'blue water' ports or facilities has been a consistent thread of modern Russian history. Soviet aspirations to global power have been reinforced by an historic expectation that the world will ultimately become Marxist. Influential though such inevitability has been, it is also clear that: 'Despite the wisdom and caution that allegedly comes with age, the Soviet leaders make the most of opportunities arising on the world stage and this includes giving a push to history now and again'.[40]

The process of decolonisation has been pregnant with opportunities. As Mr Khrushchev declared in 1956:

The present disintegration of the imperial colonial system is a post-war development of world-historical significance... The new period in world history, predicted by Lenin, when peoples of the East would play an active part in deciding the destinies of the entire world... has arrived... Today they need not go begging to their former oppressors for modern equipment. They can get it in the socialist countries, free from any political or military obligations.[41]

Few micro-states or other developing countries have availed themselves of the Soviet offer, at least on an exclusive basis; perhaps they are unconvinced of the absence of political ramifications. Given its ideological framework, Soviet policy in the Third World has, for the most part, been opportunist. In sub-Saharan Africa, for example, its initial involvement arose when it stepped into the breach in Guinea in 1959 after the French withdrew, lock, stock and barrel. It was also prepared to become heavily engaged in the more long-drawn out process in which former Portuguese colonies gained their independence: the prospect of co-operating with national liberation movements led by Marxist-orientated parties was regarded as especially promising. However, while Soviet support and Cuban troops continue to play a highly significant role in Angola, elsewhere in Lusophone Africa, in Cape Verde, Guinea-Bissau and São Tomé, Soviet activity has been of lesser importance. Links with these micro-states remain, but all three have sought to balance Soviet influence by encouraging or reverting to Western contacts. Guinea-Bissau's aid and trade links continue to be predominantly with the West and especially with Portugal. Similarly with Cape Verde where, in addition, the United States has become one of the largest aid donors. In São Tomé, despite the traffic of Angolan and Cuban troops and Soviet advisers, the government has refused to allow the Soviet Union to establish a naval base.

The search for naval bases has inevitably grown in importance with the expansion of the Soviet Navy. The tasks of the Navy have been argued as two-fold: 'one directly involving the security of the USSR itself and its maritime frontiers and the other involving Soviet state interests in the seas and in the Third World'.[42] The role of sea-power in the defence of the Soviet Union itself became of special significance in the late 1950s. The build-up of naval strength in the Pacific, for example, was 'stimulated by the USSR's break with China and accelerated by the Sino–US rapprochement and fears of an anti-Soviet US–China–Japan security coalition'.[43] Siberia, especially, with its vast resources, appeared increasingly vulnerable.

The second task allotted to the Soviet Navy has been of particular relevance to micro-states. Soviet state interests in the seas now include the protection of the greatly expanded Soviet merchant and fishing fleets and interests in the exploitation of the sea-bed. In *The Sea Power of the State*, Admiral Gorshkov, Commander-in-Chief of the Soviet Navy, discussed the auxiliary role of the Soviet merchant and fishing fleets as a constituent part of Soviet sea power.[44] He noted that between 1960 and 1974 it had moved from twelfth to sixth place in the tonnage of the world merchant marine, and that 'Yearly its stock is being replenished by a large number of new ships of the most varied types and categories. In 1973 the fleet received over 80 ships with a total carrying capacity of over 700,000 tons and in 1974 its stock increased further by almost 90 ships with a capacity of some 900,000 tons.' In another passage he pointed out that experience of two World Wars showed that fishing vessels were widely used as 'part of the navy for solving auxiliary and combat tasks chiefly in the sphere of defence and protection of ports and areas housing naval bases'. The Soviet fishing fleet had suffered severe losses in the Second World War but it had since been rebuilt and expanded so that 'in number of vessels of different functions it now occupies first place among the major fishing fleets of the world'.

The Admiral pointed out that in addition to fishing, the fleet undertook 'wide oceanographic, meteorological and other explorations of the oceanic sphere'. He claimed that 'now in the remotest areas of the world ocean one can meet fishing vessels flying our flag'. He did not mention intelligence gathering among the activities of the fishing fleet. However, some micro-states believe this does occur. Marshall Islanders, for instance, have commented that they always know when an American missile exercise is about to take place because a Soviet fishing vessel comes close in-shore.

Soviet interest in the Third World, and especially in those countries with potentially useful port facilities, has led a leading American expert to conclude that: 'showing-the-flag increased sharply after 1968, but since 1972 the task has assumed new dimensions, extending to port clearance and minesweeping, and to providing support for revolutionary forces or to regimes threatened by secessionist elements'.[45] Such measures have not always been successful in winning new bases as such. Cuba continues to be the Soviet Union's mainstay in the Caribbean. Relations with the micro-states in the area, such as Grenada, Guyana or Suriname have either been interrupted or have at least fluctuated wildly. Latin America has, however, become of importance as a growing market for Soviet arms. In West Africa, Guinea, to which the Soviet Union despatched gunboats in 1960 to counter a Portuguese incursion, provided a major base during the 1970s. Dahlak off the Ethiopian coast replaced Berbera as a major East African–Indian Ocean base in 1977 when support was switched from Somalia to Ethiopia. Soviet naval forces also use Aden. Vietnam provides major bases for the Soviet Pacific fleet, including that at Cam Ranh Bay. However, increased deployment in the Indian Ocean in the wake of the American buildup of forces after the Iran hostages crisis and the Soviet Union's own invasion of Afghanistan has heightened the importance of bases, or at least of safe deep water anchorages. No new bases have been established in any of the micro-states of the region. The Maldives Government, for example, refused a Soviet offer to lease the former British base of Gan in 1977. However, links between the Soviet Union and North Korea with the Seychelles have increased markedly in recent years. Anchorages off the Seychelles continue to be used, as are those off Diego Garcia, the Maldives and Mauritius. In the Pacific, some commentators have noted increased Soviet and Cuban influence in Vanuatu,[46] while Soviet approaches were also reported by Fiji and Tonga. The former then reached agreement with the United States on the use of port facilities in Suva and on American economic aid. So far the Soviet Union has not secured a base in the South Pacific.

Notes

1. *The Republic of Andorra* is a co-principality under the joint suzerainty of France and Spain. It has a total area of 465 sq. km. (190 sq. miles) and a population (in 1983) of 39,940. *The Principality of Monaco* originated as a buffer state between France, Savoy and Genoa; since the cession of Savoy and Nice to France by Italy in 1860 it has been an enclave in French territory. Monegasque relations with France are based on conventions of neighbourhood and administrative assistance. The area of Monaco is 190 hectares, or 467 acres, and the population (in 1980) was 28,000. *The Republic of San Marino* originated as a buffer state between the duchy of Urbino and the lordship of Rimini. Its relations with Italy, whose territory completely surrounds it, are based on a treaty of friendship and co-operation concluded in 1962, which includes a *de facto* customs union. San Marino is land-locked, though only 20 km from the Adriatic, its area is 61.19 sq. km (24.1 sq. miles) and the population (in 1981) was 21,622, though some 20,000 citizens were living abroad. *The Principality of Liechtenstein* originated as a buffer state between Austria and Switzerland, and achieved its present boundaries in the early fifteenth century. In 1923 it entered a customs union with Switzerland whereby it entrusted Switzerland with its representation abroad. It has a total area of 160 sq. km (61.8 sq. miles) and a population (in 1982) of 26,380.
2. League of Nations, 1st Assembly, *Plenary Meetings, Annex C*, p. 667.
3. As an example of the change in tempo which had taken place in a comparatively short period, it is useful to recall that a UN Visiting

Mission to Tanganyika in 1954 daringly recommended 1974 as a 'target date' for independence. In fact, Britain granted independence in 1961 following bilateral negotiations.

4. S/9836, Annexes I and II (1970). See also Gunter, 'Whatever Happened to the United Nations Ministates Problem?', *Americal Journal of International Law*, 1977, p. 110.
5. Ibid., p. 122 and S/AC. 16/Conf. Room Paper 8 (1971).
6. See Blair, *The Mini State Dilemma*, Carnegie Endowment for International Peace, Occasional Paper No. 6, 1968, pp. 6–9 and pp. 52–56, and Bowett, *The Law of International Institutions*, 3rd edn, Stevens, 1975, p. 108.
7. Ian Brownlie, *African Boundaries: A Legal and Diplomatic Encyclopaedia*, C. Hurst & Co., for the RIIA, 1979.
8. The United Nations Peacekeeping System which evolved in its place is described in Chapter 5 of this study.
9. Nehru, for instance, in his speech to the Political Committee on 22 April, after commending the principle of 'peaceful co-existence', denounced as 'degrading' the attempt to divide Asian and African countries into pro or anti communists, 'devoid of any positive position'. He criticised defence pacts in the following terms: 'I submit to you, every pact has brought insecurity and not security to the countries which have entered into them. They have brought the danger of atomic bombs and the rest of it nearer to them than would have been the case otherwise. They have not added to the strength of any country, I submit, which it had singly. It may have produced some idea of security, but it is a false security. It is a bad thing for any country thus to be lulled into security.'
10. *The Goa Declaration on International Security*, Commonwealth Secretariat, London, 1983.
11. See, for example, Gordon Connell-Smith, 'The Crisis in Central America: President Reagan's Options', *World Today*, October 1983.
12. Berhanykun Andemicael and Davidson Nicol, 'The OAU: Primacy in Seeking African Solutions within the UN Charter' in Y. El-Ayouty and I.W. Zartman (eds), *The OAU After Twenty Years*, Praeger, New York, 1984, p. 115.
13. Peter Mangold, 'Shaba I and Shaba II', *Survival*, May/June 1979.
14. Bukar Bukarambe, 'The Role and Impact of the OAU in the Management of African Conflicts', *Survival*, March/April 1983, p. 55.
15. See Julius Emeka Okolo, 'Securing West Africa: the ECOWAS Defence Pact', *World Today*, May 1983.
16. Stuart Drummond, 'Fifteen Years of ASEAN', *Journal of Common Market Studies*, June 1982, Vol. XX, No. 4, p. 315.
17. HMSO Cmnd 9227–1, p. 29.
18. See Geoffrey Edwards, 'UK and the Middle East' in D. Allen and A. Pijpers, *European Political Cooperation and the Middle East*, Martinus Nijhoff, The Hague, 1984.

50   *Micro-States and the International System*

19. Gregory Treverton, 'Defence Beyond Europe', *Survival*, September/October 1983, p. 217.
20. Sir Geoffrey Howe, 'The European Pillar', *Foreign Affairs*, Winter 1984/5, p. 335.
21. Ibid., p. 339.
22. Dominique Moisi, 'Intervention in French Foreign Policy' in Hedley Bull (ed.), *Intervention in World Politics*, Oxford University Press, Oxford, 1984, p. 72.
23. See John Chipman, 'France, Libya and Chad', *World Today*, October 1983.
24. Marie-Claude Smouts, 'The External Policy of François Mitterrand', *International Affairs*, Spring 1983, Vol. 59, No. 2, p. 166.
25. Moisi, op. cit., p. 73.
26. *Observer*, 17 April 1977, quoted by Mangold, op. cit., p. 110.
27. Moisi, op. cit., p. 69.
28. See Jeane Kirkpatrick, 'Dictatorships and Double Standards', *Commentary*, Vol. 68, No. 5, 1979.
29. Robert Pastor, 'Sinking in the Caribbean Basin', *Foreign Affairs*, Summer 1982, p. 1042.
30. *United States Overseas Loans and Grants Assistance for International Organizations, 1945–83*.
31. See Chapter 3, note 30.
32. *The Guardian*, 21 October 1981.
33. Seymour Maxwell Finger, 'The Reagan-Kirkpatrick Policies at the United Nations', *Foreign Affairs*, Winter 1983/4.
34. *International Herald Tribune*, 24 October 1979.
35. Quoted in SIPRI, *World Armaments & Disarmament, SIPRI Yearbook 1982*, Taylor & Francis, p. 179.
36. *US Grants and Loans*, op. cit.
37. Philip Windsor, 'Super Power Intervention' in Hedley Bull (ed.), op. cit., p. 58.
38. SIPRI, *World Armaments & Disarmament; SIPRI Yearbook 1982*, p. 187.
39. *Neue Zuercher Zeitung* (Zurich), 15/16 April 1984.
40. Walter Laqueur, 'United States–Soviet Relations', *Foreign Affairs*, 1984, Vol. 62, No. 3.
41. Quoted in Bruce D. Porter, *The USSR in Third World Conflicts*, Oxford University Press, Oxford, 1984, pp. 17–18.
42. Admiral Gorshkov quoted indirectly in C.G. Jacobsen, *Soviet Strategic Initiatives*, Praeger, 1979, p. 16.
43. Peter Polomka, 'The Security of the Western Pacific: the Price of Burden-sharing', *Survival*, January/February, 1984.
44. S.G. Gorshkov, *The Sea Power of the State*, Pergamon Press, Oxford, 1979.
45. M. McGwire, 'Soviet Naval Doctrine and Strategy' in Derek Leebaert (ed.), *Soviet Military Thinking*, George Allen & Unwin, 1981, p. 165.
46. *Sunday Times*, 30 December 1984, and 6 January 1985.

3 Micro-States and International Law

There are no special rules of international law governing the nature, status or relations of micro-states, still less binding principles defining what is meant by such a term. Nevertheless, certain legal norms are of particular relevance to the micro-states. For example, the principles relating to intervention are of especial concern, as the Grenada episode has emphasised. Other legal problems are also worthy of note.

By reason of their small human and environmental resource base, micro-states are of necessity rather more sensitive to external pressure than many other states and are ill-equipped to cope with the rigours of life within the international community. Paradoxically, these and other factors have not discouraged the governments of micro-states from seeking independence and membership in international organisations, as seen in Chapter 2. They reason that the international environment, with its stress on statehood and community of interest, might be more protective than isolation.

Statehood

The traditional criteria of statehood in international law have specified the need for a permanent population, a defined territory, a government and the capacity to enter into relations with other states (or independence).[1] The problems that particularly affect micro-states here concern population and independence. There is no prescribed minimum for the population requirement; the cases of Nauru (population 7,000, independent and prosperous but not a member of the United Nations) and Tuvalu (population 7,500) demonstrate that statehood can be accepted with low numbers of inhabitants. It is unclear, however, how far this can be taken; many remaining dependencies have populations of less than 7,000. Paucity of resources may theoretically affect the criterion of independence, but United Nations practice is instructive in its analysis of such criteria in the light of the principle of self-determination as set out in the Charter (article 1 (2)). In practice, the necessity for an effective government has been lowered (as can be seen, for example, in the case of Guinea-Bissau), while self-determination as an additional criterion of statehood has been increasingly stressed.[2] This was important in the cases of Rhodesia and the Bantustans. United Nations' practice has also shown clearly that size and resource levels do not affect the realisation of the right to self-determination, as can be seen, for example, in General Assembly Resolution 36/47 on the American Virgin Islands. Thus the way has been opened for the large number of Pacific and Caribbean micro-states to achieve independence and statehood.

Independence, however, is not the only option in asserting self-determination. General Assembly resolution 1541 (XV) emphasised that the right may also be validly expressed by free association with an independent state or by integration with an independent state. The acceptance of the 'Commonwealth' (i.e. political union) arrangement made by the United States with Puerto Rico and the association of the Cook Islands and Niue with New Zealand demonstrate this, as does the United Nations' approval of the integration of Greenland with Denmark and of Alaska and Hawaii with the United States.[3]

But it is true to say that the United Nations tends to regard independence as the norm and to scrutinise the other options more carefully. For example, in the case of the eleven Trusteeship Territories established after the Second World War, three opted for integration with an independent State: British Togoland (integrated with the Gold Coast to become the independent State of Ghana); British Cameroons (Southern British Cameroons integrated with French Cameroons as the independent United Republic of Cameroons and Northern British Cameroons integrated with independent Nigeria); and Australian-administered New Guinea (integrated with the Australian Dependent Territory of Papua to become the independent State of Papua New Guinea). In all three cases the wishes of the populations concerned were ascertained by plebiscites, observed and organised by the United Nations, before the termination of the Trusteeship Agreement was approved by the General Assembly.

More recently, the decisions of the four entities within the last remaining United Nations Trust Territory (the Trust Territory of the Pacific Islands) to opt respectively for a 'Commonwealth' status in political union with the United States (Northern Marianas) and 'Free Association' with the United States (the Marshall Islands, the Federated States of Micronesia and Palau) after termination of the Trusteeship Agreement, have also been the subject of a series of plebiscites under United Nations' observation. The future of Palau at the time of writing has still to be agreed. Thus, although both integration and 'free association' remain valid options,[4] statehood, irrespective of size and resources, has been and remains the favoured aim of the decolonisation process.

The Law of the Sea

The law of the sea has recently been the subject of a wide ranging and comprehensive international agreement, although one that has also proved controversial.[5] We note here briefly some of the provisions that are of special interest to micro-states. Island states will be particularly affected by developments affecting the Exclusive Economic Zone. This Zone, which may extend up to 200 nautical miles from the baselines from which the breadth of the territorial sea is measured,[6] is a recent phenomenon and reflects the need felt by many coastal states to assert their control over resources, such as fish, that were being exploited by the fleets of the economically powerful states.

Under article 56 of the 1982 treaty, coastal states possess sovereign rights in the Zone for the purpose of exploring and exploiting, conserving and managing the living or non-living natural resources of the waters superjacent to the sea-bed and of the sea-bed and its subsoil. Their sovereign rights also extend to activities for the economic exploitation and exploration of the Zone, such as the production of energy from the water, currents and winds. Under the Convention, coastal states have jurisdiction over, *inter alia*, the establishment and use of artificial islands, installations and structures, marine scientific research and the protection and preservation of the marine environment.

Such increased control clearly has considerable practical implications. The cost of asserting these sovereign rights and jurisdiction

will pose considerable problems for the states concerned, particularly in the case of small island states comprising scattered
archipelagos. The difficulties of policing such potentially vast areas
are discussed in Chapter 4. The increase in specific negotiated
arrangements will add to the burdens of micro-states, diplomatically
as well as in terms of finance and manpower.

As far as the law relating to international fisheries is concerned, it
is fair to conclude that a regime of some international regulation has
moved on to a situation of primarily coastal state control. This will
again impose considerable burdens on micro-states; their costs could
be greater than any revenue derived from fishing.

Similar problems arise in relation to the Continental Shelf. This
comprises the sea-bed and subsoil of the submarine areas extending
beyond the territorial sea. Coastal states possess sovereign rights over
the Shelf for the purpose of exploring and exploiting its natural
resources. One particular aspect of the Continental Shelf that
should be noted is article 82. This provides that where coastal states
exploit the mineral resources of the Shelf beyond 200 miles from the
base lines of the territorial sea, they are required to make payments or
contributions to the International Sea-bed Authority for distribution
to states party to the Convention, particularly the least developed and
land-locked.[7] However, in the case of developing states, there is a
significant exception: if the state is a net importer of the mineral
concerned, it is exempt from making any such payment or
contribution.

The deep sea-bed regime of the Convention, which declares that
the sea-bed beyond national jurisdiction and its resources are 'the
common heritage of mankind', is also designed to enable the benefits
of deep sea-bed exploitation to be distributed to states generally,
taking into consideration the particular interests of developing states
and their peoples who have not yet attained independence.

Economic Development

Micro-states are much involved in the evolution of new international
law provisions relating to economic development. Increasing
concern is manifest in this area and there is no doubt that it will
ultimately produce legal results. The right of states to permanent
sovereignty over natural resources is accepted, but there are problems
with regard to the issue of expropriation of foreign property and

compensation. The question of the transfer of technology to developing states has also been controversial.[8]

There has also been a wealth of state practice in the area of development assistance, both bilateral and multilateral. International institutions such as the International Bank for Reconstruction and Development and the UN Conference on Trade and Development[9] are also involved in wide-ranging discussions in this area. Such considerations have led to the argument that there is a right to development. These issues are undoubtedly on the international agenda and international law has an important role to play (see Chapter 5).

Intervention

The Context

International law operates within the framework of the dominant statist model. The framework principles of the system are those which protect sovereignty, legal equality, territorial integrity and the domestic jurisdiction of states. This, of course, presupposes that the state in question is a viable entity. The case of a micro-state, therefore, raises crucial questions for international society.

Nevertheless, the primary result of decolonisation has been the achievement of statehood rather than amalgamation, federation or association. This tendency to grant equal status in international law to increasing numbers of small territorial units has not only complicated international political processes but has also posed particular problems for micro-states in sensitive geographical locations. By virtue of the very fact of their vulnerability, the ease with which influence or pressure can be exerted upon them is increased and the threshold of intervention is thus lowered. This is particularly true of the case where a micro-state exists within the 'sphere of influence' of a much larger power. Concern for continued stability and the maintenance of the status quo in the area may lead the larger power to intervene, either directly or indirectly, in the micro-state. This kind of behaviour, of course, does not only affect micro-states, as post-war events in Eastern Europe, Latin America and Asia amply demonstrate.[10]

The heavy emphasis placed by international law upon statehood and its attributes and prerogatives is mitigated to some extent by certain general concerns or basic themes of international society. There are four that need mention here. First, there is the preservation of international peace and security. This posits the illegitimacy of aggression and argues for stability in international relations. Article 24 of the UN Charter provides the Security Council with the primary responsibility for maintaining international peace and security; in exercising this responsibility, the Council may adopt a series of binding measures varying from economic sanctions to the use of such force as may be necessary for that purpose. While the Security Council has taken action in this context, for example, the economic pressure upon Rhodesia and the armed response to North Korea's invasion of the South in 1950, it is important not to over-estimate the comprehensiveness of the cover in practice.

Self-determination is another basic theme of contemporary international society that has had an impact upon the statist concept. In practice, the right of self-determination in international law has centred around the decolonisation of the European empires, virtually ignoring the rights of other subject peoples. On colonial issues, the principle of non-intervention in matters of domestic jurisdiction (article 2 (7) of the Charter) has been so eroded that it is now rarely even advanced. Self-determination is based on the supremacy of the will of the inhabitants of the dependent territory in deciding its future political status.[11] The argument has been advanced that the right to self-determination applies beyond the colonial context, to independent countries. This is a controversial proposition within the present context of international law, and one that appears to have insufficient practice behind it. If it were to be accepted, then the question would arise as to the right of third parties to intervene to restore or place in power a government according to the freely expressed wishes of the people, irrespective of other legal considerations. Certainly this is of considerable political and ethical importance and may easily be justified in those terms, but as far as international law is concerned it would not appear consistent with current practice. Nevertheless, the principle of self-determination may be a useful supplemental guide in the context of legitimate interventions with regard, for instance, to the duration of the intervention concerned and the nature of the subsequent authority.

The third basic theme to be noted is that of the international protection of human rights.[12] Here again, the concept of non-intervention in matters of domestic jurisdiction, first breached in a human rights context on the issue of apartheid, has been modified so as to permit international concern, at least, with human rights matters. Many international instruments now exist which enshrine this and in many cases permit an offending state to be examined before an international tribunal.[13]

Finally, it is worth noting the development of international organisations, both global and regional, whose concerns range well beyond the maintenance of international peace and security, and which constitute the framework of an international welfare law of mutual existence and interdependence. Such organisations and bodies, for example, the International Labour Organisation, the UN Committee on Human Rights, the European Commission and the Court of Human Rights, in theory, and often in practice, mitigate the rigours of an unadorned statist emphasis.

This brief survey of some relevant background factors must end with a mention of the ambiguity and uncertainty surrounding the notion of intervention itself. Intervention in general can be taken to mean any external involvement in a matter regarded as being within the internal jurisdiction of a state. States are often unhappy about the domestic policies of other states, for example in the economic field, and many seek to apply pressure for their modification or change. Not every such modification can or should be regarded as illegal. In view of the range and variety of state intervention, it is often very difficult to place a marker and declare that from that point on, all external activity is illegitimate. State practice, and thus international law, is in a continual ferment; changes are taking place all the time. The rules and principles of international law are in constant flux. While foreign armed aggression is clearly illegal, what is the position with regard to economic boycotts or sanctions? To what extent are these acceptable? Practice is far from clear.

The Law Governing Resort to Force

After the First World War, attempts were made to regularise and restrict the permissible use of force in the context of a general international institution which would somehow seek to oversee the conduct of the world community. The Covenant of the League of Nations provided that members should submit disputes likely to lead to a rupture of relations to arbitration or judicial settlement or to enquiry by the Council of the League. Members were forbidden to resort to war until a cooling-off period of three months had elapsed after such a process, while the use of force against members complying with such an arbitral award or judicial decision or unanimous Council report was proscribed.[14] States party to the 1928 Kellogg–Briand Pact condemned recourse to war for the resolution of international controversies and renounced it as an instrument of national policy. Today, the essence of the doctrine of international law governing resort to force is contained in article 2 (4) of the UN Charter. This provides that all members 'shall refrain in their international relations from the threat or use of force against the territorial integrity or political independence of any state, or in any other manner inconsistent with the purposes of the United Nations'. This statement is regarded as a crucial binding principle in international law. It must be read in conjunction with article 51 of the Charter which declares that 'nothing in the present Charter shall impair the inherent right of individual or collective self-defence if an armed attack occurs against a member of the United Nations, until the Security Council has taken measures necessary to maintain international peace and security'.

The precise relationship between these provisions has occasioned considerable debate,[15] concerned to a large extent with the exhaustiveness or otherwise of the Charter in the legal regulation of force. Certain writers adopt a wide interpretation of article 2 (4) and a narrow view of article 51, while others are of the opinion that the scope of article 51 is relatively wide and that the phrase 'inherent right' in that article underlines the continuing applicability of the customary rules of international law relating to self-defence. These arguments are of tremendous importance; at stake is a state's right to resort to force when faced with threatening moves. Does a state, for example, have to wait for an actual armed attack to begin?[16]

Further disagreement concerns the meaning of the phrase 'against the territorial integrity or political independence of any State' in article 2 (4). Although these words were inserted at the San Francisco Conference in 1945 at the request of the small states, there are those who argue that any action involving force that has no serious or permanent effect upon the territorial integrity of a state would not contravene article 2 (4).[17] The legitimacy of humanitarian intervention is often predicated upon this kind of argument. It is also argued that the reference to the purposes of the United Nations in article 2 (4) would permit actions in favour of such purposes, such as self-determination and human rights, which might otherwise fall foul of the prohibition contained in the article. Such arguments have clear implications for the legitimacy of certain forms of intervention which are considered later. They also illustrate the uncertainty surrounding the subject.

International and Internal Armed Conflicts

Traditional law relating to third-party intervention in armed conflicts was founded upon the dichotomy of international and internal war. In the former case, the primary norms were exemplified in articles 2 (4) and 51 of the UN Charter and in the provisions relating to aggression.[18] In the latter case, the relevant rules depended upon the characterisation of the situation as one of rebellion, insurgency or belligerency. Rebellion was seen purely as an internal phenomenon involving only the state concerned and its domestic law. Insurgency existed as a legal phenomenon where third parties felt that the insurgent forces had succeeded to an extent that made it necessary to treat with them in order, for example, to protect nationals, or property, or trade in an area under their *de facto* control. Beyond this degree of 'internationalisation' of an internal conflict, international law remained very vague as to the consequences of such action, leaving this to the parties concerned. Belligerency was better defined and was deemed to occur where four factors were involved: firstly, the hostilities were of a general rather than local character; secondly, the insurgents occupied and administered a reasonable area of territory; thirdly, the laws governing the conduct of hostilities were applied, and, fourthly, it had become necessary for third parties to define their attitude to the situation. In such a case, the rules governing neutrality applied as did rules relating to rights and duties under the laws of war.[19]

In recent years, as the nature of internal warfare has altered, these categories have not been applied. Accordingly, international law has had to try to come to terms with these changes, particularly with the phenomenon of anti-colonial conflicts involving guerrilla operations. This has not occurred, however, and the law remains in a state of flux. What has happened as a result of these changes has been a shift in the frontier between international and domestic armed conflicts so as to include self-determination wars, or 'wars of liberation' within the former category.

This shift has come about largely as a result of the evolution of the right to self-determination of dependent peoples and the recognition of the dependent territory as separate from the metropolitan power.

Once this had been placed on the agenda, the question naturally arose as to the legitimacy of the use of force by the relevant parties. In the light of over two decades of international practice, it is clear that the use of force by the colonial or occupying power to suppress the right to self-determination of a people recognised as having that right would be illegitimate. Such a people would be entitled to use force in defence of that right.[20] Article 1 (4) of Protocol I Additional to the 1949 Geneva Convention, adopted in 1977 after much debate, provides that the concept of international armed conflicts includes 'armed conflicts in which peoples are fighting against colonial domination and alien occupation and against racist regimes in the exercise of their right to self-determination' as set out in the UN Charter and resolution 2625 (XXV). The effect of this is to make clear that legitimate struggles for self-determination fall within the concept of international relations of states and thus within article 2 (4) of the Charter and outside the domestic jurisdiction barrier of article 2 (7) of the Charter. This has implications for intervention which will be considered in the next section.

It is significant that the Protocol is not concerned exclusively with anti-colonial struggles which, by 1977, were becoming a thing of the past. It also covers resistance to 'alien occupation' and would thus be applicable to the Soviet occupation of Afghanistan, for example, and could also be raised in a Middle Eastern context.

The Lawfulness of Intervention

Although the general prohibition on intervention remains, and we are primarily considering here armed intervention in the internal affairs of other states, the legal situation is less clear where civil strife has broken out within a state. A variety of situations exist in which claims to intervene have arisen.

To Assist the Governmental Authority

Since international law does not prohibit civil wars as such, with the exception already noted of attempts to suppress the legitimate exercise of the right to self-determination, it would appear that third party assistance to a government would not be contrary to international norms. The traditional view is that a recognised government could be aided while rebels could not be until a recognition of belligerency had occurred.[21] Other views have been suggested. Wright, for example, has put forward the view that aid to either side in a conflict for control of authority structures is not permitted in international law once the outcome of the struggle has become uncertain.[22] However, practice suggests that some kinds of aid, for instance economic, technical and arms provision assistance, to existing governments faced with civil strife is acceptable. Whether this would extend to the despatch of troops is more dubious. It could also be argued that there is a form of 'cut-off' here; substantial aid to a government clearly in the throes of collapse might be considered intervention in a domestic situation that is on the point of resolution. There are considerable problems of definition here. Where a state intervenes in response to the prior intervention of another state on the side of the rebels, there seems little problem in accepting its legality; international law clearly forbids activities aimed at the overthrow of governing regimes of another state. Whether the converse can be argued, so that where third states are aiding established governments, other states may legitimately aid the rebels is more dubious. It will depend in significant measure upon whether the rebels have a right of self-determination.

In a number of cases, intervention to assist the government has been given pursuant to an existing treaty commitment, such as the British provision of troops to end mutinies in East Africa in 1964 and French action in Africa. These activities under pre-existing treaty arrangements are in general acceptable, although questions may be raised in civil war situations that have reached a certain level of intensity and in situations where the actions of the government may be deemed to be in suppression of the legitimate right of self-determination. Apart from these examples, assistance, including military assistance, to a recognised government under a treaty provision would be permissible. Of course, where the government has been overthrown and has thereby ceased to be the government, such assistance could not be given; the time element is therefore crucial.

Problems also arise where there are doubts as to who constitutes the valid authority in a given situation. In the former Belgian Congo in 1960, for example, the President and Prime Minister sought to dismiss each other and each sent a delegation to the United Nations requesting accreditation. In the event the United Nations itself made a determination.[23]

The United States intervened militarily in the small state of Grenada on 25 October 1983. It stated officially that its action was based on a combination of three legal grounds.[24] Two of these, regional peace-keeping and protection of nationals are referred to below in the relevant sections. The first legal ground noted was that the 'invitation of lawful governmental authority constitutes a recognised basis under international law for foreign states to provide requested assistance'. This would be unremarkable, except for the controversy surrounding the role of the Governor-General of Grenada, Sir Paul Scoon. According to the American statement, the Governor-General 'had used a confidential channel [on 28 October 1983] to transmit an appeal for action by the OECS [Organisation of Eastern Caribbean States] and other regional states to restore order on the island'. This appeal was accorded 'exceptional moral and legal weight' by the OECS and the United States.[25]

Doubt exists as to whether the Governor-General did issue an appeal for support and as to the date when this is said to have occurred. Be that as it may, the designation of the Governor-General as the requisite authority for such an invitation is itself problematic and depends upon a careful analysis both of the powers of a Governor-General and of the conditions in the country concerned at the time. Under the 1973 Grenadan constitution, the Governor-General could exercise certain powers vested in the Queen as the executive authority;[26] this appears to have remained the case even after the suspension of the constitution in 1979, although there is room for doubt.[27] In addition, the military coup of 12 October, the murder of former Prime Minister Bishop and others on 19 October, and the imposition of a 24-hour 'shoot on sight' curfew, inevitably disrupted the stability of the island. Whether the degree of instability was sufficient to activate the residual powers (if any) of the Governor-General is debatable.[28]

What can be said is that the episode highlights the problem of the constitution of authority when requesting external armed intervention. Significantly, the United States has been careful not to base its action solely on the alleged invitation of the Governor-General. The dangers of such an approach are clear.

Once an internal coup has been successful, the principle of effectiveness will operate, in conjunction with other relevant principles, to ensure that external armed intervention then becomes illegitimate. The establishment of a new government with effective control ends the acceptability of intervention.

Where, in effect, there is no clear authority, as in Angola in 1975, it is difficult to characterise the matter as rebellion against legitimate government. Accordingly, it is suggested that the basic principle of non-intervention should constitute the primary norm. This would enable the competing elements in the state to resolve the issue on their own in a manner consistent with the concept of self-determination, although in reality the exercise of violence may undermine this. Foreign intervention would thus be unlawful to either side, but prior external intervention could justify a counter-intervention.

To Allow for Self-Determination
Clearly, intervention by a third state in order to suppress the recognised right of self-determination in a particular territory would be unlawful. Many of South Africa's activities in Angola and Mozambique, and in pre-independent Rhodesia, may be so characterised. The crucial question is whether assistance to a people struggling to exercise self-determination would be legitimate and, if so, to what extent. A number of General Assembly resolutions have called for such assistance to be given.[29] While the principle of support is well established, and thus constitutes an exception to the general prohibition on external intervention, the extent of such permitted support is not clear. Diplomatic support and, presumably, medical and economic aid is clearly legitimate, but would the supply of arms or the provision of training and transit facilities be permissible? Indeed, could one go further and include the use of volunteer fighters or regular army units? Practice suggests elements of the former but not the latter, but the matter is very unclear.

One issue that is of considerable relevance to many micro-states is the question of the unit entitled to the exercise of the right of self-determination. More particularly, may the colonial power in the pre-independence period alter the extent of the territory over which the right is to be exercised?

This problem has arisen in a different form in the context of Diego Garcia and the Mauritian claims to sovereignty over that island. Diego Garcia was formerly administered together with Mauritius by the United Kingdom but was removed prior to independence in order to establish a military base leased by the United States.[30] The same issue has also arisen with regard to islands in the Malagasy channel and their removal from the Madagascan colonial unit by France some months before the former's independence in 1960.[31] Such action by the colonial powers runs counter to the established practice whereby the pre-independence colonial unit defines the territory over which self-determination is to be exercised. The essence of self-determination is the decolonisation of the colonially defined territory in accordance with the wishes of its people. A related issue in this context is the situation in Palau, part of the American administered Trust Territory of the Pacific Islands, which is currently facing pressure from the United States to accept nuclear substances on its territory as a condition of Free Association.[32]

Collective Security

By virtue of chapter VII of the UN Charter, the Security Council may, after determining the existence of a threat to the peace, breach of the peace, or act of aggression, impose mandatory sanctions (as against Rhodesia in 1966 and the arms embargo on South Africa in 1977) or, indeed, take action including the use of force to maintain or restore international peace and security. Collective security may also be exercised by a number of states acting together pursuant to a treaty, such as the NATO or Warsaw Pact alliances. Actions taken by regional agencies are looked at in the following section.

As Regional Peace-Keeping

Under article 53 of the UN Charter, the Security Council may utilise regional arrangements or agencies for enforcement action under its authority, but no such action may be taken under regional arrangements, or by regional agencies, without the Security Council's authorisation. No such authorisation was sought in the case of Grenada. (Since the Security Council voted 11 to 1 (United States) on 28 October deploring the armed intervention any such request would undoubtedly have been denied.)[33] However, article 52 of the Charter does provide for regional arrangements or agencies dealing with 'such matters relating to the maintenance of international peace and security as are appropriate for regional action, provided that such arrangements or agencies and their activities are consistent with the purposes and principles of the United Nations'. The United States has relied on this regional peacekeeping agreement as one of the three legal grounds for its action in Grenada.[34]

    Clearly, the line distinguishing regional peace-keeping from enforcement action has to be firmly held and an unambiguous appeal from the legitimate authority in the state concerned would appear to be of great importance. Article 52 also raises the question, important in the Grenada case, of the identity of the appropriate regional arrangement or agency. Only a cursory analysis will be attempted here, but it will suffice to underline the problems inherent in this kind of situation.

The Charter of the Organisation of American States emphatically underlines the inviolability of the territory of states (article 20) and the prohibition of any kind of intervention in the internal or external affairs of States (article 18). However, article 22 notes that 'measures adopted for the maintenance of peace and security in accordance with existing treaties ' do not violate articles 18 or 20, and article 28 notes that:

> if the inviolability or the integrity of the territory or the sovereignty or political independence of any American State should be affected by an armed attack, or by an act of aggression that is not an armed attack, or by an extra-continental conflict, or by a conflict between two or more American States, or by any other act or situation that might endanger the peace of America, the American States, in furtherance of the principles of continental solidarity or collective self-defence, shall apply the measures and procedures established in the special treaties on the subject.

Thus, the question arises as to whether the appropriate 'existing treaties' or 'special treaties' existed in the case of Grenada. The United States holds the view that the 1981 treaty establishing the Organisation of Eastern Caribbean States (OECS) functions as the requisite regional security arrangement,[35] even though it operates outside the OAS system. Article 8 established a Defence Committee to advise the Heads of Government on external defence and collective security against external aggression. The decisions of the Committee must be unanimous. This article is not really applicable in the Grenada instance since external aggression was not committed and the Committee, in view of Grenada's absence, was hardly unanimous. The other articles specifically noted by the US are articles 3 and 4. Article 3 is only relevant to the extent that among the functions and purposes of the OECS are included 'such other activities calculated to further the progress of the Organisation as the member States may from time to time decide', whereas article 4 calls on member States to carry out the obligations arising out of the treaty.[37] It is thus only with some difficulty that the OECS treaty can be interpreted to include regional peacekeeping action in the Grenada case.[38] What is obviously needed is greater precision in regional treaties if they are intended to cover such a situation.

To Protect Nationals Abroad

The third legal ground adduced by the United States to justify its action in Grenada lies in the competence of a state to take action to rescue endangered nationals abroad. The extent to which this is possible, if at all, under international law in the light of article 2 (4) of the UN Charter has been debated extensively.[39] The crucial factors would appear to be that the threat to the nationals is overwhelming and that the authorities of the state concerned are failing in their duty to protect them. The Entebbe episode of 1976 would seem to be the best model for this. It is, at the least, factually uncertain as to whether the requisite conditions were present in Grenada with regard to American students on the island. It should also be noted that, unlike the Entebbe incident, the intervening forces stayed in Grenada for some time after the rescue.[40] Some have argued for a broader right of humanitarian intervention to include non-nationals, but this must be regarded as a very dubious proposition in contemporary international law.

Mercenaries[41]

Micro-states are particularly vulnerable to mercenaries because limited numbers of trained and armed people can have a disproportionate effect upon a micro-state by reason of the latter's minimal military resources.

Under traditional international law, mercenaries were not treated separately but fell within the rules governing the conduct of international or internal armed conflicts. In the former case, mercenaries who satisfied the conditions imposed under the 1949 Geneva Conventions would be regarded as lawful combatants and would thus benefit from prisoner-of-war status if captured. If they did not fulfil the necessary criteria, they would be treated as civilians taking part in an armed conflict and might be liable for violating the laws and customs of war. Mercenaries involved in a non-international armed conflict would be subject to the laws of the state concerned; international law did not presume to regulate the conduct of internal wars.

With the emergence of self-determination as a legal principle, it was inevitable that the role of the mercenary would be looked at afresh. The impact of mercenaries on the independence and territorial integrity of states, as well as on self-determination and liberation struggles, has been particularly stressed. In General Assembly resolution 2395 (XXIII) all states were urged to take measures to 'prevent the recruitment or training in their territories of any persons as mercenaries for the colonial war being waged in the territories under Portuguese domination and for violations of the territorial integrity and sovereignty of the independent African States'. In resolution 2465 (XXIII), the Assembly declared the use of mercenaries against liberation movements to be a criminal act, the mercenaries themselves to be 'outlaws', and demanded that states enact legislation declaring the recruitment, financing and training of mercenaries in their territories to be a punishable offence and to prohibit their nationals from serving as mercenaries.

The use of mercenaries in an attack on Guinea in 1970, allegedly by Portugal, was criticised by both the OAU[42] and the Security Council, and led to an OAU Declaration on Mercenaries the following year. This reiterated its 1970 resolution and called, *inter alia*, on member-states to ensure that their territories were not used for the recruitment, drilling and training of mercenaries or for the passage of equipment intended for them. It also called on member states to hand over mercenaries present in their countries to states against which they had carried out subversive activities. The Declaration led to an OAU Draft Convention on Mercenaries which was adopted in Rabat in 1972, but which appears not to have been ratified.[43] In this document, a mercenary is defined in terms of an alien who is employed, enrols himself or links himself willingly to a person, group or organisation whose aim is to overthrow the government of a member-state of the OAU, to threaten the independence, territorial integrity or normal function of the institutions of a member-state, or to oppose by any means the activities of an OAU recognised liberation movement.

In 1973, the General Assembly stressed that mercenaries acting against liberation movements were criminals and thus could not benefit from the laws of war.[44] This approach was taken up at the 1976 Geneva Diplomatic Conference on International Humanitarian Law, which eventually resulted in the adoption of Protocols I and II to the 1949 Geneva Conventions. The issue was introduced to the Conference by Nigeria, which proposed a new article to deal with mercenaries. This resulted in article 47 of Protocol I.[45] Protocol I, it should be noted, deals with international armed conflicts, which according to article 1 (4) are also deemed to include wars of self-determination. Article 47 emphasises that a mercenary does not have the right to be a combatant or a prisoner-of-war, and defines a mercenary as any person who:

(a) is specially recruited locally or abroad in order to fight in an armed conflict;
(b) does, in fact, take part in the hostilities;
(c) is motivated to take part in the hostilities essentially by the desire for private gain and is promised, by or on behalf of a party to the conflict, material compensation substantially in excess of that promised or paid to combatants of similar ranks and functions in the armed forces of that party;
(d) is neither a national of a party to the conflict nor a resident of a territory controlled by a party to the conflict;
(e) is not a member of the armed forces of a party to the conflict; and
(f) has not been sent by a state which is not a party to the conflict on official duty as a member of its armed forces.

Despite a number of ambiguities and imperfections, this article constitutes the most authoritative statement on mercenaries to date.[46]

The problem of mercenaries reappeared in 1977 in a complaint by Benin of an aggressive attack by imperialists and mercenaries. In resolution 405 (1977), adopted by consensus, the UN Security Council reaffirmed the provisions of resolution 239 (1967) which condemned states permitting or tolerating mercenary recruitment. In 1982, following a complaint by the Seychelles of a mercenary attack, the Council condemned all forms of external interference in the internal affairs of member-states, 'including the use of mercenaries to destabilise states and/or to violate the territorial integrity, sovereignty and independence of states' (resolution 507 (1982) which was adopted unanimously).[47]

A variety of problems in international law are raised by this issue. For example, does 'mercenarism' constitute an international crime; what responsibilities do states have with regard to the recruitment of mercenaries on their territories or of their nationals; what is the legal position as regards the use of facilities on their territories; how precisely may one define mercenaries so as to permit the use by governments of foreign instructors and advisers? Indeed, could it be maintained that mercenaries themselves are without meaningful protection under the laws of war?

States are under a duty not to intervene in the internal affairs of other states and this would clearly cover the use by them of mercenaries for such activities.[48] The responsibility of states may well be evolving to include not only organising the sending of mercenaries but also toleration in their territories of other preparatory mercenary activities. The use of mercenaries to suppress the legitimate exercise of the right to self-determintion would also be regarded as unlawful. In cases of civil war the issue is rather more clouded, but the internal use of mercenaries by the parties to the conflict may well be regarded as falling outside the current concern and regulation of international law. Where mercenaries are used by external forces to overthrow a government, this would be regarded as contrary to international law, and the mercenaries concerned would be treated as in the internal armed conflict model.

The functional approach to the problem is thus a more acceptable method of analysing the issue, particularly as many states do not accept that serving as a mercenary constitutes a crime in international law.[49] A number of states rely on public and private foreign assistance in various governmental capacities including military personnel. The more reasonable view would be that in international armed conflicts the provisions of articles 47 and 75 would apply with respect to parties bound by the 1977 Protocols. In other cases, the traditional law would apply; mercenaries would thus be able to claim combatant status if the relevant provisions were applicable in the circumstances. What is clear is that the point of pressure has moved to states that are deemed to be encouraging or tolerating or simply refraining from acting with regard to mercenary recruitment or training.[50]

Notes

1. See article I of the Montevideo Convention on the Rights and Duties of States, 1933; Crawford, *The Creation of States in International Law*, Clarendon Press, Oxford, 1979, and Higgins, *The Development of International Law Through the Political Organs of the United Nations*, Clarendon Press, Oxford, 1963, pp. 11–41.
2. See Shaw, *Title to Territory in Africa*, Clarendon Press, Oxford, 1985, chapter 4.
3. See General Assembly resolution 748 (VIII), 849 (IX), 1469 (XIV) and 2064 (XX).

4. See the case of the trust territory of the Pacific Islands, Clark and Rolf, *Micronesia: The Problem of Palau*, Minority Rights Group Report, no. 63, 1984.

5. See, for example, Churchill and Lowe, *The Law of the Sea*, Manchester University Press, Manchester, 1983; and O'Connell, *The Law of the Sea*, Oxford University Press, Oxford, 2 vols., 1982–4. See also the UN Convention on the Law of the Sea, 1982 and the 1958 Conventions on the Law of the Sea, text in Brownlie, *Basic Documents in International Law*, Clarendon Press, Oxford, 3rd edn, 1983.

6. Article 57 of the 1982 Convention. The Convention has not yet entered into force. Under article 3, each state may extend its territorial sea, over which it has full sovereignty, up to twelve nautical miles.

7. See also articles 69, 70, 87, 148, 160 and 161 with respect to the advantages to be enjoyed by such states under the 1982 convention regime.

8. See General Assembly resolution 1803 (XVII) and the Charter of Economic Rights and Duties of States, 1974. See also Hossain (ed.), *Legal Aspects of the New International Economic Order*, Frances Pinter, London, 1980.

9. See, for example, Rich, 'The Right to Development as an Emerging Human Right', *Virginia Journal of International Law*, Vol. 23, 1983, p. 287, and *Development, Human Rights and the Rule of Law*, Pergamon Press, Oxford, 1981.

10. See Hall, *International Law*, Clarendon Press, Oxford, 8th edn., 1924, p. 153 and McDougal and Reisman, *International Law in Contemporary Perspective*, Foundation Press, 1981. See also *International Legal Materials*, Vol. VIII, 1968, p. 1299.

11. See, for example, Rigo Sureda, *The Evolution of the Right of Self-Determination*, Sijthoff, Leiden, 1973 and Johnson, *Self-Determination Within the Community of Nations*, Sijthoff, Leiden, 1967. But note the arguments put by Morocco, in the *Western Sahara* case, Shaw, 'The *Western Sahara* case', *British Year Book of International Law*, Vol. 49, 1978, p. 119.

12. See, for example, McDougal *et al.*, *Human Rights and World Public Order*, Yale University Press, New Haven, 1980; Lillich and Newman, *International Human Rights*, Little, Brown, Boston, Mass., 1979 and Lauterpacht, *International Law and Human Rights*, Praeger, New York, 1950.

13. See, for example, the International Covenants on Human Rights and Optional Protocol, 1966; the International Covenant on the Elimination of All Forms of Racial Discrimination, 1965; the European Convention of Human Rights, 1950; the American Convention on Human Rights, 1969 and the African Charter on Human and Peoples' Rights, 1981.

14. See articles 10, 15 and 16 of the Covenant.

15. See in particular Brownlie, *International Law and the Use of Force by States*, Clarendon Press, Oxford, 1963 and Bowett, *Self-Defence in*

International Law, Manchester University Press, Manchester, 1958. See also Brierley, *The Law of Nations*, Clarendon Press, Oxford, 6th edn., 1963, pp. 417–18, and O'Connell, *International Law*, Stevens, 2nd edn.,1970, vol. 11, p. 317.

16. Note the Middle East experience of 1967, see, for example, Moore (ed.), *The Arab–Israeli Conflict*, Princeton University Press, New Haven, 1974, 3 vols. The *Caroline* case provides the following formulation: 'a necessity of self-defence, instant, over-whelming, leaving no choice of means and no moment for deliberation', *BFSP*, Vol. 29, pp. 1137–8.

17. See Lillich, 'Humanitarian Intervention' in Moore (ed.), *Law and Civil War in the Modern World*, Johns Hopkins University Press, 1974, pp. 229, 236–7.

18. See General Assembly resolution 2131 (XX), 1965, which declares that no state 'has the right to intervene directly or indirectly, for any reason whatsoever in the internal or external affairs of any other state.' See also resolutions 2625 (XXX) and 3314 (XXIX).

19. See, for example, Higgins, 'International Law and Civil Conflict', in Luard (ed.), *The International Regulation of Civil Wars*, Thames & Hudson, London, 1972, pp. 169, 170–1 and Lauterpacht, *Recognition in International Law*, Cambridge University Press, Cambridge, 1947.

20. See, for example, General Assembly resolutions 2625 (XXV), 1908 (XXVII), 3103 (XXVII) and 3314 (XXIX).

21. Lauterpacht, op. cit., pp. 230–3.

22. 'US Intervention in the Lebanon',*American Journal of International Law*, Vol. 53, 1959, pp. 112, 122. See also Hall,*International Law*, op. cit., p. 347; Akehurst, *A Modern Introduction to International Law*, George Allen & Unwin, London, 4th edn., 1982, pp. 240–7 and Falk, *Legal Order in a Violent World*, Princeton University Press, NJ, 1968, pp. 227–8, 273.

23. See Higgins, op. cit., *supra* note 1, pp. 162–4.

24. See statement of Deputy Secretary of State Dam of 2 November 1983 quoted in *American Journal of International Law*, Vol. 78, 1984, pp. 200, 203–4. See also Gilmore,*The Grenada Intervention*, Mansell, 1984; Moore, 'Grenada and the International Double Standard', *American Journal of International Law*, Vol. 78, 1984, p. 145 and *Law and the Grenada Mission*, Center for Law and National Security, 1984; Joyner, 'Reflections on the Lawfulness of Invasion', *American Journal of International Law*, Vol. 78, 1984, p. 131; and Vagts, 'International Law Under Time Pressure: Grading the Grenada Take-Move Examination', *American Journal of International Law*, Vol. 78, 1984, p. 169. Note also American Bar Association Section of International Law and Practice, Report of the Committee on Grenada (10 February 1984) and Second Report from the House of Commons Foreign Affairs Committee, session 1983–4. In addition, see the letter of the State Department Legal Adviser of 10 February 1984, reproduced in Moore, *Law and the Grenada Mission*, Center for Law and National Security, p. 125.

25. Statement of Deputy Secretary of State Dam, op. cit., p. 203. See also Gilmore, op. cit., p. 64 and Appendices 7, 11 and 14.
26. See Articles 57, 61, 62 and 69 of the 1973 Constitution of Grenada. However, it is fair to say that 'the text of the constitution and the operation of constitutional convention left the Governor-General without real power', Gilmore, op. cit., pp. 65–6.
27. See American Bar Association Section Report, op. cit., *supra* note 24, pp. 23–5 and Moore, *Law and the Grenada Mission*, op. cit., *supra* note 24, pp. 51–4 and Moore, *American Journal*, op. cit., *supra* note 24, pp. 159–61, cf. Joyner, op. cit., pp. 137–9 and Gilmore, op. cit., pp. 66–8.
28. See Gilmore, op. cit., pp. 67–8. See also Gilmore, op. cit., pp. 68–73 and article 46 of the Vienna Convention on the Law of Treaties, 1969, for the rules of international law dealing with the apparent authority of state agents. Note in addition *Yearbook of International Law Commission*, 1969, Vol. II, pp. 240–2, the *Eastern Greenland* case, PCIJ series A/B, no. 53 and the *Free Zones* case, ibid., no. 46.
29. See, for example, General Assembly resolutions 2625 (XXV) and 3314 (XXIX).
30. See Madeley, *Diego Garcia: A Contrast to the Falklands*, Minority Rights Group Report, no. 54, 1982 and Shaw, *supra* note 2, pp. 130–2. It should, of course, be noted here that agreement was made with a constitutionally elected government and accompanied by an offer of compensation.
31. Ibid., pp. 132–4.
32. Official Records of the Trusteeship Council, Fiftieth Session, Supplement No. 3. (T/1851), UN, New York.
33. In fact, the resolution was not adopted by virtue of the veto exercised by the United States, see *UN Chronicle*, December 1983, pp. 15–22.
34. See *supra* note 24.
35. See the statement by Deputy Secretary of State Dam, *supra* note 49, p. 203.
36. See Gilmore, op. cit., pp. 42–55 and Moore, *Law and the Grenada Mission*, *supra* note 24, p. 47.
37. Ibid., pp. 45–50. Article 6 of the OECS Treaty provides that the Heads of Government of the Member States constitute the supreme policy-making institution of the organisation and that this 'Authority' may make such recommendations and give such directions as it deems necessary for the achievement of the purposes of the organisation.
38. See also General Assembly resolution 38/7, calling for an immediate cessation of the armed intervention in Grenada, see *UN Chronicle*, January 1984, p. 4.
39. See, for example, Akehurst, 'Humanitarian Intervention' in Bull (ed.), *Intervention in World Politics*, Clarendon Press, Oxford, 1984, p. 95 and Higgins, 'Intervention and the International Law', ibid., pp. 29, 38–40. See also Lillich (ed.), *Humanitarian Intervention and the United Nations*, Virginia University Press, Chapel Hill, 1973, see, for example,

Knisbacher, 'The Entebbe Operation: A Legal Analysis of Israel's Rescue Mission', *Journal of International Law and Economics*, Vol. 12, 1977, pp. 57–83.

40. See Gilmore, op. cit., pp. 55–64 and American Bar Association Section Report *supra* note 24, pp. 72–4. It should also be noted that the American troops remained at the request of the Governor-General and of the regional organisation. Following the elections in December 1984, resulting in a landslide victory for the New National Party, the new Prime Minister asked the United States to keep troops on the island indefinitely. He also asked the Caribbean governments which had contributed forces to allow them to remain.

41. See Cassese, 'Mercenaries: Lawful Combatants or War Criminals?', *Zeitschrift fur Auslandisches Offentliches Recht und Volkerrecht*, Vol. 40, 1980, p. 1; David, 'Les Mercenaires en Droit International', *Revue Belge de Droit International*, Vol. 13, 1977, p. 197; Green, 'The Status of Mercenaries in International Law', *Israel Yearbook of Human Rights*, Vol. 8, p. 9; Tercinet, 'Les Mercenaires en Droit International', *Annuaire Français de Droit International*, 1977, p. 269; Burmeister, 'The Recruitment and Use of Mercenaries in Armed Conflicts', *American Journal of International Law*, Vol. 72, 1978, p. 37 and Mockler, *The Mercenaries*, MacDonald, 1970.

42. ECM/Res. 17 (VII). This *inter alia* requested member-states to outlaw, arrest and hand over all mercenaries to the country against which they were active. See also Security Council resolution 289 (1970). This demanded the 'immediate withdrawal of all external armed forces and mercenaries, together with the military equipment used in the armed attack against the territory of the Republic of Guinea.' See also S/10009 and Add. 1, and resolution 290 (1970). See also Security Council resolutions S/4741, S/5002 and 239 (1967) regarding the Congo and mercenaries.

43. CM/433/Rev. 1, Annex 1. See also the Report of the OAU Committee of Experts, CM/1/33/Rev. 1. See also Elias, *New Horizons in International Law*, Sijthoff & Noordhoff, Leiden, 1979, pp. 201–5; Green, op. cit., pp. 45–6 and Cassese, op. cit., p. 13.

44. Resolution 3103 (XXVIII). See also resolutions 31/34, 32/14, 33/24, 34/44 and 34/140.

45. CDDH/III/GT/82. See also CDDH/III/SR. 57, paras. 13–57 and CDDH/236/Rev. 1, paras 95–108 and CDDH/III/363.

46. The OAU Convention does not appear to have come into effect. Note the 1976 trial of thirteen mercenaries in Angola and the judgement of the Tribunal which declared mercenarism to be 'a crime in the view of nations', see Cassese, op. cit., p. 17. Angola established an International Commission of Enquiry on Mercenaries, which produced a draft convention on mercenarism, see Green, op. cit., pp. 9, 55–8. This had little effect upon article 47.

47. See *UN Chronicle*, May 1982, pp. 35-7; ibid., July 1982, pp. 25-32 and resolution 419 (1977). See also Chapter 2 on the Caribbean with respect to the Barbados complaint of 1979.
48. See, for example, Assembly resolution 2131 (XX). Resolution 2625 (XXV) of the 1970 Declaration on Principles of International Law, noted that all states were under 'the duty to refrain from organising or encouraging the organisation of irregular forces or armed bands, including mercenaries, for incursion into the territory of another state'. See also article 3 (g) of the 1974 Definition of Aggression but cf. article 7. See also Security Council resolutions 239 (1967), 405 (1977) and 507 (1982).
49. See, for example, *Digest of US Practice in International Law 1976*, Department of State, Washington, DC, 1977, p. 714 and ibid., *1977*, 1979, p. 931. See also the statement by Belgium on behalf of the members of the EEC, A/C.3/32/SR.28, para. 31 and the statement by the British Minister for Foreign and Commonwealth Affairs, *House of Commons Debates*, Vol. 915, cols. 44-5, 12 July 1976. Note the *Report of the Diplock Committee into the Recruitment of Mercenaries*, 1976, cmnd. 6569, HMSO, London. Note also that mercenarism is not declared a crime under Protocol I, nor are mercenaries defined as criminals.
50. The United Nations established an Ad Hoc Committee in 1981 on the Drafting of an International Convention against the Recruitment, Use, Financing and Training of Mercenaries, see resolutions 35/48 and 36/76. See also the reports of the Committee, for example A/36/43 and A/37/43 and *UN Chronicle*, October 1983, p. 21.

4 The Maintenance of Adequate Security Forces

The first part of this chapter discusses in broad terms some of the problems faced by micro-states in maintaining security forces adequate to their needs. The second considers practical means by which indigenous security forces may be made more capable of performing their functions. The chapter concludes with a detailed discussion of maritime security, a subject of increasing concern to very small island states which lack the means to protect their large and economically important maritime resources.

In this context, the term 'security forces' includes not only the armed forces but also all other forces concerned with the maintenance of law and order and defence against internal and external threats to the state. Thus, for example, those concerned with policing, coast guard, fishery protection, paramilitary and specialist military forces all fall within the definition, as do the intelligence organisations that serve their needs.

The chapter addresses two general situations: firstly, maintaining the security of a state that is stable and, secondly, where the legitimate government has been overthrown but subsequently restored. In the latter circumstance it would be necessary to consider means of creating new security forces.

The Problems

The threat to the security of micro-states is both internal and external. The latter is generally more expensive to guard against since, to be successful, external aggression will require a fairly sophisticated military capability on the part of the invader, and the small state in its turn will require an almost equally sophisticated response in order to defend itself.

A significant difficulty encountered by a micro-state seeking to ensure its security is the high cost of equipment, and of its subsequent operation and maintenance. With the exception of the oil-rich Gulf States and Brunei, no micro-state can afford to buy much military equipment from overseas, or to manufacture it in sufficient quantities to secure itself from any likely external threat. The resource base of such a state is extremely limited and the first task for any government must be to set out clearly its spending priorities. Experience indicates that both internal and external intervention is less likely if a state is demonstrably stable. The first priority must therefore be to assure, as far as possible, the state's internal stability.

A further difficulty for micro-states concerns personnel. Demographic factors can impose significant limitations on the size of the indigenous forces that can be recruited. The pool from which recruits may be drawn for the security forces is necessarily small, and demand for the services of members of this pool is not confined to the security forces. This applies not only to the number of reasonably fit young people required but also to the number of capable leaders and managers available to run the affairs of micro-states. This latter category will be particularly in demand; indeed it can reasonably be argued that its members would be more usefully employed in more productive areas of the state's economy. In addition, states may decide, for ethnic or religious reasons, to exclude certain sections of the population from serving in their security forces. Low overall standards of literacy and education can be a further problem in recruiting men able to handle increasingly complex military equipment.

There is always the danger that the security forces of a state may seek to take over the running of the country and history shows that small states are particularly susceptible to this form of political instability. A system of checks and balances is necessary to counter this threat, the most usual method being the division of the security forces into units with separate functions and power bases to prevent any one element of the force becoming too powerful. However, this solution brings with it some additional problems, not least that separate organisations require separate control structures and administrative services, the provision of which is expensive in both financial and human resources. Moreover, fragmentation of the security forces tends to reduce their cohesion and effectiveness.

Of particular importance in making best use of inadequate resources is the ability to target them effectively; in other words, the less effective the security forces, the more important the intelligence services become. But the provision of effective intelligence services in small states is both difficult (because the skills involved are hard to learn) and dangerous (because the power accruing to the intelligence service can readily be abused).

Alleviating the Problems

Financial Assistance

As has already been stated, the creation and maintenance of adequate security forces is costly. Very few of the states considered in this study are sufficiently wealthy to be able to bear this expense wihout doing untoward damage to their economies and hence their development in other fields. The vast majority are presented with a problem they are unable to resolve by themselves. On the one hand they could have strong security forces at the cost of inadequate development in other sectors, and on the other hand, their security will be compromised. Either situation is potentially unstable.

Faced with this dilemma the micro-state must first analyse clearly the nature of any security threat and set its defence priorities accordingly to deal with the most likely threats. The history of instability in small states shows that the internal security threat is the most immediate in the majority of cases; it is also fortuitously the least expensive to cope with since it does not require the state to maintain the expensive array of weapons necessary to cope with a serious external threat. However, it is probably also true that the leaders of newly emergent small nations, rightly proud of their recent achievements, tend to play up the external and play down the internal threats. This natural reaction can result in priorities being wrongly set; one function of aid donors must be to discourage this.

However, even the maintenance of adequate internal security forces will be a severe economic burden for most micro-states, and aid, both financial and material, will probably be necessary. If it is necessary to create forces capable of resisting external aggression, even only in token form, the aid required is likely to be substantial.

Demographic Problems

A micro-state can reduce the impact of the demographic factors mentioned earlier in several ways. These include various forms of conscription, the use of reserve forces and voluntary and part-time organisations. Such devices allow the state to have larger forces available in an emergency than they need in normal times. But all such schemes have costs, both financial and in terms of diverting human resources that could probably be better used elsewhere.

It is possible to hire the services of foreign nationals to bolster the indigenous security forces. This method is used on a significant scale by some wealthy small states; indeed, in some cases foreign nationals significantly outnumber indigenous members. However, it is a device that is unlikely to be available except to the wealthy, since few aid donors have so far been prepared to allow their aid to be used to pay for the services of nationals of a third state or for security services provided by a commercial agency, and it seems unlikely that this attitude will change. Furthermore, the existence of large numbers of non-indigenous members of the security forces can cause resentment among the native population. This can pose problems particularly for countries without a democratic system of government.

However, some states, among them the United Kingdom, have proved willing to lend limited numbers of their own security forces for service in the forces of micro-states. This has several advantages since, as well as helping to bolster numbers, it is also possible to introduce skills and experience not normally available within the recipient country. In particular, the loan of senior staff (and in some cases commanders) and skilled technicians can do much to sustain the standards of local security forces while at the same time releasing indigenous experts for use elsewhere. Another significant advantage of the presence of numbers of expatriates in key positions is that it becomes difficult to plan the misuse of the security forces without their knowledge, thereby making more difficult the use of the security forces to overthrow the government. Thus the problem of 'checks and balances' alluded to earlier is to some extent eased. In addition to the loan of personnel in management appointments, aid donors may also choose to lend their servicemen to assist with the introduction of new weapons into service.

The function of servicemen on loan is to train local forces to take over, rather than to remain indefinitely, though the process may take a long time and may indeed be deliberately prolonged at the request of the recipient government in an attempt to enhance stability. Friendly nations will be able to assist in the development of local skills in several other ways, for example in the provision of advice and training. The former will often involve sending experts to the micro-state to examine problems *in situ* before preparing reports; the latter can be provided either in the donor's training establishments or in the recipient state. Experience has shown that technical training is usually best carried out where the best facilities exist, which is more usually in the donor country; basic skills are generally more effectively passed on in the environment in which they are to be used.

It is difficult to generalise about the scale of support individual micro-states require, since this depends on so many factors, few being common to all. But it is probably true to say that the effect for good in the recipient country is out of all proportion to the burden on the donor. Donors need to look carefully at the extent to which they seek to recover their costs since even relatively small costs are likely to be a significant burden on the majority of micro-states and this could prove destabilising.

Other Devices

Of particular interest to micro-states is the protection afforded by defence treaties with one or more friendly powers and by membership of international and regional organisations in order to cope with perceived threats, particularly external ones. In this context, friendly larger states can provide help in various ways, ranging from moral support to guarantees of sovereignty. Among the more helpful measures are the stationing of forces in the threatened state (for example, Belize) and the loan of otherwise unavailable military capabilities (for example, mine counter-measures in the Red Sea). It is also mutually beneficial to set the affairs of the micro-state in a wider context by arranging for exchanges of information on matters of common interest, most particularly intelligence. Friendly nations can also encourage the creation of alliances and regional security systems by channelling the help discussed earlier in this chapter through the central organisation.

Restoring the Status Quo

When seeking to recreate the security forces after the overthrow and subsequent restoration of a legitimate government, the problems faced would be similar to those already discussed. However, they would all be present to a much greater degree, principally because the old security forces would have demonstrably failed and would therefore be discredited. They would also be likely to have lost most of their equipment or had it destroyed. Given sufficiently generous donors, equipment is not too difficult to replace. However, the recruitment of trustworthy new members of the security forces is likely to be very difficult in the short term; even if their recruitment can be effected, it must be assumed that their experience will be negligible and a great deal of time will therefore be needed for their training. The most practical solution is likely to be for friendly nations to provide adequate numbers of men on loan. Such forces might well be required, as in Grenada, to hold the ring until elections can be held. They could also provide a framework of experienced personnel to sustain the forces as they gain experience and also to make up numbers while new recruits are trained. To be effective, this would require a substantial commitment of resources over a prolonged period. Indeed, the most likely cause of failure of such a project would be the withdrawal of participating nations for political reasons before the task was successfully concluded.

Maritime Security

Since the majority of micro-states are islands, maritime security is a major concern when considering not only their vulnerability to external attack, but also the protection of their economic resources.

Historically, fishing has always constituted an important source of food and revenue in most small island states. But from the late 1960s onwards, their maritime resources have assumed a new importance as the concept of the 200-mile Exclusive Economic Zone (EEZ) has become increasingly accepted. These new resources include not only fish, but also in many cases valuable minerals, and, as land resources world-wide become scarcer, offshore resources will almost certainly become increasingly significant. Thus, in the long term a small island's prosperity may depend crucially on what is in, or under, its EEZ.

However, the potential value of these new maritime resources is in most cases jeopardised by the inability of micro-states to protect and exploit them. To illustrate the size of the problem, a small island with a 200-mile EEZ has jurisdiction over some 125,000 square miles of sea, though only a comparatively limited number of islands are so isolated as to have to cope with such a large sea area. For example, some island states are less than 400 miles apart and their individual EEZs will therefore be somewhat less. The problems of agreeing common boundaries, particularly of the Continental Shelf, are highly complex and much scope is thereby provided for disagreement, especially if high value resources are involved. Such disputes can exacerbate already unstable situations.

The security of small island states may also be threatened from the sea in a number of ways:

(a) the landing of subversive elements with a view to the forcible overthrow of the government for either political or commercially dubious motives;

(b) internationally financed smuggling of drugs, arms and other contraband;

(c) illegal fishing (leading to loss of revenue, possible food shortages and, in some instances, the destruction of fish stocks);

(d) illegal exploitation of other natural resources, such as minerals;

(e) occupation of, or damage to, offshore installations (most usually oil or gas);

(f) piracy (with consequent disruption and damage of lawful trade);

(g) illegal dumping of harmful materials (leading to pollution);

(h) local smuggling.

If such threats are to be contained, islands require an effective maritime policing capability. This demands a force which is capable of both surveillance and timely interception, and good intelligence in order that the force may be used to best effect. There needs to be close co-operation between maritime and on-shore security forces, particularly in the exchange of information and in coastal operations. To achieve this, sound equipment, good communications, well-trained personnel and good links with the intelligence service and security forces ashore, are essential.

The major difficulty for most micro-states in establishing an effective maritime security capability is, of course, its cost. Vessels and maritime patrol aircraft, their equipment and support facilities are all relatively expensive, both in absolute terms (including initial cost and subsequent running costs) and in their demand for technically capable personnel to man and maintain them. Furthermore, the necessary degree of co-operation between security forces can be difficult to achieve where inter-island rivalries prevent regional co-operation.

The main equipments needed for effective policing of an EEZ are:

(a) aircraft for surveillance out to 200 nm and beyond;
(b) vessels of sufficient seakeeping capability and with good navigation and communication equipment, which can sustain patrols out to 200 nm, ideally with helicopters to extend their surveillance capability;
(c) fast, armed craft for interception and arrest;
(d) boats for in-shore, lagoon and harbour work.

This list illustrates the scope of the problem for island micro-states. Very few can afford to buy and run all of them; even minimum protection will be out of the economic reach of most individual states. There is therefore a need to look for cheaper solutions. Co-operation and information exchange between states, as recently introduced in the Pacific, can provide a reporting system which is the first stage in achieving surveillance and control. The next step is for each member state of a regional organisation to contribute what it can (boats, aircraft, facilities, personnel) towards a regional security force, as is happening in the East Caribbean. As developments such as these continue around the world, small states, either individually or in regional groups, will be looking for low-cost equipment for maritime security work. Some examples of the cost of equipment are given at the end of this chapter.

The priorities for expenditure on maritime control of a micro-state's EEZ will depend on the economic value of the EEZ, together with an assessment of the threat of subversive or illegal activities. A micro-state with extensive offshore oil or gas resources (such as Brunei and Qatar) will need sophisticated maritime defence forces.

Such a country will probably be able to finance equipment procurement but may have difficulty in providing manpower and will almost certainly require training support. On the other hand, most small island states, with few resources but substantial fish stocks on which their populations depend for subsistence, have an urgent need to defend these stocks but no resources with which to do so. (It is a regrettable fact that illegal fishing is often carried out by nationals from relatively wealthy and more sophisticated states, some of which claim traditional rights to fish in such waters.) Some islands are subject to threat from politically subversive, or criminal elements, others are not. The requirement for maritime forces therefore will vary with each state. The first essential is for the state to define its priorities and, hence, its force requirements; this is one of the areas in which a country like the United Kingdom could provide valuabe practical advice.

Among the more important aspects of assistance that can be provided by well-disposed developed states are:

(a) assessment of the threats to be faced and definition of the size and shape of the maritime forces required to counter these threats;

(b) provision of equipment and the resources necessary subsequently to sustain it in operation (subsidised if necessary);

(c) provision of training (in the micro-state and at donor countries' training establishments);

(d) provision of shore support and logistic facilities (subsidised if necessary);

(e) the loan of expert personnel to assist with the management of forces until sufficient indigenous personnel are trained and gain the required experience; in other words, to provide an expert framework within which a new and inexperienced force can develop its capabilities;

(f) direct help, for example in policing EEZs, by friendly forces (such as New Zealand maritime patrol aircraft provide in Fijian waters);

(g) assistance with framing appropriate laws to provide the legal basis for maritime operations;

(h) political and diplomatic support in protection of micro-states' EEZs from more powerful countries;

(i) encouragement and material help to facilitate the formation of regional security arrangements.

Vehicles for Policing Micro-State EEZs

Aircraft for Surveillance cut to 200 Nautical Miles

Very few micro-states can afford to operate aircraft exclusively for maritime surveillance. Aircraft utilisation is often shared between government, civil, coastguard and military roles. The effort devoted to each is usually expressed in terms of planned flying hours; by applying the appropriate cost per hour figure, the annual cost attributable to each role can be calculated.

The minimum requirement for flying over the sea are two engines, good navigation and communications equipment, reasonable speed, range and endurance. Obviously a search radar greatly enhances the surveillance capability. Choice of aircraft will depend not only on the maritime requirement and other roles but also on the cost and availability of local resources for maintenance, training and support.

Vessels Capable of Sustaining Patrols Out to 200 Nautical Miles

Purpose-built patrol vessels for this task are usually 50 metres long or more. If they are to operate helicopters in a seaway they need flight-deck facilities, a reasonable freeboard and stabilisers, all of which leads to increased size and cost.

An alternative approach adopted by some states is to use converted trawlers which are seaworthy and capable of providing a presence. It is a relatively cheap option but the penalties are lack of speed and probably no helicopter deck.

Fast Armed Craft for Interception and Arrest

Speed costs money. Hulls which are designed for high speed (30–40 knots) are generally inefficient at lower speeds. While marine versions of truck engines can drive craft up to about 25 knots, above that speed specially designed high performance engines are needed. The speed requirement therefore needs to be very carefully assessed because it will significantly affect both the price and running cost.

Small calibre weapons, perhaps up to 20mm, are generally quite sufficient. More important for boarding and arrest is a tough wellfendered hull for going alongside vessels. A semi-rigid inflatable craft which is easy to launch and recover is needed for shallow waters, for example in estuaries, and on reefs.

Craft of about 20 metres are widely used for this work. An annual running cost is difficult to assess, even approximately, because it will depend on so many variables: crew costs, operating pattern, usage, fuel, base facilities, etc.

Boats for In-Shore, Lagoon and Harbour Work

In this category there are many different types and makes which are suitable. Very often, traditional locally-built craft are the best and cheapest for the job. The speed–cost equation applies as for larger craft.

Costs

As an indicator of the heavy financial burden the defence of their EEZs imposes on the economies of micro-states, some very rough estimates of the cost of equipment (and running costs, where appropriate), contrasted with the GDPs of a representative sample of the states concerned are given below.

Surveillance Aircraft
These figures are for basic aircraft, i.e. without navigation systems or weapon systems of any kind, and with the cheapest engine option.
$330,000–$430,000, with running costs of $90–$100 per hour.

Patrol and Attack Craft
Fast Attack Craft (56 metre). This would be the top of the range for EEZ patrol with a heavily armed fast boat with good sea keeping qualities. With 6 Exocets, 1 x 76mm gun, 4 diesel engines giving 40 knots and a complement of 59, the cost would be £16–£20 million. With no weaponry, such a craft would cost about £4–£5m.
Fast Patrol Boat (37.5 metre). Lightly armed with a 20mm gun and a speed of perhaps 24 knots, this would cost £5.3 million. With no weaponry, fire control system or modern navigation system, the cost would be about £3.5m.
Patrol craft (20 metre). Fitted with truck type engines and capable

of 24 knots, this would cost about £500,000–£600,000, excluding armament.

The Gross Domestic Products of some Micro-States
Bahamas (1979) $1.08 bn.; Brunei (1981) $4 bn.; Cape Verde (1979) $57 m.; Fiji (1978) $937 m.; Mauritius (1981) $988 m.; Oman (1983) $7.6 bn.; Qatar (1981) $6 bn.; Seychelles (1979) $86 m.; Tonga (1976) $40 m.

It is clear from the above that no micro-state outside the Gulf and Brunei could afford to buy new patrol vessels suitable for constant EEZ surveillance or control.

5 Prevention, Anticipation and Cure

In the factors of vulnerability outlined in Chapter 1, it was suggested that while micro-states may be subject to a variety of external pressures, internal factors need to be given the higher priority. Micro-states are, of course, far from a homogeneous group. They range from oil-rich sheikhdoms, such as Qatar with a GNP per capita of some $27,720, to the economically beleaguered Equatorial Guinea with a GNP per head of only $180.[1] They also run the gamut of political systems from democracies to harsh dictatorships.

In Chapter 6, a range of specific measures are put forward which could be taken by the international community to improve the security of micro-states. Few of these are novel; that so few have been implemented is a reflection of the fact that it is relatively easy for larger, more prosperous states to overlook or ignore the problems arising from the lack of size. There is also ignorance, not confined to micro-states, of what options might be available, as well as failure to estimate what the consequences of neglect can be – until, usually, it is too late. While the proposals which are discussed here are necessarily made in general terms, their adoption will need to be tailored carefully to particular cases.

The options available to micro-states, whether individually or acting in concert with other states, and to outside bodies and states, can best be considered under two broad headings: firstly, prevention – the longer-term measures that promote stability – and anticipation; and secondly, cure – the restoration of peace when violence has broken out.

Prevention and Anticipation

In Chapter 4 we discussed the military steps which might be taken to protect micro-states from both external attack and armed *coup*, the latter possibly preceded by a policy of destabilisation. In this chapter, in considering preventive measures, we wish to stress the importance of political stability and economic development as bulwarks against subversion.

Political Stability

Although we do not advocate any specific political system, we believe that a state is more likely to remain politically stable under a system where there is: first, freedom of speech and of assembly, including some means of voicing criticisms of the government, whether at public meetings, or through the media; secondly, some form of democratic process enabling the political leadership to be changed by peaceful means; thirdly, respect for human rights (including provisions for the protection of the rights of minority groups, where applicable).

In many newly independent micro-states, traditional forms of government and customary law have been incorporated into constitutions and judicial systems based on western models; and traditional leaders have, like Shaw's King Magnus, often successfully competed for political power under democratic systems of government. This blending of local and Western political concepts has been particularly widespread in the island states of the Indian Ocean and the Pacific and in Africa where strong ethnic traditions survive; for example in the Marshall Islands, Palau and Tonga in the Pacific, and Lesotho in Africa. This can often be a source of strength and stability and help to bridge the transition from a traditional society to a modern one.

A multi-party system is not an essential element in political stability. In many traditional societies decisions are reached by consensus and, provided there is a sufficient degree of popular participation in the decision-making process, such a system can provide opportunities to express opinions and air grievances. In the case of micro-states with small populations and a limited leadership to draw upon, it has been argued that it makes little sense to confine half the political talent available to the negative role of opposition. Instead, all should work together for the good of their country.[2] Governments of micro-states can also enhance their stability and security by strengthening their links with friendly states, especially neighbouring states, through personal contacts, through promoting regional arrangements, and through improved communications in order to insure that in their hour of need they have allies to call upon for aid, and the necessary means to do so expeditiously. Modern communications can prove invaluable in building up a sense of community and of nationhood in newly independent states. Their importance in combatting subversion or external aggression is obvious. Their educative and training role can also be highly significant.

Economic Development as a Factor in Political Stability

For many developing micro-states the most important threats to their political stability are economic and social in nature. Uneven rural and industrial development, the resentments created by poverty and inequality of wealth, and the dislocation and uncertainties caused by social, cultural and environmental changes brought about by the development process itself can have profoundly important consequences for political stability and security. Such problems are not, of course, confined to micro-states; they are often shared by other developing states. However, the evidence suggests that many micro-states are particularly disadvantaged economically because of their size; for example, because of the narrowness of domestic markets and remoteness from world markets which raise trading costs, poor internal communications which hamper the movement of produce, and their special vulnerability to natural disasters.

Micro-states in the process of development tend to be very much more dependent on international trade than larger ones. The scope for creating an internal market of a size large enough to benefit from economies of scale is obviously limited. Costs would be higher if they attempted to be self-sufficient and meet domestic requirements internally; they therefore need to export to achieve scale economies. This greater dependence on trade makes micro-states particularly exposed to variations in relative prices. The great majority of micro-states export only a few products or commodities. Thus stable prices and unimpeded access to foreign markets are of critical importance. The majority have few natural resources and lack the funds and expertise to exploit those which they do have. As a result they are heavily dependent on imports, and inflationary pressures have therefore been high. Energy prices have often weighed especially heavily; in 1980, for example, some two-thirds of Western Samoa's foreign exchange earnings went on imported fuel. Yet while micro-states are peculiarly susceptible to changes in the international trading system, they can exert little influence on its workings.

Given the small population of the states we are discussing the pool of skilled labour is inevitably also small and those with technical expertise are at a premium. Moreover, the use to which such expertise may be put may not be particularly efficient if, for example, the expert is under-employed because of a lack of investment or if he or she is obliged to try to undertake too many functions. And yet, since a large number of micro-states are as yet underdeveloped, with little in the way of infrastructure, they can also suffer from problems of unemployment. This has caused many to seek work overseas. For example, many nationals of the Solomon Islands and Kiribati work in foreign merchant fleets. While their remittances may contribute significantly to the national income, the effects of their absence on the social fabric of a small community may be severe.

One of the areas where expertise is often lacking is knowledge of the international capital markets. Here, too, micro-states are at a disadvantage as the cost of small loans is relatively high. But even if the expertise to tap the capital markets did exist, although many micro-states are dependent on inward capital flows, they are not in a position to offer many inducements to private capital. The number of tax havens remains few and they are largely confined to dependent territories which are considered economically more stable.

If, because of their size, micro-states are restricted in what they themselves can do economically, the question arises of what they might do together. There have been numerous attempts at closer co-operation on a regional basis: examples in the Caribbean, the Pacific and in Southern Africa are examined in the Annexes. The possible benefits of co-operation, as well as the sometimes all too real difficulties of reaching agreement, are discussed there in greater detail. The distribution of costs and benefits has been an issue bedevilling all regional organisations; it is one exacerbated by disparities in size and resources. It also demands a great deal of newly independent states, still attempting to build up a national identity, to join with others in a similar position but who are also real or potential competitors. However, the significance of transport and other infrastructure projects is clear. Consideration should also be given to establishing more common services. The regional develop-ment banks can play an important role, not simply because of their physical presence but also because they are usually closer to the needs as well as to the aspirations of micro-states. They can also play a useful intermediary role between micro-states and the larger agencies and institutions.

In recognising the importance of economic factors in contributing to stability and in emphasizing the great dependence of micro-states on the international system, we acknowledge the role that the West and Western dominated trade and aid agencies can play. It is clear that whilst many micro-states are heavily dependent on aid, aid by itself is not enough. There is, for example, little point in providing aid for improving animal husbandry if restrictions are then imposed on exports of beef – as they were under the first Lomé Convention against Botswana and Swaziland. Similarly, it is not particularly generous for Western donors first to tie aid to the purchase of, say, textile machinery and then to subject exports of clothing to quotas under the Multi Fibre Arrangements. Too often so far, whether under the Generalised System of Preferences, the Lomé Convention or the Caribbean Basin Initiative, preferences extended to developing countries have had only a marginal impact on trade flows.[3] It is unfortunately the case that preferences have often been extended to cover goods that are not imported by the industrialised countries; restrictions on 'sensitive' goods, i.e. those that are imported, remain in place. The example of Mauritius, a Lomé signatory, is a case in point. Although Mauritius has been attempting to diversify its exports and so end its dependence on sugar, it has found itself obliged to sign a 'Voluntary Export Restraint' agreement with the Community for certain of its new textile exports. In the case of textiles, it is theoretically possible that if all micro-states became textile producers, this would have an impact on Western producers; although the combined populations of all independent and still dependent micro-states would still not add up to half the Japanese population. On the other hand, the effect of unrestricted access for the textiles of states such as Barbados or Mauritius could have a beneficial impact on those countries out of all proportion to the effect on the Western economies. If the principle of discrimination on the basis of size is accepted, lifting restrictions and extending preferences could be a valuable way of assisting in the economic development of micro-states.

Most micro-states remain more heavily dependent on their exports of commodities than on manufactures. Indeed, there have been cases, such as Mauritius in the mid-1970s, where states have been dependent on a single commodity for up to 90 per cent of their foreign earnings. Stable prices have been regarded by them as vital for reasonable economic planning, let alone for growth and development. The West, however, has tended to see calls for stable prices as calls for higher prices. Few of the existing international commodity agreements have been of particular assistance to micro-states. They have either been dominated by the big producers or have been ineffective in the face of big consumer countries. The hopes pinned on UNCTAD's Integrated Programme for Commodities have been dashed not only because of opposition from many Western countries but also because of continued divisions among developing countries themselves.

Given the problems surrounding commodity agreements, two other schemes have taken on a greater significance which may be of more relevance to the needs of micro-states. These are the IMF's Compensatory Financing Facility and the Stabex Scheme of the Lomé Conventions. Both seek to compensate for loss of earnings when prices of commodities fall below certain levels, by means of loans in the case of the IMF and grants in the case of Stabex. It is not necessary to go into the details of the schemes except perhaps to note that they have strict criteria and somewhat complex procedures. The impact of the IMF Facility is particularly limited by the size of each member country's quota and, since 1984, loans under the Facility have been tied more closely to observance of IMF policy guidelines. The major limitation of Stabex has been the lack of capital allocated unilaterally to it by the Community. In 1981–2 the amount available was considerably less than the demands made upon it; only some 40 per cent of claims were in fact met, and EC member states advanced more funds only on an *ad hoc* basis. The number of products covered has been extended under the third Lomé Convention and its capital increased, although only marginally. In view of the positive impact that such a scheme could have on recipient countries, which is out of all proportion to the financial burden imposed on the Community member states, this was extremely disappointing, and consideration should be given to further capitalisation of the fund. Stabex procedures already allow for an element of discrimination in favour of least-developed, land-locked and island states which should be used as flexibly as possible.

Whatever changes are made in the international trading system, many micro-states will continue to depend on aid for their development, some, indeed, for their continued viability. The UN Specialised Agencies are important sources of aid and technical assistance to developing countries. Two of them, the International

Bank for Reconstruction and Development (IBRD) and the International Monetary Fund (IMF) play a crucial role in most states' development. Other UN Agencies of particular relevance to micro-states are the Food and Agriculture Organisation (FAO), the World Health Organisation (WHO) which was, *inter alia*, responsible for the eradication of smallpox throughout the world, and the United Nations Children's Fund (UNICEF), a particularly successful UN agency which assists in the development of child welfare and health services primarily in developing countries. The United Nations Educational, Scientific and Cultural Organisation (UNESCO) has provided valuable assistance in the educational field in developing countries, including an effective programme against illiteracy. Most of the Specialised Agencies were set up after the Second World War to organise post-war reconstruction, mainly in Europe. However, from about 1960 onwards they have concentrated their main efforts on economic development projects, aid and technical assistance in Third World countries.

However, the ways in which both multilateral and bilateral aid could be better geared to the particular needs of micro-states are numerous, although they do raise some fundamental questions. Micro-states have been critical of the World Bank and other international agencies for taking too little account of the inherent constraints on their development. Most organisations focus their attention primarily on levels of development: the World Bank uses GNP figures to determine eligibility for its IDA loans while the UNDP uses the criteria of GDP per capita, share of manufactures in GDP and literacy rates. Using GNP criteria means that only nine micro-states – Cape Verde, Comoros, Djibouti, Equatorial Guinea, Gambia, Guinea-Bissau, Maldives, São Tomé, and Vanuatu – are eligible for Least-Developed Country status, and therefore additional assistance. The limitations imposed by reason of a small population should be recognised by development agencies.

If aid for development is regarded as a major factor in preventing insecurity, the actual use to which aid is put needs to be closely examined. The effectiveness of much aid, especially bilateral aid, has often been adversely affected by the overall approach of donors and the conditions they impose on their assistance. As the Swazi Deputy Prime Minister has declared:

> Inevitably aid donors and international agencies have concentrated on giving help based on their own experiences. However,

these experiences are not always relevant to Africa. They are derived from experiences of a system geared to high technology, large markets, high volume production runs and high production costs. As a result, African countries are being equipped with goods and services which the developed world can easily supply but which, regrettably, add more to the superstructure of African economies but are contributing very little to the base.[4]

Unfortunately, such strictures apply equally in other developing countries, particularly low-income ones. On the other hand, there have been cases where the governments of developing countries, particularly of newly independent ones, have been unrealistic in asking for aid in the form of prestige projects of little or no benefit to their citizens. Realism and a sense of proportion are required from both donors and recipients.

At a bilateral level, much of the problem has been caused by aid that is conditional on purchases of the donor's own manufactures or equipment. The economic recession has made this problem of tied aid worse, as Western governments have sought to provide additional stimuli for their own industries. Not only does this perpetuate the dependence of the economies of recipient states on the host, but it also ties them to what is, in many cases, inappropriate technology. The introduction of sophisticated Western technology can also bring in its wake the difficult and expensive tasks of maintaining the equipment and acquiring spare parts. All such aid should include provisions for the training of local staff in the operation and maintenance of equipment and the cost of maintenance over an initial period should be included in aid agreements.

While capital intensive technology may be appropriate for some developing states, it is equally clear that labour-intensive technology is more appropriate for others. Where states are suffering from under-employment or unemployment, the latter technology is obviously beneficial for political stability. There are, then, difficult choices for developing states necessitating a clear assessment of priorities and ensuring that the aid offered is appropriate to their individual needs.

Of crucial importance in any assessment of different technologies is information on the choices available. Most micro-states lack the trained manpower necessary to make those choices. This is an area where a technical adviser can often prove valuable. Funds such as the Commonwealth Fund for Technical Co-operation, and especially its

Technical Assistance Group, could therefore usefully be expanded (see Chapter 2).

One of the concerns of the Substantial New Programme of Action which emerged from the 1981 Paris Conference on Least Developed Countries was the need for simpler, as well as more effective and responsive, aid programmes. There have been some moves towards co-ordinated programmes by, for example, the Nordic countries and the European Community. However, more could usefully be done to co-ordinate activities, either through multilateral agencies or in association with them. If the former, a precondition might be a greater element of flexibility in their eligibility rules.

External Threats

However significant the role of economic development in preventing internal unrest and instability in the longer term, other measures are required where states are at risk from external attack. Among these measures are those that seek to reduce tension and build mutual confidence or which are geared towards anticipating and identifying factors which might lead to an outbreak of hostilities. It is obviously much less costly in terms of lives and resources if preventive measures can be taken before a crisis develops rather than waiting until one has occurred. Many of these measures can be taken on a regional basis as well as by the parties directly involved in a dispute. Some could be dealt with more appropriately by the UN or other international organisations.

Confidence Building Measures

Considerable attention has been given to the concept of 'confidence-building' in recent years, notably in Europe within the context of the Conference on Security and Co-operation in Europe but latterly also in the United Nations and elsewhere. While interest has been growing, Confidence Building Measures (CBMs) remain fairly ill-defined. In European terms they are almost exclusively military in character, the aim being to increase transparency through such measures as the notification of troop movements, and thereby to reduce the threat of surprise attack. For the most part they are practical steps which are relatively easily verifiable. However, in discussions on extending the concept, the Soviet Union and its allies have laid some stress on more declaratory measures such as non-first-use of nuclear weapons. In the UN context, many Third World countries also wished to extend the concept to include economic and social measures, not least because such factors have frequently given rise to disputes. However, in thus extending their scope, CBMs perhaps become too all-encompassing and may lose their impact.

None the less, even within a relatively restricted definition, some measures have been proposed which are of considerable relevance to a number of micro-states. The Contadora Group, for example, has put forward a number of objectives in the light of the conflicts in Central America. These include: keeping registers of military installations, troops and weapons in the area; preparing censuses of foreign military and security advisers; eliminating illegal arms traffic, and establishing mechanisms for resolving inter-state disputes.

The usefulness of Confidence Building Measures inevitably relies on the willingness of states to renounce the use or the threat of force. But they depend also on the capacity of states to implement them; an obvious prior condition would be a state's ability to control its armed forces. For micro-states, outside assistance in monitoring implementation would be crucial, whether it is in the form of technical assistance (not least in gathering statistics) or in the provision of information transmitted by satellite. (The latter might have important civil purposes, as in spotting possible poachers in a state's EEZ, as well as military uses.) External financial help would also be necessary. In the case of micro-states, Confidence Building Measures could probably best be organised by, and channelled through, regional bodies.

Crisis Anticipation

The UN Charter sets out a number of ways of settling disputes peacefully. The parties are enjoined first of all to:

> Seek a solution by negotiation, enquiry, mediation, conciliation, arbitration, judicial settlement, resort to regional agencies or arrangements, or other peaceful means of their own choice. [article 33.]

Any member state, not only those party to the dispute, may alert the Security Council to a potential trouble-spot,[5] and parties to a dispute have a duty to take it to the Security Council if they have failed to resolve their differences (article 37).

This is not the place to examine at length the means available to states to settle their disputes before taking them to the United Nations. This has been done by others, including the David Davies Memorial Institute which published a report on the peaceful settlement of disputes in 1972.[6] The methods outlined in this and other studies include both diplomatic and judicial means of settlement. The former include bilateral negotiations between the parties to the dispute; the use of good offices, such as those of the UN Secretary-General; mediation, an example being that attempted by Secretary of State Haig during the Falkland Islands conflict; inquiry, a UN example being the 1982 fact-finding commission set up by the Security Council to investigate the attempted coup in the Seychelles; and conciliation. Judicial settlement includes arbitration as well as recourse to the International Court of Justice. There is, as the 1972 DDMI study put it:

> a vast network of international institutions designed for the judicial settlement or conciliation of disputes . . . the character and functions of which are extremely varied. Some are organs of regional political organisations, e.g. the African Commission of Mediation, Conciliation and Arbitration . . . Others are independent of any political organisation, e.g. the Permanent Court of Arbitration and numerous bilateral commissions of arbitration or conciliation. Some are standing tribunals; others have to be established as and when occasion arises. In some the tribunal is elected by a group of States; in others it is appointed by the parties to the dispute. Some have a general competence in regard to any dispute or any legal dispute; others are limited to disputes with respect to particular matters, e.g. human rights, foreign investments . . . In some the tribunal may be seized of a dispute only by agreement of both parties; in others the agreement has been given in advance and the act of one party alone will suffice to establish the tribunal's jurisdiction to deal with the dispute.[7]

Since the means exist, therefore, it is clear that the problem lies with governments in not using them.

Numerous efforts have been made officially and unofficially to improve these procedures and to make them better known and more available to governments. In the field of conciliation, for example, the Swiss government has been particularly active in promoting new procedures to complement those that already exist. Various non-governmental bodies exist, including the Foundation for International Conciliation based in Geneva. Within the UN system itself, proposals for reform or improvement have been frequent. Most recommendations have concentrated on the functioning of the Security Council and the office of the Secretary-General. Both were, for example, prominent in the Manila Declaration on the Peaceful Settlement of Disputes between States adopted by the General Assembly in November 1982. Among other proposals, the Declaration suggests greater use by the Security Council of its fact-finding capacity. It is also encouraged to act without delay in cases where international disputes may develop into armed conflict. This latter point was taken further by the distinguished American lawyer, Louis B. Sohn, who has suggested that the Security Council has been too constrained by its own Rules of Precedures to be able to act quickly enough. He proposed various procedures which would involve the Council at an earlier stage, including the use of regional monitoring groups acting in co-operation with the Secretary-General to bring disputes to the Council's attention.[8]

The present Secretary-General, Sr. Perez de Cuellar, has also announced his intention to play 'a more forthright role in bringing potentially dangerous situations to the attention of the Security Council' (within the framework of article 99). He noted that although he tried to keep watch for problems likely to result in conflict and to do what he could 'to pre-empt them by quiet diplomacy', the diplomatic means open to him were 'quite limited'. He therefore intended:

> to develop a wider and more systematic capacity for fact-finding in potential conflict areas. Such efforts would naturally be undertaken in close co-ordination with the Council. Moreover, the Council itself could devise more swift and responsive procedures for sending good offices missions, military or civilian observers or a United Nations presence to areas of potential conflict. Such measures could inhibit the deterioration of conflict situations and might also be of real assistance to the parties in resolving incipient disputes by peaceful means.[9]

This proposal of the Secretary-General should be supported. Fact-finding and the gathering of intelligence are essential means of anticipating crises at an early stage. Since few micro-states have the resources to undertake this, we further recommend that intelligence is a fruitful field for co-operation which friendly developed states might undertake. We also suggest that it is often a false economy on the part of developed countries to cut down on overseas posts which could keep them in close touch with local problems and developments, thus giving them early warning of potentially dangerous situations in remote areas.

The Report of the Palme Commission contains some interesting suggestions for strengthening the UN security system. Their suggested 'anticipatory procedures', in response to a request from at least one of the parties, would consist of three consecutive steps: (a) a fact-finding mission; (b) a military observer team; and (c) a UN military force within the likely zone of hostilities to act as 'a visible deterrent to a potential aggressor'.[10]

There is little doubt that the introduction of UN forces before the outbreak of hostilities would in many cases prevent an attack from taking place. But, as the Report recognizes, acceptance of this procedure would depend on a concordat among the Permanent Members of the UN not to exercise their right of veto. Accepting a request from only one of the parties would also be controversial. It therefore seems unlikely that agreement could be reached on this scenario in the present political climate.

Cure

Consideration has been given in this chapter to preventive measures which can be taken to make micro-states less vulnerable either to an internal coup or to an external attack. What action can and should be taken – and by whom – once violence has broken out remains to be discussed.

Economic Sanctions

The range of policy options available to the international community and its individual members in the event of a crisis is, of course, considerable, from doing nothing to military intervention. Within these limits, measures may include: an individual state making confidential representations to the state (s) concerned; the imposition of an arms embargo; the withdrawal of aid; the freezing of assets, and the imposition of trading sanctions, unilaterally, by a regional grouping, or by the United Nations.[11]

Interest in the use of sanctions as a means of exerting pressure on a delinquent state without resort to military force has grown in recent years. The United States has a long tradition, dating back to Thomas Jefferson, of using economic sanctions as a policy instrument. It has also, as a 'major supplier of raw materials as well as of industrial equipment and technology, . . . made trade embargoes an instrument of its foreign policy to a greater extent than other countries'.[12] In some cases it enlisted OAS support, for example in Cuba and the Dominican Republic. In the former case, sanctions were a failure and Cuba became even more dependent on the Soviet Union. Sanctions may have had an effect on the Dominican Republic; they were, in any case, lifted as soon as the Trujillo dictatorship was overthrown. Other countries have also used sanctions, including the Soviet Union against Yugoslavia and Albania; without achieving the desired political objective in either case. AOPEC has also used sanctions in the aftermath of the 1973 Arab–Israeli War.

The UN Charter (in articles 41 and 42) lists various measures 'not involving the use of armed force' which the Security Council may apply in respect of 'threats to the peace, breaches of the peace and acts of aggression'. These include 'complete or partial interruption of economic relations and of rail, sea, air, postal, telegraphic, radio and other means of communications'. Article 42 includes provision for a blockade. The sanctions imposed against Rhodesia by the UN Security Council, at the request of the United Kingdom, constituted the most widely supported use of sanctions to date. The extent of their role in persuading the Rhodesians to negotiate a settlement remains a matter for debate.

The impact of sanctions is always uncertain. In many instances the imposition of an embargo has had such a marginal impact that the objective was clearly symbolic, reflecting the desire to appear to be doing something rather than nothing. The example of the European Community's limited sanctions against the Soviet Union in the aftermath of the Soviet invasion of Afghanistan is a case in point. However, sanctions have, on occasions, had a more significant impact. In the case of the Argentinian invasion of the Falklands, for example, the fact that the members of the European Community first imposed an arms embargo and then, collectively, introduced sanctions on Argentine exports was important, for the United Kingdom, the Community itself and, potentially at least, for Argentina.[13] However, in assessing their importance, the EC's sanctions have to be set in the context of the United Kingdom's despatch of forces to retake the Islands. The imposition of sanctions raises numerous difficult questions and conflicts of interest.[14] Should they, for example, be mandatory or voluntary? To have any effect must they be comprehensive or are embargoes on selected goods sufficient? Economic sanctions often have a boomerang effect, damaging trade and causing unemployment in the countries imposing sanctions. Ideally, of course, they should be universally applied in order to be effective. But universality of support is usually difficult to achieve. It was significant that the United Kingdom did not seek UN sanctions against Argentina; the likelihood of a Soviet veto was too great. Lack of universality in the Cuban case allowed the Soviet Union to support that country and South Africa did the same when sanctions were imposed on Rhodesia.

Economic sanctions, according to one commentator, may well have economic effects but 'one of the most serious flaws in sanctions policies has been reliance on the theory that they can be depended on ... to have a corrective effect – to bring about the desired political changes'.[15] Sanctions remain one policy option and obviously need to be considered seriously as an internationally more acceptable means of exerting pressure than armed intervention. Used alone, however, they may well be ineffectual.

It is inconceivable that a micro-state would itself seek to impose sanctions. There might, however, be circumstances in which, for example, a regional organisation might choose this method of exerting pressure in support of a micro-state which was the victim of an act of aggression, as in the case already mentioned of the arms embargo and sanctions imposed on Argentina by the European Community after the former's invasion of the Falkland Islands.

The Problems of Intervention

Theoretically, this should be a problem for the United Nations, since its founders envisaged that it would be the body that would keep the peace, and member states in adhering to the Charter undertake not to use force except in self-defence (including the right of collective self-defence). But in practice the collective security system set out in the Charter has remained largely a dead letter owing to the failure of the permanent members to agree. The system of UN peacekeeping which has evolved in its place, is dependent upon the consent of the warring parties and is only set up after the start of hostilities although there is no reason under internaional law to prevent steps being taken to meet a threat to the peace. UN peacekeeping forces (excepting the unique circumstances of the Korean War) are not designed or equipped to enforce a solution. With the exception of the setting up of UNEF I after the Suez War of 1956 and UNSF in West Irian, all peacekeeping operations have been set up by the Security Council and are thus subject to the veto.[16] Their primary role has been to maintain effective cease-fires, keeping parties apart until negotiations can take place. Their success clearly depends on the cooperation of the parties to the dispute and a clearly defined mandate.

As Professor Rosalyn Higgins pointed out in her 1984 Grotius Lecture:

> At the heart of the Charter was the intention that it would be realistic to enjoin states not to use force save in self-defence, because collective security would be provided to ensure that rights would not be denied in a manner which might threaten international peace. The reality is that the UN collective security system has totally failed, and I believe that it is of critical importance frankly to acknowledge this and to address our minds to the consequences that flow from this reality. From the outset the UN has been unable to set up the forces with which it was envisaged the Security Council would provide collective security. The umbrella which was to encourage members to limit their use of force to self-defence has never really been in place.

The consequences of the failure of the UN collective security system, as Professor Higgins pointed out in a later passage, is that: 'sometimes interventions for utterly unacceptable purposes are made; and sometimes unlawful interventions for more acceptable purposes are made'.[17]

There would thus appear to be a need to identify more precisely the principles governing the circumstances in which intervention is justified and the form that it should take. Is it possible to identify objective criteria to determine whether self-determination has ceased to exist? How, for instance, is the line to be drawn between respecting the principles of sovereignty and non-interference in the domestic affairs of states on the one hand, and, on the other, making it possible for the strong to go to the defence of the weak when they are attacked, or to intervene in circumstances where serious violations of human rights are taking place, without the intervening powers opening themselves to charges of illegality'[18]

The two most recent examples, worth considering since both involved the invasion of a micro-territory, are the Falkland Islands and Grenada. In the first case the aggressor was Argentina and the victim a dependent territory of the United Kingdom. The latter immediately reported the Argentinian invasion and occupation of the Falkland Islands to the Security Council and tabled a resolution calling for the withdrawal of the invader. However, since the United Nations lacked the means to evict the Argentinians, United Kingdom forces exercised their right of self-defence and liberated the Islands. As the votes in the General Assembly indicated, the reaction of the world community to the British intervention was for the most part favourable (apart from the predictable Communist and Latin American votes). The Argentinian invasion was seen as a clear violation of such key UN principles as non-intervention, the non-use of force, and the right of self-determination of peoples (particularly colonial peoples). The British action was thus welcomed as likely to discourage other would-be aggressors.

In contrast, the American invasion of Grenada was more controversial, for a number of reasons. First, while the obligation of the United Kingdom to go to the defence of its dependent territory, the Falkland Islands, was clear cut, the American invasion of Grenada following an internal coup was seen by many as violating the principle of non-intervention in the domestic affairs of an independent state. Secondly, one of the justifications advanced – the invitation from the Governor-General – was difficult to substantiate.[19] In the event, it became clear that the great majority of the population had welcomed their liberation by the Americans from an unpleasant political regime which had seized power by force. Elections were subsequently organised, as the Americans had promised, which were widely held to have been conducted fairly.

This question of intervention is highly emotive. The Charter and many subsequent UN instruments enshrine the principle of non-intervention and non-interference in the domestic affairs of states, and most small states, particularly those which are newly independent (but also many states in Eastern Europe), understandably attach great importance to this provision. The Western democracies, on their part, have also welcomed it as providing some safeguard against the Brezhnev Doctrine of the limited sovereignty of Socialist states which was advanced in justification of the Soviet invasion of Czechoslovakia in 1968.[20]

One of the great virtues of the Charter has been its flexibility and adaptability to a changing world. There has, for instance, already been some modification in practice as regards article 2 (7) which precludes intervention in matters of domestic jurisdiction. In the early years of the United Nations, this was strictly interpreted and any discussion, let alone intervention, in the domestic affairs of states, was ruled out of order. This prohibition was first breached in the cases of apartheid and colonial issues, largely because this principle was seen as an obstacle to the promotion of another United Nations principle, the right of self-determination of peoples.[21] Issues that had previously been perceived as solely within domestic jurisdiction became classified as issues of international concern.

In judging cases of intervention, self-determination should be taken into account, as well as the Charter obligation 'to promote and encourage respect for Human Rights and for fundamental freedoms'. The Charter clearly allows for collective intervention in response to a government's call for help. Given the limited resources available to a micro-state to resist an external armed attack, outside help will be critical. Such help should be confined to repelling or capturing the aggressors, and restoring peaceful conditions. Sanctions by the United Nations itself are only permitted where there has been a finding by the Security Council of 'a threat to the peace, breach of the peace, or act of aggression' (article 39). Normally, gross violations of human rights, while deplorable, will not be perceived as constituting a threat to or breach of international peace.

Where there is a broad consensus that sanctions are necessary and desirable, then the possibility exists of authorising military, economic and diplomatic sanctions through the technique of declaring the situation a threat to peace, and then providing for sanctions under article 41 of the Charter. This was what was done over the Rhodesian Unilateral Declaration of Independence in 1965. However, for quite different reasons beyond the scope of this book, the United Nations will not itself through this route be able to mount military intervention against a state violating human rights.

As for military intervention by individual states, the possibilities are even more limited. The United Nations Charter only permits the use of force in self-defence. It is clearly not permissible under the Charter to intervene militarily in another country to redress a gross violation of human rights. While this has the result of allowing deplorable conditions to continue, it is also true that military intervention for human rights purposes would be open to abuse by states using it as a pretext for territorial ambitions. A number of states, including the United Kingdom, apparently take this view of Vietnamese intervention in Kampuchea. The reality is that when intervention to end human rights abuses is generally perceived as bona fide it is widely tolerated, notwithstanding legal difficulties. This was the case, for example, with Tanzania's military action in Uganda in 1978/9, which, however, occurred after Uganda's attack on Tanzania.

The bona fides of a state's motives for intervening on alleged human rights grounds will turn upon a cluster of factors, all especially relevant to a micro-state. These include: whether the help has been confined to capturing or repelling those responsible for the excesses; whether democratic elections are rapidly organised, under United Nations, or possibly Commonwealth, supervision (in the case of a member state) which would allow the local people to exercise their right to determine their future government; whether the period preceding the election is short and the time-limit announced in advance (i.e. in time for political campaigning, the drawing up of electoral rolls etc.); whether the intervening state has withdrawn immediately after the elections, or before if its peacekeeping role could be taken over by a United Nations, Commonwealth or regional force.

This, together with pressure for United Nations economic and diplomatic sanctions on 'threat to peace' grounds against major human rights violations, is probably the best that one can reasonably hope for, at least at present. It is, of course, open to states to construct their aid programmes with human rights compliance by recipients to the fore as a factor in deciding whether aid, and what type of aid, should be given. In our view this is to be encouraged, notwithstanding the very real difficulties that the Carter Administration experienced with such a policy, and the failure of the European Community to negotiate the inclusion of a human rights clause to the Lomé Convention.

Peacekeeping

The United Nations
As already stated, the United Nations as at present constituted cannot undertake coercive action. Thus, if the initial phase of evicting the invader is beyond the defence capability of the victim (as is likely in the case of a micro-state), this must be carried out by an external source. The first objective of the victim must therefore be to secure outside aid. This could come from a single state which it trusted, or from a group of states, such as fellow members of a regional or sub-regional organisation if arrangements already existed for joint operations, although the legal problems of intervention, already discussed, militate against such aid being easily, or quickly, forthcoming. However, once the coercive action is over, a UN peacekeeping force can play a valuable role in supervising a cease-fire, policing, observing (and if necessary organising) elections and emergency care of the civilian population, the last with the help of appropriate UN specialised agencies. The UN has wide experience in all these fields and its reputation for impartiality is a particular asset in the observation of elections.

At present Cyprus is the only micro-state where a UN peace-keeping force is in operation. The UN involvement in Cyprus is an example of both its strengths and limitations. A UN peacekeeping force (UNFICYP) has been in Cyprus since 1964, sent there originally to keep the peace between the Greek and Turkish communities following serious inter-communal fighting in December 1963. However, it was powerless to prevent the Turkish invasion of the north of the island in 1974 in support of the Turkish community, although the UN force successfully prevented the Turkish capture of Nicosia airport.

UNFICYP has otherwise continued to play a valuable role within its mandate and limited military capabilities. It controls a buffer zone between the two cease-fire lines that have divided the island since the Turkish invasion. It has some 150 posts along the buffer zone and undertakes round-the-clock surveillance. It also monitored the evacuation of Greek civilians from the Turkish area to the extent that verification was permitted. UNFICYP includes political as well as military personnel, an economics section and a police adviser. The military contingents have over the years been drawn from a number of countries, but the chief-of-staff position alternates between the British and Canadians, thus providing continuity. Logistic support is provided by the British forces from the sovereign base areas. Sr. Perez de Cuellar, the present United Nations Secretary-General, has been particularly active in encouraging a settlement in Cyprus.

Although it is sometimes argued that the continuing presence of a UN force in Cyprus tends to encourage the status quo, there can be little doubt that its withdrawal would precipitate a resumption of the fighting. There would thus appear to be little alternative to its continuance while efforts are pursued to arrive at a political settlement.

The credibility of UN peacekeeping has been seriously questioned – from the eviction of UNEF 1 in 1967 via the Turkish invasion of Cyprus (1974) to Israel's treatment of UNIFIL (1982). This reaction is in many ways unfair, since it is based on a misconception of the United Nations' severely circumscribed mandate. UN peacekeeping is extraordinarily cheap, in money and human lives; its positive achievements are seldom noticed. Although the Congo operation was controversial, 'international peacekeeping not only survived the challenge but established beyond any doubt that, without its involvement, the Congo would have ceased to survive as a unified nation and could easily have become a battleground of economic and ideological warfare'.[22] In the Middle East, too, UN forces have played an important role. Henry Kissinger, who otherwise has little use for the United Nations, was quick to call for the assistance of UNEF II in negotiating the Israeli withdrawal from the Sinai.

The strengthening of the United Nations' peacekeeping capabilities is very much in the interest of micro-states which lack the means to defend themselves. It is also in the longer-term interest of the major powers. The experience of the Multinational Force in the Lebanon in 1982 illustrated the political and military hazards of operating without a clearly defined mandate and without the agreement of the parties to the dispute.

Both the Secretary-General of the UN, and the Palme Commission have taken a new critical look at existing peacekeeping machinery and made a number of interesting suggestions for reform which deserve further study. One means of strengthening UN peacekeeping operations suggested by the Secretary-General is: 'to underpin the authority of peacekeeping operations by guarantees, including explicit guarantees for collective or individual supportive action'.

The Palme Report, stressing the need 'to bridge the huge gap between the active security concept envisaged by the Charter and the limited peacekeeping role that has evolved in its place', urged, as a start:

international agreement in support of collective security operations for all Third World disputes which are likely to cause, or actually result in, a breach of the peace – it being clearly understood that the decision to initiate collective security action would not prejudge the substantive issues causing the conflict.[23]

The proposal envisaged the existence of standby forces set aside for such operations; states committed in advance to accept such action; and the Permanent Members of the Security Council agreeing to co-operate, at least to the extent of voluntarily refraining from using the veto.

Greater consideration should be given to these suggestions. Meanwhile, credibility in UN peacekeeping will best be restored if member nations are more prepared to accept: automatic earmarking of men and weapons for this purpose; automatic funding; guarantees by the larger states that they will underpin the operations to which they have committed themselves; more evaluations of past lessons; more advanced planning, and a clearer understanding of what constitutes a practicable mandate and what (like UNIFIL) does not.

In some circumstances, peacekeeping could be more appropriately carried out by a Commonwealth or regional force if such were available. These latter would have the advantage of not being subject to a veto in the Security Council in cases where East–West rivalries may arise.

The Commonwealth

The most successful example of Commonwealth involvement in peacekeeping was Zimbabwe (Rhodesia). Since there has been no instance of a Commonwealth observer/peace force operating in a Commonwealth micro-state, the Zimbabwe case is worth citing as evidence of the effective use of a Commonwealth force. The means by which Zimbabwe should be brought to independence were discussed exhaustively at the Commonwealth Conference in Lusaka (August 1979). This was followed by a Constitutional Conference in London (September–December 1979) at which the detailed plans were agreed. These included the setting up of a Commonwealth monitoring force (CMF) to monitor and observe the cease-fire, maintain contact with the Commanders of the Rhodesian and Patriotic Front forces and monitor agreed crossing lines. In addition to the British contingent, the CMF included 150 Australians, seventy-four New Zealanders, fifty Kenyans and twenty-four Fijians. In spite of the very great difficulties which had to be overcome, this Commonwealth operation was totally successful; the cease-fire was maintained and, contrary to prognostications, free and fair elections were held under Commonwealth observation.

General Indar Jit Rikhye, in his authoritative book on peace-keeping, considers the possibility of extending the Commonwealth peacekeeping capacity in the light of the successful Zimbabwe operation. His proposals are worth considering in view of his unrivalled practical, as well as theoretical, experience in UN peacekeeping operations:

> The Commonwealth monitoring force [in Zimbabwe] was not exactly a Commonwealth operation because it was a British responsibility and not under the Commonwealth organisation. Yet it indicated a capability which the Commonwealth could easily develop. The Commonwealth has a common language and there is a commonality of military organisations, procedures and training. Several Commonwealth countries have UN peace observation experience, and Australia, India, Nigeria, Ghana, Canada and Britain have had experience in peacekeeping forces. Thus there is knowledge and capability to have contingents on a standby arrangement. In the absence of an agreement on the implementation of Article 43 of the UN Charter, such an arrangement could prove useful in creating a Commonwealth component just as one had been set up during the Korean War. A Commonwealth peacekeeping force is also a practical possibility if it is politically desirable. The Commonwealth Secretariat would have the ready availability of the Commonwealth's military attachés in London and could call for support from Common-wealth nations for logistics and administration.[24]

The Commonwealth Heads of State might consider authorising the Commonwealth Secretary-General to prepare advance contingency plans for such a force (possibly in co-operation with Commonwealth Defence attachés in London, as General Rikhye suggests). These might include undertakings by individual states members to provide 'standby' forces and/or services, provisions for co-monitoring of forces, joint exercises etc. Contributions from the wealthier members might include assistance with communications, transport, patrol boats and so on. Commonwealth peace observer forces should operate, like their UN equivalent, 'with the consent of the parties' who should also agree to the national contingents participating in the force. A Commonwealth force would, of course, only be appropriate in the case of a dispute between Commonwealth member states, or involving a Commonwealth dependent state.

Regional and Sub-regional
Regional and sub-regional peacekeeping forces are other possible options open to micro-states. (The security provisions of the various regional organisations are discussed in Chapter 2.) The UN Charter (Chapter VIII) authorises regional arrangements relating to the maintenance of International Peace and Security provided these are consistent with the Purposes and Principles of the United Nations. It also lays down that no enforcement action shall be taken at a regional level without the authorisation of the Security Council and that: 'The Security Council shall at all times be kept fully informed of activities undertaken or in contemplation under regional arrangements by regional agencies for the maintenance of international peace and security' (article 54).

In practice, however, despite a number of exceptions (e.g. the Arab League Security Force in Kuwait, the Arab Deterrent Force in the Lebanon, the OAS Inter-American Peace Force in the Dominican Republic and the OAU peacekeeping force in Chad), the main regional organisations have concentrated more on mediation than on peacekeeping. As far as micro-states are concerned, discussions taking place in the Caribbean on sub-regional security arrangements appear to be more promising (see Annex B). The possibility of sub-regional security arrangements in the South Pacific is discussed in Annex C. These two areas would seem to offer the most suitable conditions for contingency planning at a sub-regional level in joint peacekeeping and other security matters.

The Palme Report included useful comments on the regional security dimension. It noted that regional peacekeeping efforts were often hampered not only by political differences but also by lack of funds (as in Chad). It stressed the need to develop close co-operation between the UN and regional organisations designed to provide UN financial and logistical support to back up regional security measures. The Report concluded that:

> a more effective role for regional organisations could contribute to international peace and security by providing a framework and mechanism for the prevention, or at least containment, and resolution of local conflicts. Stronger regional organisations also could improve the capacity of the countries in a region or sub-region to withstand pressures from outside powers, thus reducing opportunities for the latter to aggravate local conflicts or disrupt intra-regional relations. By the same token, this could serve the interests of the major powers, helping them to withstand pressure from inside a region to become involved in a local dispute and reducing the risk of extending the geographical area of potential East–West confrontation.[25]

Other Multilateral Peacekeeping Operations

Two other attempts at peacekeeping which may have useful lessons for our study, are the Multinational Force and Observers in the Sinai (MFO) and the Multinational Force in Beirut (MNF). The former undertook a successful peacekeeping role as an integral part of the Egypt–Israel Peace Treaty of March 1979; the latter was sent (twice) to Beirut in the aftermath of the Israeli invasion of Lebanon. Its peacekeeping operation ended in failure and withdrawal.

In neither case was a United Nations' or regional solution possible. Both were undertaken because there was no prospect of agreement in the UN Security Council. In the case of the MFO, for example, the Soviet Union, in response to calls from many Arab countries, intimated early on that it would apply a veto to any proposal to extend the life of the UN Emergency Force in the Sinai, which had been regarded as the possible peacekeeping body. Both the MFO and the MNF were initiated by the United States and included contingents from a number of other countries: the MFO had forces from ten countries with a force commander (General Bull Hansen of Norway) from an eleventh; the MNF had a more limited make-up with contingents from only four countries, France, Italy, the UK and the United States, all of which had traditional links with the Middle East.

The success of the MFO was due primarily to the willingness of

Egypt and Israel to execute their treaty obligations. The role of the United States was also crucial in encouraging both sides to hold to their commitments. In addition, the MFO was established as an international body under a Director-General who had considerable leeway within the terms of the Treaty. No such body, nor even more than day-to-day co-ordination, was established by the forces in Beirut. The MFO had a more neutral composition than the MNF and a clear mandate to inspect and verify Israel's withdrawal. It was regarded as impartial by both sides. It has perhaps added interest for micro-states since it included forces from Fiji which received help in the matter of equipment and training from the United States and 'an attractive financial arrangement was also worked out which took account of Fiji's economic needs'.[26]

Admittedly the MNF had a near impossible task. But the ignominious outcome was made even more certain by its failure to gain acceptance as an impartial body, and by the level of its military activities which went well beyond what has come to be accepted for a peacekeeping force. The lessons of the MFO operation are interesting in the context of this study because they indicate some of the basic conditions that are required for any non-UN multilateral peacekeeping force to be successful.

Finally, the potential role of the European Community in a peacekeeping capacity deserves a mention. For the most part, relations between the EC and micro-states are limited to economic matters under the Lomé Convention or bilateral aid agreements. However, a number of developments over the last decade have suggested at least the potential for a greater political role and even for military action. The development of European Political Co-operation, whereby the ten member states of the Community co-ordinate their foreign policies, has created the incentive for several states and groups of states to seek a political dialogue: in the case of ASEAN, for example, the EC–ASEAN co-operation agreement allows for discussion of political as well as economic matters. The agreement by the Ten on the so-called Venice Declaration on the Arab–Israeli dispute in 1980 included the statement that they 'were prepared to participate within the framework of a comprehensive settlement in a system of binding guarantees including [guarantees] on the ground'.

Although the Community as a body has not as yet undertaken a peacekeeping role, a number of its member states have security arrangements with former dependent territories and have come to their aid on request. With the agreement of their partners, individual member states participated in the MFO in Sinai. Several also contributed to the MNF in Lebanon, and many have participated in UN peacekeeping forces. They thus have considerable experience to offer in the right political circumstances.

Notes

1. Both figures are for 1981. See *World Development Report 1983*, Oxford University Press for the World Bank, 1983, p. 204.
2. See *Report of the Study Group of the Commonwealth Parliamentary Association on the Security of Small States*, co-chaired by Senator the Hon. Sir Arnott Cato, KCMG (President of the Senate, Barbados) and Senator Wesley M. Barrett, JP (President of the Senate, Fiji), 19–21 September 1984.
3. See Joanna Moss and John Ravenhill, 'Trade between the ACP and EEC during Lomé 1' in Christopher Stevens (ed.), *EEC and the Third World: A Survey 3*, Hodder and Stoughton, 1983.
4. Fred Fluitman and John White, *Technology and Employment Programme: External Development Finance and Choice of Technology*, International Labour Office, Geneva, 1981, p. 20.
5. A non-member state may alert the Security Council to any dispute to which it is a party 'if it accepts in advance, for the purposes of the dispute, the obligations of pacific settlement provided in the present Charter'. (article 35 (2)) Further proposals on this subject are contained in the Manila Declaration (1982) on the Peaceful Settlement of International Disputes.
6. *International Disputes: the Legal Aspects*, Report of a Study Group of the David Davies Memorial Institute, Europa Publications, 1972.
7. Ibid., p. 19.
8. Louis B. Sohn, 'The Security Council's role in the Settlement of International Disputes', *American Journal of International Law*, April 1984, Vol. 78, No. 2, p. 403.
9. *1982 Annual Report of the UN Secretary-General on the Work of the Organisation*.
10. *Common Security: A Programme for Disarmament*, Report of the Palme Commission, Pan Books 1982, p. 130.
11. For a useful discussion of such measures, see Evan Luard, 'Human Rights and Foreign Policy', *International Affairs*, Autumn 1980, Vol. 56, No. 4, p. 598.
12. Robin Renwick, *Economic Sanctions*, Harvard University Centre for International Affairs, 1981, p. 60.
13. See Geoffrey Edwards, 'Europe and the Falklands Crisis 1982', *Journal*

of Common Market Studies, June 1984, Vol. XXII, No. 4.

14. James Barber, 'Economic Sanctions as a Policy Instrument', *International Affairs*, July 1979, Vol. 55, No. 3.

15. Renwick, op. cit., p. 91.

16. The 'Uniting for Peace' Resolution (adopted in 1950 in a Korean context) provides for action by the General Assembly in cases where action in the Security Council has been blocked by a veto. It was challenged by the United Kingdom and France in the Suez context and has always been opposed by the Soviet Union.

17. Rosalyn Higgins, 'Grotius and the United Nations', in *International Social Science Journal*, No. 103, April 1985.

18. See Chapter 3 for the legal argument on Intervention.

19. See Chapter 3.

20. The Soviet representative in the UN Security Council at the time defended his Government's action as having been taken in response to an 'invitation' (which the Czechoslovakian Government denied) and claimed that the Warsaw Pact forces had undertaken regional action in collective self-defence in accordance with articles 51 and 52 of the UN Charter.

21. It is also beginning to be breached on Human Rights issues, see Chapter 3.

22. Indar Jit Rikhye, *The Theory and Practice of Peacekeeping*, Hurst, 1984, p. 89.

23. *Common Security: A Programme for Disarmament*, Report of the Palme Commission, Pan Books, 1982, p. 131.

24. *The Theory and Practice of Peacekeeping*, op. cit.

25. Report of the Palme Commission, op. cit., p. 130.

26. Alan James, *Symbol in Sinai: The Multinational Force and Observers*, paper presented to the International Peace Academy, October 1984, p. 7.

6 Recommendations

The security and stability of a micro-state is primarily in the hands of the state itself. We do not suggest that states should adopt a particular system of government, although it is clear that systems which do not allow for grievances to be aired and satisfied are likely to lose popular support; they may also alienate potential aid donors. If the government of a micro-state is notable for its abuse of the rule of law and absence of representative institutions, the international community should, we suggest, be reluctant to intervene on its behalf. Nor do we advocate any specific economic system, although it is obvious that a safe and predictable investment climate is likely to be more attractive to foreign investors, and in some cases to aid donors. The policies which a micro-state adopts are ultimately the responsibility and choice of its people. However, a micro-state may need help in preserving its independence and integrity and it is generally in the interest of friendly democratic countries to aid them in these objectives.

There is much that a micro-state could and should do for itself to strengthen its own individual security before looking to the international community for assistance. Such measures cannot be restricted simply to orthodox defence arrangements; they need also to be designed to promote political stability and the welfare and prosperity of its people. None the less, throughout this study we have been conscious of the particular dependence of micro-states on external assistance, whether military, political or economic, and whether provided bilaterally or through multilateral bodies. We have also been aware of the possible repercussions of instability in micro-states on the international system as a whole.

This study therefore has a two-fold purpose: it aims to elucidate the difficulties caused by a state's lack of size and also to suggest ways in which the Governments of micro-states might seek to avoid or overcome these difficulties. Beyond this it also seeks to raise the consciousness of others, especially decision-makers in the developed world, to measures that could be of practical value to micro-states as means of promoting their own security from both external attack and internal *coups*. These measures can be bilateral or multilateral, economic, political or military.

Defence Assistance

Among the more important aspects of assistance that can be provided bilaterally by well-disposed states are:

(a) An assessment of the internal and external threats to be faced and a definition of the size and shape of the forces required to counter these threats.

(b) The provision of equipment and the resources necessary, subsequently, to sustain it in operation (subsidised if necessary).

(c) The provision of training (in the micro-state and at donor countries' training establishments).

(d) The provision of support and logistic facilities (subsidised where appropriate).

(e) The loan of expert personnel to assist with the management of forces until sufficient indigenous personnel are trained and gain the required experience; in other words, to provide an expert framework within which a new and inexperienced force can develop its capabilities.

Specifically related to maritime security, further aid might be provided in the form of:

(a) direct help, for example in policing EEZs, by friendly forces (such as New Zealand maritime patrol aircraft provide in Fijian waters); and assistance in setting up systems for the exchange of information between micro-states regarding the policing of EEZs;

(b) assistance with framing appropriate laws to provide the legal basis for maritime operations;

(c) political and diplomatic support in protection of micro-states' EEZs from more powerful countries.

Given the economic constraints under which most micro-states exist, donors should seriously consider the provision of such assistance at no cost, or very little cost, to recipients. Well-disposed states may also wish to consider, favourably, requests from micro-states to station forces in their territory as a deterrent against aggression or perhaps to enter into treaty arrangements to provide forces in time of need.

Intelligence is of such importance if limited resources are to be well used that donors may also wish to consider arrangements to provide recipients with material they cannot gather for themselves. And, given the intelligence required to respond appropriately and effectively to any requests for aid in defence matters, we consider it a false economy for developed states to cut back too far their overseas posts in small states.

Trade and Economic Assistance

In acknowledging the often heavy dependence of micro-states on exports of commodities, the developed world, whether acting through regional or global organisations, should support measures which encourage stability in both commodity markets and prices. Developed countries should encourage the diversification of micro-states' exports. This could be done by easing existing restrictions, both tariff and non-tariff barriers, on that trade. Many of our findings coincide with those approved by the Commonwealth Heads of Government at their meeting in Lusaka in 1979.[1] The majority of these have a wider application than that of the Commonwealth and their lack of implementation, for the most part, is much regretted. The recommendations in the Lusaka Memorandum will doubtless be reiterated and augmented in the Report of the Commonwealth Secretariat's Study Group on Small States which will be presented to the meeting of Commonwealth Heads of State in the Bahamas in October 1985.

From our study we would stress the following:

(a) International financial institutions and other development agencies need to recognise the inherent constraints on a micro-state's development imposed by the size of its population and adjust accordingly their categories for lending or their conditions for assistance.

(b) In view of the small-scale funding required for micro-states, the role of the Regional Development Banks could be further developed, both by specifically earmarking and increasing loans to micro-states and by acting as intermediaries between micro-states and the larger multilateral agencies.

(c)   There remains a need for donors to take special care not to exacerbate the problems of uneven development between urban and rural areas; agricultural and rural development schemes are as important as, and sometimes more important than, industrial development.

(d)   Donors need to increase the amount of aid that is not tied to purchases in their own countries since these have often created problems because of the inappropriateness of the technology involved. Perhaps one of the major contributions that donors can make is the provision of information on the kinds of technology available so that more rational choices can be made in response to the micro-state's needs.

(e)   Donors should look favourably on the opportunities for the development of transport and communications, especially in scattered island states which depend on sea and air links for their basic needs. The building of roads linking the interior with ports and population centres should also be given priority. All such measures can have a direct bearing on the state's stability and security.

(f)   We recommend that technical assistance should be increased and that greater provision be made for professional, technical and managerial training schemes both in the donor's and in the recipient's countries. In many micro-states 'on the job' training, or short courses in electrical and engineering maintenance could be valuable. Agencies and institutions such as the Technical Assistance Group of the Commonwealth Fund for Technical Co-operation, which have proved particularly successful should be given additional funding. Their services should be publicised; they could also provide a model for others. The extra funds involved would not be large.

(g)   Donors should consider the possibilities of co-ordinating their aid and assistance, whether through multilateral agencies or in association with them, in order to reduce the sometimes heavy administrative burden on recipients.

(h)   Donors should, to quote the Lusaka recommendations, 'ensure that adequate attention within their aid programmes is devoted to projects which promote regional co-operation and which take particular account of the needs of island, developing and other specially disadvantaged countries'.

Co-operation at Regional Levels

There has been a growing recognition by many micro-states that they lack the financial means, the expertise and the manpower to carry out all the tasks normally undertaken by states individually. They have therefore shown increasing interest in associations for mutual help and co-operation at regional and sub-regional levels. This trend should be welcomed and encouraged.

Many of the policy recommendations outlined above could also be executed at a regional or sub-regional level. The policing of EEZs by friendly forces is a case in point; joint transport services is another. The provision of training facilities for police forces at a regional level as well as co-operation between individual police forces should also be encouraged.

Few micro-states can afford to maintain adequate defence forces to guard against external threats; their limited financial and human resources are undoubtedly better deployed in ensuring internal law and order. Regional and sub-regional defence treaties and understandings have therefore assumed a greater importance. In these circumstances we recommend the following:

(a) Developed countries should encourage the formation of regional security arrangements, and if requested should be willing to provide the material help to service them.

(b) Where regional defence arrangements include provision for peace-keeping, expertise and financial and logistical support should be extended, preferably through the United Nations.

(c) Greater attention should be focused on crisis anticipation, mediation, conciliation procedures and confidence building measures in the future resolution of disputes at the regional level. States outside the region can play an important part in providing technical and financial assistance, particularly in support of confidence building measures.

Multilateral Peacekeeping

The Commonwealth

We recommend that the Commonwealth should be encouraged to play a greater security role in view of the number of micro-states that are members. Further consideration should be given to General Rikhye's proposal for a Commonwealth capacity for contingency planning for a peacekeeping role if called for by parties to a dispute.

We recommend the establishment of watchdog committees on the lines of that set up by the Commonwealth to monitor the situation in Belize whether at a regional or a global level. Alternatively, standing commissions might be preferred to these *ad hoc* watchdog committees; the issue rests largely with the states of the region involved. Standing commissions might also be useful in forewarning the UN Security Council of possible trouble spots.

The United Nations

We remain convinced that the best long-term hope for collective security remains the United Nations. A number of proposals have been put forward for strengthening its peacekeeping capacity. These include:

(a) Further consideration should be given to the 'anticipatory' procedures put forward by the UN Secretary-General and by the Palme Commission in relation to the use of 'good offices', observers and fact-finding missions. Such collective action need not prejudge substantive issues but could be used where possible when conflict threatens.

(b) Support should be given to the Palme Commission's proposals for attempting to bridge the gap between the security concept envisaged by the Charter and the limited peacekeeping role that has emerged, by, for example, member states earmarking stand-by forces and offering services (such as transport) and facilities for peacekeeping operations. Member states should also guarantee funding for those operations to which they have committed themselves. Much could also be gained if there was more advanced planning, based on the evaluation of past operations.

International Law and Intervention

Under the UN Charter, the right of intervention is strictly limited to collective self-defence. Intervention by a single state or regional body under a defence agreement in response to a call for help against an external armed attack would also appear to raise few problems. We recommend, however, that micro-states which wish to have the option of securing military support in time of need, either from a friendly power, or from a regional/sub-regional organisation should enter into formal and clear-cut agreements before a crisis occurs. Great care, however, should be taken in the drafting of the provisions. An agreement by which external intervention would take place not upon external attack, but upon certain internal events taking place, may still raise problems under contemporary international law.

We also note that although international law does not recognise the right of intervention except on very limited grounds, intervention to end major human rights abuses has sometimes been widely tolerated, notwithstanding the legal difficulties. In such cases, the bona fides of a state's motives for intervening on alleged human rights grounds will turn upon a cluster of factors, all especially relevant to a micro-state. These include confining the help to capturing or repelling those responsible for the excesses; swiftly organising democratic elections under United Nations, or possibly Commonwealth, supervision; and withdrawal immediately after the elections, or before if its peacekeeping role could be taken over by a United Nations, Commonwealth or regional force.

Draft Declaration on Micro-States

We believe that the security of micro-states could be furthered if the United Nations General Assembly were to agree on a declaration on micro-states. A draft declaration follows.

The General Assembly

Noting the special vulnerability of micro-states with respect to their sovereign equality and territorial integrity, and noting further the right of their people to self-determination,

Emphasising the particular responsibility of the international community with regard to the need to assist micro-states in the political, economic, social and other fields,

Reaffirming that the maintenance of international peace and security and the development of friendly relations and co-operation between nations are among the fundamental purposes of the United Nations,

Bearing in mind the importance of maintaining and strengthening international peace founded upon freedom, equality, justice and respect for fundamental human rights and developing friendly relations among nations irrespective of their political, economic and 'social systems or the levels of their development or their size,

Recalling the duty of States to refrain in their international relations from military, political, economic or any other form of coercion aimed against the political independence or territorial integrity of any State,

Convinced that the principles of equal rights and self-determination of peoples constitutes a significant contribution to contemporary international law, and that its effective application is of paramount importance for the promotion of friendly relations among States, based on respect for the principle of sovereign equality,

Convinced that international, regional and sub-regional institutions can play a significant part in aiding micro-states,

Deploring the use of mercenaries and proxies against freely elected governments,

Reaffirms the following principles of international law of particular relevance to micro-states:

1. Under the United Nations Charter, All peoples have the right to self-determination. By virtue of that right they freely determine their political status and freely pursue their economic, social and cultural development. The exercise of that right is not dependent upon adequacy of political, economic, social or educational preparedness nor upon size.

2. All States enjoy sovereign equality. They have equal rights and duties and are equal members of the international community, notwithstanding differences of an economic, social, political or other nature, such as size.

3. Any external attempt aimed at the partial or total disruption of the national unity and the territorial integrity of a country is incompatible with the purposes and principles of the Charter of the United Nations.

4. All States shall refrain in their international relations from the threat or use of force against the territorial integrity or political independence of any State, or in any other manner inconsistent with the purposes of the United Nations.

5. Subject to this Declaration and to Clause 8 below, no State or group of States has the right to intervene, directly or indirectly, for any reason whatsoever, in the internal or external affair of any other State. Consequently, armed intervention and all other forms of interference or attempted threats against the personality of the State or against its political, economic and cultural elements, are in violation of international law.

6. No State shall organise, assist, foment, finance, incite or tolerate subversive, terrorist or armed activities directed towards the violent overthrow of the regime of another State or interfere in civil strife in another State.

7. All States have the right to seek aid from international, regional and sub-regional institutions and from other States, and to make treaty arrangements to this end.

8. All States have the right of individual and collective self-defence as enshrined in the Charter of the United Nations. States may call for and receive assistance in exercising this right until the Security Council has taken measures necessary to maintain or restore international peace and security. In providing such assistance, States must bear in mind the need to respect the right to self-determination based on the freely expressed wishes of the people.

Note

1. The Lusaka recommendations are quoted in the House of Commons First Special Report from the Foreign Affairs Committee: *The Economic and Political Security of Small States*, May 1984.

Annex A: The States of Southern Africa*

Introduction

Although only two of the states in Southern Africa – Botswana and Lesotho – plus the dependent territory of Namibia have populations of one million or less, special consideration is given to this region for the following reasons. Although they share the economic and political vulnerability common to other micro-states, the principal factor with which the small states here have to contend is the overwhelming economic and military dominance of South Africa. This dependence on South Africa is shared, to a greater or lesser extent, by their larger neighbours – a situation which has led to the formation of the Southern African Development and Coordination Conference (SADCC).[1] This exercise in regional co-operation may well have useful lessons for other micro-states attempting to escape from a wide degree of dependence on a dominant regional power.

Until 1980 the smaller states in the region had little alternative but to deal with South Africa on a unilateral basis, although one exception to this trend is the periodic renegotiation of the Customs Agreement linking South Africa with Lesotho, Botswana and Swaziland. In general, however, continental regional bodies such as the Organisation of African Unity (OAU) – while sympathetic to the political and economic difficulties facing the Southern African states in their unequal relationship with South Africa – can do little beyond

---

* The author's debt is gratefully acknowledged to the excellent study of the Southern Africa Development Coordination Conference by Professor Gavin Maasdorp, Director of the Economic Research Unit of the University of Natal, South Africa. The assistance of Professor John Barratt, Director of the South African Institute of International Affairs is also acknowledged with pleasure.

rhetorical denunciation of this dependence to help solve the difficulties in a practical way.

With the establishment of SADCC, a multilateral approach to the problems of the region became apparent, based on the premise that the security and economic problems of the small Southern African states cannot be considered in isolation from the weighty influence of South Africa and its hegemonic aspirations. SADCC consists of nine states – Angola, Botswana, Lesotho, Malawi, Mozambique, Swaziland, Tanzania, Zambia and Zimbabwe. The organisation is designed to promote economic co-operation within the region, enhance bargaining power for investment and increased aid from the outside world, and over the long run reduce dependence on South Africa.

Table 1   Population, national product and per capita income – SADCC countries and South Africa, 1980

Country	Population (mill.)	GNP ($ mill.)	GNP per capita ($)
Angola	7.1	3,320	470
Botswana	0.8	730	910
Lesotho	1.3	520	390
Malawi	6.1	1,390	230
Mozambique	12.1	2,810	230
Swaziland	0.6	380	680
Tanzania	18.7	4,780	280
Zambia	5.8	3,220	560
Zimbabwe	7.4	4,640	630
Total SADCC	59.9	21,490	359
South Africa	31.0	66,960	2,290
Note: Namibia =	1.0	1,420	1,410

Source: Africa Insight, Vol. 13, No. 8, 1983.

The South African Challenge

The signing of the Nkomati Accord between Mozambique and South Africa on 16 March 1984 is a concrete and dramatic manifestation of the current economic and political balance of power in Southern Africa.[2] While all the black states in the area have expressed their repugnance for apartheid in a variety of international forums, the gravitational pull of the South African economy has proved difficult to resist. The latter's transport and communication systems, its availability as a market for exports and a source of imports for foodstuffs and manufactured goods, the dependence of South Africa's mines and industries for employment on large numbers of foreign black workers – all these linkages have given Pretoria powerful levers for the maintenance of economic hegemony, which it regards as the key to political dominance, despite profound differences in the complexion of domestic political systems.

Where South Africa's neighbours have been tempted to offer aid and comfort to liberation movements such as the African National Congress (ANC), retaliation has been swift involving military intervention in pursuit of a policy of destabilisation. The self-conscious manipulation of the neighbouring states by the use of economic and military instruments is a relatively recent phenomenon, dating back to 1975 when South Africa intervened in Angola in support of its proxy, UNITA, in the civil war following Angola's independence. Pretoria's strategy became even more aggressive after Zimbabwe's independence in 1980 and the use of Lesotho, Mozambique and Swaziland as sanctuaries by the ANC for the launching of a sabotage campaign within South Africa.

Hence the significance of the Nkomati Accord which was construed, both at home and abroad, as a major diplomatic triumph; the product of a deliberate, controlled military strategy designed to demonstrate who was to be master of the Southern African region. (A similar agreement had been signed with Swaziland in less publicised circumstances in 1982.)[3] Simultaneously, Pretoria was involved in launching a new *regional* (as distinct from UN-sponsored) initiative designed to end the war in Namibia; this was the result of close diplomatic collaboration between Angola, South Africa, Zambia and the United States.

These developments – the consequence of a confident South African diplomacy clearly influenced by the expanded role of the military in decision-making – were hailed abroad in Western capitals as presaging a new and more productive era in Southern African politics in which regional economic co-operation would increasingly come to replace ideological discord and guerrilla violence.

Nor must the symbolic significance of the Nkomati Accord be underestimated: South Africa has long aspired to gain *de jure* as distinct from *de facto* recognition of its regional hegemony, an ambition which historically expressed itself in a variety of modes of external behaviour veering from short-lived diplomatic co-operation to military intervention. These changes in policy can be summarised as below.

A straightforward imperialism: this was the external manifestation of a maturing Afrikaaner nationalism and found expression in the aspiration to round off territory, i.e. incorporate the High Commission Territories of Lesotho, Swaziland and Botswana in the years before they achieved independence in the 1960s.

The outward movement of the 1960s: a thrusting diplomacy designed to break down South Africa's isolation on the African continent. It stemmed from the mood of post-Sharpeville confidence following the virtual elimination of black opposition within the country and a remarkable burst of economic growth. The government sought to capitalise politically on the economic dependency of its neighbours seeking diplomatic recognition and aimed at the eventual creation of a Southern African Economic Community. Malawi was the one state in the region prepared to enter into formal ties with South Africa. Although Zambia's dependence increased during the period of Rhodesian UDI, the guerrilla conflicts in progress in Rhodesia, Namibia and the Portuguese territories effectively wrecked Pretoria's grandiose vision of a community of states in which the latter would fulfil its self-appointed role as the manager of regional security and promoter of economic development in line with the Nixon Doctrine of 1968.

Détente: following the collapse of Portuguese rule in Angola and Mozambique in 1974, Prime Minister Vorster collaborated briefly with the 'front line' states (Botswana, Mozambique, Tanzania and Zambia) in the hope of engineering a negotiated transfer of power from white to black in Rhodesia. This foundered on the ill-fated military intervention in Angola early in 1975, and South Africa, preoccupied with the aftermath of the Soweto disturbances, the reform debate and the war in Namibia, appeared to play a largely passive role in the events leading to the independence of Zimbabwe.

The Constellation of Southern African States (CONSAS): this notion was first defined in detail in 1979 by Mr Pik Botha, South Africa's Foreign Minister, though Mr Vorster gave the idea currency as early as 1975. In essence this was a revival of the Southern African Economic Community and was originally designed to include all the states south of the Kunuene and Zambesi Rivers though candidates further north were not precluded. Obvious candidates were Namibia under the rule of the South African-sponsored Democratic Turnhalle Alliance, Rhodesia–Zimbabwe under the premiership of Bishop Muzorewa, and the 'independent' homelands within South Africa. But Robert Mugabe's victory in the pre-independence elections for the new state of Zimbabwe, together with a blunt refusal of participation by Lesotho, Swaziland and Botswana, ended any immediate prospect of locking the neighbouring states into a 'constellation' of diplomatic pawns acknowledging their dependence on Pretoria as the guarantor of order and stable economic growth throughout the region. However, the assumption of a co-ordinated regional development plan based on industrial decentralisation still operates with respect to South Africa in its relations with the homelands. (The homelands, incidentally, represented an attempt by the South African government to create, over time, some seven sovereign, ethnically-based states, but none have received external diplomatic recognition. All the homelands are profoundly dependent upon the South African 'metropolis' for security and economic needs, and the SADCC states share the general perception of critics abroad that their sovereignty is spurious, disguising their true status as satellites of the South African political economy.)

Mugabe's success at the polls profoundly disturbed South Africa's leaders. Perceived as a Marxist, a pawn – like his counterparts in Angola and Mozambique – of the Soviet Union, Mugabe's openly declared hostility to apartheid and the impact this made on domestic black opinion prepared the way for a more aggressive policy, namely:

Destabilisation: by 1980, with the independence of Zimbabwe – the last of the 'white' buffer territories – South Africa's traditional bulwark against intervention from the north had gone. In the late 1970s the first such intervention occurred as the African National Congress began to infiltrate armed bands into South Africa. These were committed to a programme of sabotage directed at symbolic

targets of apartheid such as police stations, power and communication systems, and the more dramatic manifestation of the state's
military and industrial power (the SASOL plant, the Voortrekker-
hoogte base, and the Air Force headquarters in Pretoria). (This
strategy of armed propaganda had as its political objective 'the mass
politicisation through demonstrations, boycotts, strikes and con-
frontations'. Ultimately the goal was 'a mass based armed insurrec-
tion aimed at seizing political power'.[4]) The ANC clearly did not
expect the state to totter; nor did the government. For the ANC it was
crucial to demonstrate that it was no mere debating society operating
in far off exile; it was an organisation with teeth capable of forcing the
government to react – indeed over-react – to antagonise black
opinion still further, and promote a climate of downright hostility to
government-sponsored reform measures.

For Mr Botha and his colleagues, ANC sabotage contributed to a
condition of 'violent equilibrium' in which the constraint of
repression outweighed the incentive to reform and in the process
strengthened the position of the government's right-wing critics.
Hence the policy of destabilisation which had as its prime motive the
destruction of ANC power in the host states of Lesotho, Mozambique
and Swaziland. Hence also, the more aggressive military posture
adopted by South Africa during the 1980–4 period: the raids on
guerrilla bases in Mozambique (January 1981 and May 1983), and
Lesotho (December 1982), together with diplomatic and economic
pressure on the Swazi government to desist from providing sanctuary
for the ANC. Hence the use and support of proxies: the Lesotho
Liberation Army and the Mozambique National Resistance Movement (MNR) as well as UNITA in Angola (where, over the last fifteen
years, SWAPO has moved from Mao's first stage of guerrilla war
– demonstrations, strikes, political education of the masses, establishment of cells and bases both within and outside the territory – to the
second stage of substantial hit-and-run guerrilla activity).

It has been argued that the policy of destabilisation concealed a
hidden agenda of objectives: the use of military force to demonstrate
who is the master in Southern Africa; to dislocate the economies of
the target states in order to promote their permanent weakness and
vulnerability; to distract their leaders from external 'adventures' and
ultimately replace them with client elites willing to do South Africa's
bidding; to cripple the long-term aspirations of SADCC as an
'alternative constellation'; and finally, to 'turn back the tide of

"foreign" or "Marxist" influence' – that 'total onslaught' (as the government has defined it) which requires a 'total strategy' capable of countering the threat whether it emanates from indigenous front organisations such as the United Democratic Front (UDF) or external ones such as the front-line states.

No doubt all these motives were at work in the prosecution of the destabilisation strategy. Certainly any assessment of South Africa's motives and intentions towards its weaker neighbours must take into account the growing role of the military in the formulation and execution of both domestic and foreign policy. There is now a 'security establishment' responsible for major decision-making, the apex of which is the State Security Council, the membership of which includes, *inter alia*, the Prime Minister and the Ministers of Foreign Affairs, Defence, Police and Justice. It is this body which defines the 'total strategy' and every aspect of state policy is perceived in terms of its significance for the maintenance of white security: 'regional planning, economic planning, manpower planning, constitutional planning – the whole gamut is influenced by security and internal stability considerations'.[5] Thus, ANC sabotage, township unrest, labour disputes, overseas propaganda are all part of the same insidious design – a total war involving political, diplomatic, religious, cultural and social instruments of coercion by South Africa's enemies, whether internal or external. Hence the enhanced role of the military in the State Security Council, the senior members of which are all versed in the literature on counter-insurgency in the Third World. The soldiers see themselves as social engineers filtering domestic and foreign policy through a security lens. White security is thus indivisible: military action in the black townships and pre-emptive strikes across South Africa's borders are both justified as rooting out 'revolutionary elements' – a view which clearly derives from the overriding assumption that South Africa is threatened by a 'total onslaught'.

The military have also been influenced by Israeli military doctrines for dealing with regional threats; indeed, the parallel with Israel is often cited by way of analogy: a foreign policy which, for much of the post-war period, was defensive in tone and substance, relying on the traditional instruments of diplomacy and propaganda abroad, slides into one employing military force on a tit-for-tat or increasingly pre-emptive basis as guerrilla infiltration mounts. Eventually there is the temptation to engage in Lebanon-style incursions, support for indigenous proxies and – perhaps as a last resort – occupation of border zones.[6]

There is substance in this analogy, although scholarly prudence inhibits making too much of it. South Africa's armed forces have, after all, been in occupation of the southern part of Angola for several years. There is, too, the example of the joint collaboration – following the Nkomati Accord – with Mozambique in the attempt to arrange a cease-fire between the MNR and President Machel's government. In other words, Pretoria has made it absolutely clear that it is not averse to a forward military strategy should other instruments of coercion fail.

The Nkomati Accord

It is against this background that the Accord between Mozambique and South Africa and the relatively unpublicised agreement with Swaziland must be assessed. The Accord has significance in the context of this paper because it is perceived by the South African government as a model for future relations with several of its neighbours. In addition, and more importantly, the manner in which it was achieved, by a Clausewitzian combination of force and diplomacy, indicates a fundamental shift in the locus of decision-making in Pretoria as well as a willingness to be uninhibited about the use of armed intervention when circumstances appear to justify that last resort. Certainly Mr Botha's reliance on his senior military advisers, most notably the Minister of Defence, General Magnus Malan, indicates an impatience with the 'cocktail' diplomacy of the Departments of Foreign Affairs which failed in the 1960s to translate the promise of *détente* with the front line states into concrete achievement.

It is fair to say that the Accord surprised most foreign observers of the Southern African scene. At one stage in the early 1980s, military stabilisation seemed to be a policy in which military objectives were paramount, namely, the destruction of the ANC as a vehicle for political liberation. The rebuff administered by the SADCC states in rejecting the invitation to join CONSAS, and the need to reassure white opinion at home during a period of intense constitutional debate that the government was not going 'soft' in external relations, were cited as partial explanations of the destabilisation strategy which was seen to owe more to domestic political constraints than any firm aspirations to create a new structure of regional order.

In other words, destabilisation was seen to be an end in itself – the first stage of that 'race war' which some commentators have predicted for Southern Africa's future.

What this analysis left out of account was the parlous state of the Mozambique economy: the impact of the Rhodesian war and the emigration of skilled Portuguese workers had taken their toll, while South African policy – though ambivalent in some respects – had not helped. Mr Vorster, after all, had publicly declared his government's wish for peaceful co-existence with the new Machel government and some assistance had been forthcoming over the years to reorganise Maputo's harbour facilities – an example of South Africa's 'transport diplomacy' in action. But the decision to cut down migration labour from 100,000 to some 40,000 and the ending of migrant mineworkers' payments in gold at a preferential price, together with a reduction in the use of Maputo as a port of outlet for rail traffic from the Witwatersrand all contributed to the 47.5 million Rand loss out of a total of 700 million Rand lost in revenue since independence.

Nor can the disruptive influence of the South African-backed MNR be left out of account: road and rail links had been attacked while supplies of electricity from the Cabora Bassa project had also been cut off. Finally, the Soviet Union had made little effort to restore the Mozambique economy, confining its aid programme to supplies of arms.

All these factors help explain Mozambique's shift in attitude towards South Africa, its willingness to depart radically from the orthodox view of the Organisation of African Unity in relations with Pretoria. Well before the signing of the Accord, President Machel had made overtures to Western Europe for help in reviving the economy, but the lack of substantial assistance from this quarter in effect compelled the Mozambique government to turn south for assistance.

The key clause in the Accord is the undertaking made by both parties to desist from supporting 'irregular forces or armed bands . . . whose objective is . . . to plan or prepare to commit acts of violence, terrorism or aggression against the territorial integrity or political independence of the other'. The agreement also provided for a joint security commission to monitor its operation.

Clearly the Accord had long-term economic implications: Mozambique gained a promise of assistance (August 1984) with the task of repairing road and rail links between the Witwatersrand and Maputo, the prospect of a revival of the tourist trade and an end to the disruption of the Cabora Bassa electricity supply lines. The private business sector in both South Africa and the West was also expected to play its part in reviving recovery via investment in Mozambique, but a favourable response in this context depends on the restoration of order in Mozambique and a revival of the South African economy. Here the success in bringing the MNR to heel is crucial: the Republic has already made one attempt (October 1984) to mediate between the warring factions, but the war continues despite South African promises to cease aiding the rebel movement, and there are signs of disillusion with the Accord in Maputo. (The continued operation of the MNR is made possible by stock piles built up before March 1984 and alternative sources of supply.) Thus there are still uncertainties surrounding the successful implementation of the Accord and the implicit hope of economic growth following a resolution of the security problem. And South Africa does have much to gain from its success:

(i) the favourable reception from domestic sources prepared the ground for the initiative launched on the Namibian issue in 1984, strengthening the incentive to find regional solutions free of involvement by extra-regional agencies such as the United Nations or the great powers;

(ii) a *Pax Afrikaaner* dictated by Pretoria would give the government a 'shield of stability', free of guerrilla incursion, and behind which the current reformist strategy could – it is argued – gather impetus;

(iii) a replication of Nkomati-style pacts would strengthen South Africa's standing in the West – especially in the eyes of conservative administrations already on record as approving South Africa's efforts to promote peace and economic growth throughout the region;

(iv) similarly a network of non-aggressive treaties, while not meeting the aspiration of the 1960s to establish an integrated community type structure along the lines of the EEC, would at least realize the ambition to compel the smaller states to acknowledge in a 'public' and official way their dependence on South Africa – an advantage in propaganda terms far superior to the 'passive' acceptance of South Africa's domination which hitherto had characterised their relations with the white South.

Thus Pretoria has much to play for in the 'great game' of Southern African politics, but we must be careful not to over-estimate the government's capacity to manipulate the external environment at will. There are constraints on what it can do in its search for recognition – both regional and external – as the hegemonic power:

(i) Nkomati could collapse if MNR activity increases in scope and undermines efforts to restore the Mozambique economy (the parallel with UNITA's role in Angola is disturbing). Direct military intervention in Mozambique – albeit at the invitation of the Machel government – would be expensive and possibly counterproductive, if only because it would confirm the worst fears of South Africa's critics and the governments of neighbouring states that the former was bent on an Israeli-type solution to its security problems;

(ii) large-scale economic assistance from both the public and private sectors of the South African economy may prove difficult to generate in a climate of economic recession;

(iii) promulgation of the new constitution and the exclusion of blacks have – together with the impact of recession on black living standards – created a new militancy, reflected in the disturbances that have continued, unabated, since early September 1984.

It could be argued that a condition of 'violent equilibrium' at home is a poor base from which to launch radical new initiatives in foreign policy – especially if these involve massive injections of economic aid and possible military involvement to deal with dissident groups who show no sign of accepting the implications of non-aggressive pacts between their host countries and South Africa. It should, after all, be remembered that the agreements with Swaziland and Mozambique were signed in an atmosphere of euphoria induced by the massive majority accorded Mr Botha's constitutional proposals in the referendum of November 1983. At that time the domestic scene was quiescent and the government had the flexibility to launch a variety of initiatives. Of course troubles at home might suggest a more aggressive policy abroad, but the record of earlier South African initiatives in the region indicate that Pretoria only undertakes dramatic foreign policy moves when the domestic base is reasonably secure.

The SADCC Response

The remainder of this Annex will examine the responses of the smaller states in the region to the fact of South African dominance and the options open to them.

When SADCC was established in 1980, the signatories eschewed a grandiose commitment to economic integration, preferring the more modest initiative to promote economic interdependence through 'regional co-operation . . . with particular reference to transport and communications infrastructure, the co-ordination of foreign aid and the promotion of industry and trade'.[7] The headquarters of the organisation is in Gaberone in Botswana and is serviced by a small secretariat which *inter alia* organises the annual summit when progress on previously agreed projects is assessed and proposals for new ones are put forward. Donor states and development organisations such as the EC, the World Bank, and the United Nations Development Programme are represented: their financial assistance is essential for the funding of the projects agreed upon.

Each member state has been given a priority area in which to prepare plans for co-ordination by the organisation as a whole: Mozambique, for example, is responsible for transport and communications; Angola for energy conservation; Zambia for the development fund and mining; Zimbabwe for food security, and Tanzania for industry. The funding for and control over specific development projects is the responsibility of the country on whose territory the development is planned or which is charged with that particular development portfolio.[8]

Transport and Communications

The Southern African Transport and Communications Commission (SATCC) was established in 1980 largely because dependence on South Africa was particularly strong in this context. Transport infrastructure is regarded as the most important area for co-ordination and Table 2 lists the estimated costs and amounts committed by donors for projects the Commission believes are crucial if East–West links are to be improved. It is hardly surprising that Mozambique was given responsibility for co-ordinating transport and communications. The ports of Maputo, Beira and Nacala and the connecting rail and road links require drastic improvement if they are to be an effective outlet for the trade of Zimbabwe, Malawi

Table 2 Project costs and commitments

Project group	Total costs		Total committed	
	US$ mill.	%	US$ mill.	Col. (3) as % Col. (1)
	(1)	(2)	(3)	(4)
Operational co-ordination	9.4	0.4	3.8	40.4
Training	2	0.1	1.6	80.0
Port Transport Systems:				
Maputo	552	21.7	160	29.0
Beira	414	16.3	58	14.0
Nacala	235	9.3	101	43.0
Dar-es-Salaam	339	13.4	22	6.5
Lobito	90	3.5	14	15.6
Intra-regional surface transport	404	15.9	41	10.1
Civil aviation	258	10.1	155	60.1
Telecommunications	235	9.3	108	46.0
TOTAL	2,538.4	100.0	664.4	26.2

Source: Overview, Maseru: SADCC, 1983, p. 9.

and Swaziland; similarly, the Benguela railway linking Zambia to the Angolan port of Lobito needs extensive modernisation if Zambia is to reduce its dependence on the South African rail and port system.

Food Security

This is a high priority area given the drought that has ravaged the region in the 1980s. In the past, Zimbabwe and South Africa have exported maize to their neighbours, but the problem has become more acute as the crops of the latter have proved insufficient for local consumption, let alone to meet the shortfall in neighbouring states. Here the emphasis is on early warning systems, food planning, the establishment of reserves and joint action on imports.

Industry

In this context some sixty-six projects were discussed at the Maseru meeting of SADCC in 1983; subsequently, in 1984, a vote for investment of $1,209m was made in fields as diverse as salt, textiles, pesticides and fertilisers, paper and cement. Industrial co-ordination, however, has proved difficult: many of the early projects were regarded as unsatisfactory and it was clear that 'further investigation was required to produce a particular product and whether that product could be marketed in competition with current suppliers'.[9] Lack of consultation with the private sector – the main source of industrial investment – also proved an obstacle to significant progress with co-ordination in this area.

The Patterns of Dependence

The task facing SADCC is a formidable one, especially in view of the commitment to reduce dependence on South Africa over the long term. It is, therefore, appropriate to consider current north–south linkages in some detail before examining the pattern of incentives and constraints that operate upon the SADCC members as they attempt to achieve their prime objective.

Transport

About 75 per cent of the region's rail system lies in South Africa. The imports of Botswana, Lesotho and Swaziland are carried by South African Railways (SAR) as well as the exports of Botswana and Lesotho. Because of guerrilla disruption to the Angolan and Mozambique systems, much of the foreign trade of Zambia, Zaire and Zimbabwe is also carried.

Economic recession and drought account for the drop in tonnage between 1979 and 1983. Even so, some 50 per cent of Zimbabwean trade is likely to be carried by SAR in 1985/86, although the figure will drop to 30 per cent if and when improvements take place to the Mozambique rail and port structure. Supplies for the drought-stricken smaller states are also landed at South African ports for dispatch onwards. Other factors making for transport dependency include a shortage of skilled staff and rolling stock, especially in Mozambique.

Table 3   Rail freight traffic between South Africa and neighbouring
countries: 1979/80, 1980/81 and 1982/83 (tons)

To/from	1979/80	1980/81	1982/83
Botswana, Zimbabwe, Zambia, Zaire, Malawi			
Northbound	1,529,791	2,866,452	1,575,816
Southbound	2,654,063	2,472,982	1,460,394
Swaziland, Mozambique			
Eastbound	2,932,533	2,581,792	1,391,862
Westbound	1,267,435	1,518,469	1,385,350
Total	8,383,822	9,439,695	5,813,422

Source: South African Transport Services, Johannesburg. See Maasdorp,
SADDC – A Post-Nkomati Evaluation, p. 52.

The land-locked states north of the Limpopo could make
increasing use of the Benguela line to Lobito in Angola but this
depends on a settlement of the Namibian issue and South Africa
giving up possession of Walvis Bay, which could be the terminus for a
proposed trans-Kalahari railway. Similarly, better use could be made
of the TAZARA line linking Zambia with Dar-es-Salaam in
Tanzania, but this assumes a radical improvement in the administration at the Tanzanian end. By the same token, Malawi's problems
in using the line to the ports of Nacala and Beira would be eased if
order were restored in the disputed areas of Mozambique. At present
Malawian goods are forced to make the long journey south by road
and rail to South African ports. The proposed new rail link between
Botswana and South Africa will increase dependence and possibly
encourage Zaire and Zambia to do the same, in the short run at least
while the east–west lines remain prey to disruptions. In the longer
run, the dependence of Malawi, Zambia and Zimbabwe on South
Africa could be reduced if the rail and port system was restored. As
Maasdorp points out 'dependence in this context is artificial' as,
'South African ports are not the natural or traditional outlets for the
land-locked SADCC countries north of the Limpopo'.[10]

Trade

South Africa trades with forty-six of the forty-nine OAU countries. Detailed figures of trade with individual countries are not available, but the total figure is some 2,438 million Rand, of which 1,000 million Rand is with Botswana, Lesotho and Swaziland. According to Maasdorp this trade has declined in recent years because of drought and foreign exchange difficulties. These states are heavily dependent on South African trade; Lesotho takes 95 per cent of its imports from South Africa; Swaziland 90 per cent; and Botswana 86 per cent. Some 40 per cent of Lesotho's exports go to South Africa and the figures for Botswana and Swaziland are 14 per cent and 20 per cent respectively. Zambia is also dependent on South African trade (28 per cent and 22 per cent of its imports and exports respectively). For Zambia, South Africa is the second most important source of imports, while it is the main source for Malawi and Mozambique. The bulk of Angola's trade is also allegedly with South Africa.

The major obstacles to co-ordinating trade policy and reducing dependence on South Africa are, firstly, that the latter at present produces a large range of manufactured goods more cheaply than its neighbours and, secondly, the difficulty those states face in trying to diversify their products significantly to meet each other's needs. As one observer claimed 'everything from project management to heavy equipment naturally comes cheapest and, above all, quickest from South Africa'.[11]

With respect to food production, much depends on whether it will keep pace with population growth. The SADCC area is expected to grow at a rate of 3.1 per cent per annum, i.e. from 58 to 78.4 million people. Drought has, however, played havoc with food production; South Africa until recently has been willing and able to meet the shortfall, but this is unlikely to be the case in the near future as the government has had to import maize to cope with the effects of the drought on its own agricultural economy.

Angola, Zambia and Zimbabwe no longer export mine labour to South Africa, and Table 4 shows the decline in supplies from Botswana, Malawi and Mozambique. The figures for Lesotho and Swaziland, however, have increased. The trend overall is downwards: the Republic is committed to giving preference to homeland workers and demand for labour in the mines is likely to drop significantly by the year 2000.

SADCC policy is designed to reduce and ultimately end the export

Table 4   South African Chamber of Mines labour recruitment, September 1972, 1977 and 1982

Country	Mines						All sectors
	1972		1977		1982		1983 (no.)
	No.	%	No.	%	No.	%	
Angola	3,097	0.8	645	0.2	—	—	68
Botswana	21,250	5.5	24,676	5.9	18,328	4.2	25,967
Lesotho	69,950	18.2	92,875	22.2	96,416	22.0	145,797
Malawi	116,307	30.2	6,131	1.5	15,943	3.6	29,622
Mozambique	82,837	21.5	41,667	9.9	44,785	10.2	61,218
Swaziland	4,800	1.2	9,696	2.3	10,555	2.4	16,773
Zambia	—	—	—	—	—	—	743
Zimbabwe	2	—	15,910	3.8	—	—	7,742
Total SADCC	298,243	77.4	191,600	45.7	186,027	42.4	287,930
Namibia	799	0.2	2,757	0.7	1,313	0.3	
South Africa	86,213	22.4	224,622	53.6	251,398	57.3	
Total	385,255	100.0	418,979	100.0	438,738	100.0	

Sources: The Employment Bureau of Africa Ltd.; Department of Cooperation and Development. See Maasdorp, *SADCC – A Post Nkomati Evaluation,* p. 69.

of labour. In the short term, however, it has concentrated on improving, on a multilateral basis, the terms on which such labour is employed; at the same time, work is under way to find projects to absorb the migrant labour back into the local economies. The success with which this goal is achieved will clearly vary from country to country: Lesotho – the most dependent of all the SADCC states – could absorb at best no more than 20 per cent of those coming into the labour market within the country and it is, therefore, unlikely to be able to break this particular dependency link. The remittances sent home by workers account for 40 per cent of GNP and it is clear that even a phased reduction would severely damage living standards in Lesotho. The position of Botswana is less desperate, and there are apparently possibilities for absorbing a reasonable proportion of the migrants into the local economy. Certainly Malawi and Mozambique are better placed than Lesotho in this respect; both countries appear to have coped rather better than many observers expected, though the loss of foreign exchange was considerable. SADCC is, however, on record as saying that further reduction is 'manageable, albeit difficult and costly'.[12]

In general, Maasdorp's conclusion seems relevant:

> there is an asymmetry in the relationship in Pretoria's favour. The extent of SADCC's dependence on South Africa in the areas of transport, trade and employment is likely to be substantial for some years to come, but the potential undoubtedly exists for overall reduction of links. However, this potential varies from country to country and the costs of a reduction might be substantial.[13]

Conclusion

SADCC has only been in existence for five years and it is too early to make a definitive judgement about its long-term prospects for success. The organisation has rightly eschewed a fully fledged programme of economic integration, preferring instead to work piecemeal on those linkages where there is some real prospect of reducing dependence on South Africa. Its ambitions are therefore modest and cautious, based on a realistic understanding that the work of co-ordination will take time and impose costs.

The member states are at different stages of economic development and have been plagued by natural hardships such as drought
and the impact of a world recession. Several (Angola, Lesotho,
Mozambique and Zimbabwe) face violent opposition from within,
from dissident groups which gravely handicap economic growth
and absorb resources and energy which could be put to more
productive use. Nor can there be any doubt that in the vital area of
transport and communications the restoration of order and
stability in Angola and Mozambique in particular is crucial both
for the declared aim of reducing dependence on the Republic and
for the generation of growth in the regional economy. Paradoxically, the Nkomati Accord, in so far as it leads with South African
assistance to the rehabilitation of the rail and port system of
Mozambique, may, over the long run, reduce dependence on the
white south.

Nor can these states – in the medium term at least – be free of the
threat of economic and military manipulation by Pretoria, as several
have found to their cost. At best South African policy remains
ambivalent: at worst potentially aggressive. Zimbabwe's experience
in the early 1980s, as South Africa used its economic strength to bend
the Mugabe government into accepting Pretoria's hegemony, is a
case in point. The threat to terminate the preferential trade
agreement, the return of Zimbabwean workers, the withdrawal of
locomotives and wagons on loan, delays in the despatch of foodstuffs
and oil – all are examples of a self-conscious exertion of economic
pressure co-existing with a willingness to engage in 'transport
diplomacy' to help restore shattered rail links and modernise port
facilities in Mozambique.[14]

Within South Africa there is a clear division among influential
elites about the course regional policy should take. On the one hand,
those, especially in business circles and *verligte* elements in the
Nationalist Party, welcome the economic prospects held out by
Nkomati-type agreements; for this group peace and order are good
for trade and investment. As Anton Rupert once said: 'If they do not
sleep, we do not eat.' On the other hand there is the perception among
some of the military and influential members of the Afrikaaner
establishment that the SADCC states are the tools of a 'total
onslaught' instigated by the Soviet Union. (There is evidence that this
view is less prevalent among the senior military than was the case five
years ago.) Wielding a big stick or, at the very least, holding it in
reserve to punish neighbours who give aid and comfort to liberation

groups, remains for this group an important option – even if only one of last resort.

Nor do the polarisation of black–white relations within South Africa and the manifestation of increasing militancy and violent disturbances necessarily weaken the government's commitment to maintain its grip on the region. If anything, the temptation to be seen as powerful abroad may be stronger when the domestic system is under stress. In these circumstances, the constraint of external approval for a policy of peaceful regional co-operation no longer operates with quite the same force.

Finally, there is the attitude of the external world to SADCC, and in particular the relationship with donor states and international development agencies. The latter, too, are likely to remain cautious in their aid-giving until a modicum of order emerges in Angola and Mozambique in particular.

But it is hoped that Western governments – all of which have a crucial economic and political stake in the stability and orderly development of the region – will recognise the advantage of doing all within the scope of their resources to help the SADCC states – both individually and collectively – to realise their potential.

To date, both Western and COMECON governments have tended to give aid on a bilateral basis rather than funding it through multilateral agencies such as SADCC. This is understandable, given the attraction of projects which relate specifically to a particular state's economic needs rather than those which are concerned with the more general needs of the region. Nevertheless, there are areas – especially with respect to transport and communications – which are transnational in scope and utility, and it is here that Western help could most usefully be channelled through SADCC.

In this context, South Africa is the crucial actor: a settlement in Namibia, and the potential economic benefits this would confer on states such as Zambia and Angola, depends on Pretoria's willingness finally to release its grip on that territory. The constraints against doing so have weakened in recent years, but many remain sceptical about South Africa's commitment to decolonise the territory. Similarly, the rejuvenation of the Mozambique economy assumes that South Africa can and will force the MNR into submission so that the work of reconstruction can begin, with all the advantages this would bring in terms of efficient and secure transport and communications for the land-locked states with the outside world.

It may be, of course, that the South African state is in danger of over-reaching itself. Within, it is attempting to combine repression with reform. Without, it seeks to be the guarantor of a peaceful regional domain in which the member states – SADCC notwithstanding – will acknowledge that their economic and political destiny lies in closer association with it, and in an end to ideological discord. Certainly this self-image is an important one in the thinking of key political and economic elites in South Africa, if only because it would allegedly improve South Africa's standing in the West and be a first and major step towards the ending of pariah status.

But whether South Africa has the resources to engage in large-scale provision of aid and technical assistance is open to question: the homelands and the urban blacks alike cry out for help to alleviate their economic and social distress. Defence expenditure remains high and the war in Namibia is increasingly expensive. Providing South Africa with 'guns and butter' is less easy than it was fifteen years ago; providing them abroad may simply be wishful thinking.

Taken together, uncertainty about South Africa's ultimate intentions in the region, its record of intervention in the past, and its sharpening internal conflict, provide a disturbing background for the successful development of SADCC as an instrument of economic and social change in the region. There is a further paradox. Even if South Africa were to be transformed by either constitutional or violent means into a black-governed state, the dependency of the neighbouring states would not necessarily or easily wither away.

The Role of Namibia

Although Namibia is a small territory in terms of our study's general definition, its position in Southern Africa warrants separate treatment:

(i)   because of its key geographical position in relation to the rest of the region (and we have already remarked upon the implications for SADCC – especially in the field of transport and communication – of independence for the territory from South African rule); and

(ii) because it is certain to join SADCC once statehood is achieved.

The territory has long been the subject of intense and bitter dispute between South Africa and the United Nations.[15] Namibia's status was raised at the first meeting of the General Assembly in London in 1946 and, ever since international pressure – from the Third World in particular – has built up to compel South Africa to 'de-colonise' the territory. In the late 1960s the United Nations voted to terminate South Africa's mandate over the territory and subsequently voted to regard SWAPO as the 'sole and authentic representative of the people of Namibia'.

Stalemate on this issue persisted until the late 1970s when the Contact Group of five Western powers (Canada, France, Germany, the United Kingdom and United States) initiated discussions with Pretoria designed to reach a solution. In the course of the next four years a variety of initiatives were launched, invariably preceded by informal diplomatic discussions between the Contact Group, the front line states, South Africa and SWAPO. However, such agreement as was reached on the outlines of a stage-by-stage settlement floundered, as both South Africa and SWAPO engaged in a stop–go process with both parties back-tracking on seemingly firm commitments.

These negotiations have taken place against a background of increasing violence. Since 1969 SWAPO has been fighting a war of liberation against South African forces in the northern part of the territory. The former operate from bases in neighbouring Angola which have been the object of a series of military raids by South African forces over the last decade. Angola itself is racked by civil war between the Luanda government and UNITA forces led by Jonas Savimbi and supplied in the main by South Africa. Nor has the presence of some 20,000 Cuban troops in Angola eased the course of long drawn-out negotiations between the parties to the dispute.

As noted earlier, the war in Namibia has had a deleterious effect on both Angola and the economies of the land-locked states north of the Limpopo. Until the Namibian issue is settled, there is little that can be done to improve rail communications across Angola to the sea. This difficulty inevitably complicates SADCC's general aspiration to modernise the region's transport infrastructure and reduce economic dependence on South Africa.

What are the prospects for a settlement in the short term?[16] Hopes were raised in July 1984 by the launching of a new American initiative, and discussions were held in Lusaka in February at which agreement was reached to establish an Angola–South Africa Joint

Commission to monitor the withdrawal of South African troops from Angola. In July 1984 SWAPO and South African representatives met in Cape Verde, but talks collapsed over the latter's insistence on Cuban withdrawal for a settlement.

At the time of writing, there are reports that South Africa is considering an internal settlement of the Namibian issue. This would be contrary to the only internationally agreed basis for a settlement, i.e. Resolution 435 of the United Nations Security Council which calls, *inter alia*, for UN supervised elections in the territory. While it is true that South Africa appears to have new-found incentives eventually to give up control of the territory (e.g. the mounting cost of the war; the belief that even a SWAPO-governed Namibia would be amenable to Pretoria's control, and the relative unsuitability of Namibia as a sanctuary from which to prosecute insurgency within South Africa), the domestic constraints operating upon President Botha seem all-compelling. Right-wing elements in South Africa would make much of a government decision to 'appease' SWAPO – an enemy which has always been construed as an important 'agent of the Kremlin'. In addition, the impact on black opinion of a SWAPO victory in re-independence elections would be to raise expectations of a similar outcome in South Africa and make social control more difficult.

Thus a comprehensive realisation of SADCC's objectives has to wait for the transfer of power from white to black Namibia. While the struggle continues, two key members of the organisation – Zambia and Angola – cannot play their full and effective role in the social and economic transformation of the region to which SADCC as a whole aspires. By the same token, Namibia's accession to SADCC will have three important consequences:

(i)   the end of a major and destabilising phase of violence in the Southern African region;

(ii) the incorporation of a new state with considerable economic and social resources; and

(iii) SADCC states will be able to concentrate on the productive tasks of development, free of the scourge of regional conflict and with a new confidence deriving from South Africa's retreat from a traditional bastion of power.

As things stand at present, however, this must remain a long-term aspiration.

Notes

1. Cited in Gavin Maasdorp, *SADCC - A Post-Nkomati Evaluation*, The South African Institute of International Affairs, Johannesburg, 1984, p. 33.
2. See J.E. Spence, 'South Africa: Between Reform and Retrenchment', *The World Today*, November 1984, Vol. 40, No. 11, pp. 471–80.
3. Note the statement by Prince Bhekempi, the Prime Minister of Swaziland, in his opening address to the SADCC Conference in January 1985: 'Swaziland will continue to talk to South Africa and would do so in the light and openly.' *South African Press Association Report*, 1 February 1985.
4. Thomas Karis, 'The Resurgent African National Congress: the Struggle for Hearts and Minds in South Africa' in T.M. Callaghy (ed.), *South Africa in Southern Africa*, New York, 1983, p. 192.
5. Kenneth Grundy, *South Africa's Security Establishment*, South African Institute of International Affairs, Johannesburg, 1983.
6. See Simon Jenkins, 'Destabilizing Southern Africa', *The Economist*, 16–22 July 1983.
7. Maasdorp, *op. cit.*, p. 12.
8. *Ibid*, p. 16 for a complete list of portfolio allocations.
9. *Ibid.*, p. 26.
10. *Ibid.*, p. 26.
11. *The Economist*, *op. cit.*, quoted in Maasdorp, p. 117.
12. *Ibid.*, p. 73.
13. *Ibid.*, pp. 76–7.
14. *Ibid.*, pp. 81–2.
15. Namibia (together with other former German colonies) was made a Mandate of the League of Nations after the First World War. It was administered by South Africa on behalf of the League. After the Second World War, all the other mandated territories which had not meanwhile become independent were placed voluntarily under the UN Trusteeship system. South Africa, however, informed the United Nations that it had annexed Namibia and refused all subsequent appeals from the United Nations to place it under the Trusteeship system.
16. See J.E. Spence, *op. cit.*

Annex B: The Caribbean

The Caribbean is an area of extraordinary political, cultural and economic diversity. Indeed, it could be said that the only factor that all its 30.5 million people have in common is an insistence by the outside world that they be described as Caribbean.

Geographically, the region is spread across some 1.5 million square miles of ocean. Racially, its peoples come from all ethnic backgrounds. Politically, the region contains virtually all governmental models. There are, for example, Westminster-style liberal democracies, such as Barbados, small federal systems such as that in St Kitts/Nevis, Marxist-Leninist Cuba, oligarchical Haiti and a military-appointed government in Suriname. In addition there are *départements d'outre mer* of Metropolitan France, five British dependencies and a complex and fragile federation of Dutch dependencies drawn together into the kingdom of Netherlands Antilles. There are also integral parts of the United States in the form of Puerto Rico and the US Virgin Islands operating systems similar to those of individual American states. Culturally, the area is equally diverse. Spain, Britain, France, the Netherlands and Denmark were the colonising powers and this background is reflected in the national values of each nation. More recently, American cultural influences, while not always welcome, have come to dominate the region. Economically, the area is also diverse, ranging from Haiti with a GNP per capita of just US$212, St Lucia with $840, to oil rich Trinidad and Tobago with a per capita GNP of $5,670 per annum.

To a large extent, this diversity is the result of the rivalry between the early colonising powers. From the seventeenth century onwards, control of the Caribbean ensured great influence over the political and economic fortunes of Europe and the United States.

Today, the over-riding importance as expressed both by Eastern and Western military planners is strategic, principally because hostilities in Europe will involve the resupply of NATO forces from the US through the Caribbean Basin. Put at its most extreme, one element of nuclear strategy envisages an East–West war beginning with a land battle of limited duration in Europe. It is argued that if such a land battle is to remain non-nuclear for an acceptable period, then material and supplies must be able to pass swiftly and unimpeded from the United States through the deep water channels between the Caribbean islands to Europe. There are also other strategic concerns expressed principally by the United States. These are cited as: the passage of up to 60 per cent of all crude or refined oil for the United States through the region; the presence of Cuba on the United States' undefended southern sea borders; illegal immigration into the United States; the existence of large American investments in the region; the presence of a substantial number of American nationals in the region, and the use of the area by organized criminals involved with narcotics.

Regional Instability

Recent Western governmental analysis of the region's problems and its 'instability' has largely stemmed from these strategic concerns. This has meant that American considerations about a security policy for the region have originated primarily in reaction to perceived threats; they have so far failed to concentrate on the needs and aspirations of the governments of the area. As a result, recent economic policies that have been developed in response to this analysis – which, in effect positively discriminate in favour of governments deemed to be friendly and against those seen as 'enemies' – have tended to divide the region economically and politically along new lines and have resulted in fresh uncertainties.

   Despite this, the chief factors contributing to instability in the region remain economic. The high cost of energy imports and imported foodstuffs, the falling world prices for regionally produced commodities and raw materials, a decline in tourist arrivals and the recession in the region's main metropolitan markets have all combined to create, in most cases, substantial balance of payments deficits and high levels of inflation. At the same time, governments have been under increasing pressure to find employment for steadily growing numbers of school leavers and a population which is relatively well educated and has come to expect quite sophisticated levels of social services. Given the small amounts of local capital available and low incomes, governments have been increasingly unable to meet the expectations and aspirations of an increasingly young electorate. In some cases this has enabled subversive or criminal elements to manipulate local political events. However, most political pressure reflects legitimate aspirations for social and economic change.

It is also argued that another recent contributory factor to regional instability has been the development of ideologically different systems in the region. This, however, may have been overstressed in the Commonwealth Caribbean. By late 1982 it had become increasingly clear that despite Grenada's presence at most regional meetings, a consensus could be reached on regional issues and that the concept of an ideologically pluralist region had been accepted. Other concerns were centred on the existence of a complex network of links between the Cuban Communist Party and often small opposition political parties throughout the region.

There also remain a range of other concerns that have the ability to generate regional instability. These include: border disputes, such as those between Guyana and Venezuela and Belize and Guatemala; the introduction of the new phenomenon of military coups in Suriname; problems over political relations between nations in respect of illegal migration; the establishment of bilateral trading relations at the expense of inter-regional relationships; and differing perceptions as to the regional role of Cuba.

The 'Threat' and the Micro-States

Turning specifically to the security problems faced by Commonwealth Caribbean states with a population of less than 1 million, it is not easy to determine common issues that pose potential security threats. Although many Caribbean countries exhibit structural similarities, it is difficult to determine any common dynamic for political, economic or social change.

Change, when it does occur – as opposed to the often vocalised desire for change – invariably reflects the needs of the country in question, not of the region. In matters of security it is consequently difficult to analyse the nature of the threat to which either a domestic, sub-regional or other security mechanism must be designed to respond. In a sense, events in Grenada in October 1983 indicated just this. A parochial dispute within the Central Committee of the New Jewel Government led to an unpredictable series of domestic, sub-regional and regional crises and ultimately to an international crisis, in a manner that could not have been forecast or planned for.

The present decision to look more closely at the whole question of the security of small states stems partly from the problems raised by events in Grenada. But this preoccupation may be diverting attention from the real issues. For the Caribbean, the greater value lies in attempting to assess the likely nature of the present and future security threat faced by regional nations.

It is therefore worth looking at the recent problems and weaknesses of each micro-state in the Caribbean in an attempt to try to determine whether moves to establish a security mechanism that can respond to all eventualities are realistic. An outline of pertinent political aspects which could have an impact on security follows.

Antigua and Barbuda

Political Factors

In general elections held in 1983, the ruling Antigua Labour Party won all the seats on Antigua, leaving an already fragmented parliamentary opposition in complete disarray and with no voice in the lower house of parliament. In addition, the leftist Antigua Caribbean Liberation Movement, which has never polled more than 2 per cent of the votes, maintains close party-to-party ties with the Cuban Communist Party, but largely restricts its activities to verbal and printed attacks on Government. There are signs that a new opposition centrist party is likely to emerge, but it is not clear that this will gain electoral support.

American Presence

Antigua houses three American bases involved in underwater communications, electronic relay and information gathering, and the monitoring of satellite transmissions. In addition, its inter-national airport is used by the United States military as an essential staging post for flights to the strategically important island of Ascension and onwards to other facilities covering the South

Atlantic for Western interests. Also located within one of the American bases is a *Voice of America* relay which, during the Grenada crisis, was used to broadcast programmes specifically aimed at encouraging an early end to hostilities. In addition, the island has an unusually large American consulate and a substantial number of resident American expatriates.

Secession

The ward island of Barbuda with a population of only 1,500 has on occasions indicated its desire to secede. Economic neglect, and more recently arguments over land tenure and policing, have all added fuel to local complaints about the government in St Johns. While this issue has been temporarily defused by the unusual expedient of making the only elected member from Barbuda the leader of the opposition in a Parliament in which the government holds all the other seats, the Barbuda question remains open.

Other

In addition, there are a number of other factors that encourage instability leading to possible threats to security. In summary these are: the alleged presence of elements of organised crime syndicates who may use the island for complex financial transactions; the alleged use of the island for narcotics trafficking; an unclear succession in the leadership of the ruling Antigua Labour Party, and inter party factionalism and allegations of widespread corruption. However, the extent to which any of these factors could be deemed a threat might be judged by the previous ability of the ALP Government successfully to defuse a crisis in 1979 when it was revealed that advanced military equipment had been tested in Antigua and subsequently shipped to South Africa.

Bahamas

Although not strictly part of the Caribbean, the Bahamas are considered here as their security concerns are bound up with the region as a whole.

Political Factors

The Bahamas has had the same government since independence, with an equally conservative opposition.

Narcotics

The Bahamas has become a major centre for the trans-shipment of drugs destined for the United States and for the laundering of allied funding. Because the country consists of literally hundreds of inhabited, under-inhabited and uninhabited islands, it has been almost impossible to police effectively. In 1984–5 a Royal Commission investigated allegations that senior ministers and officials in the security services were in the pay of organised crime. Such allegations led to resignations and at one point threatened the stability of the government. In early 1985 the Bahamas government and the US Drug Enforcement Agency acted in concert in a series of anti-drug trafficking operations and there were indications that this co-operation might achieve substantial results.

American Bases

In the past, the Bahamas has formed a part of a satellite monitoring and weapons testing system. Although it is now the case that only one major western facility still operates out of the Bahamas, the islands' location, close to the United States, makes it of strategic importance.

Cuba

The Bahamas normally has good relations with its nearest neighbour, Cuba. However, in 1980 Cuban aircraft attacked and sank a coastguard vessel. Although formal explanations suggest the incident was an accident, some sources suggest that it related to regular clandestine passage through the outer islands by Cuban officials.

Barbados

Political Factors

Barbados traditionally changes its government every two terms. Whilst there is a great similarity between the present governing Barbados Labour Party and the opposition Democratic Labour Party, this may be changing. The opposition DLP have already expressed serious reservations about funding for both the Barbados Defence Force and a Regional Security System and in government it may, like other East Caribbean oppositions, not be prepared to continue to support agreed security mechanisms. There is, in addition, in Barbados a small leftist party, MONALI, which maintains contacts with the Cuban Communist Party.

Attempted Coup

In 1979 Barbados was to have been 'invaded' from Dominica by a group of mercenaries headed by a Barbadian. The plot was foiled and had no chance of popular support. However, it indicated a potential threat not previously considered.

Grenada Intervention

The late Prime Minister Adams adopted a high profile in regional politics, particularly in his commitment to the Grenada intervention. This led to conflict with the Caribbean left and a claim by the Prime Minister that Cuba had adopted a policy of attempting to destabilise the Barbados Government and posed a threat to his life.

Airport

The strategic nature of Barbados' international airport has been demonstrated on three separate occasions. It was used by Cuba to build up its forces in Africa and subsequently to service its troops fighting in Angola. During the South Atlantic crisis it was used by both Britain and the United States to re-fuel aircraft and carry vital equipment and *matériel* out of the United States. It was again used by the United States and others to mount the Grenada intervention. In 1979 the danger of allowing a Caribbean airport to be used for political purposes was demonstrated when a commercial Cuban air service was sabotaged; after take-off from Barbados, it crashed, resulting in a total loss of life.

Belize

Political Factors

The new United Democratic Party Government of Belize is likely to pursue a policy towards Guatemala similar to that of its predecessors. While making clear its desire for a continuing British military presence it has not ruled out the possibility of American military support if a long-term British presence is not provided. Should this occur it could bring Belize into a new range of conflict in the context of Central American political change.

External Threat

Belize still faces the possibility of invasion by Guatemala in view of the latter's outstanding claim to the whole of the country. However, while the threat is real and border incursions and periods of heightened tension have occurred, military action by Guatemala remains remote. A substantial British military presence, United Nations' support for Belize, American pressure on Guatemala wherever possible, a growing realisation in Guatemala City of the need to resolve the dispute, and Guatemalan military pre-occupations with guerrilla activities, all lessen the likelihood of direct action and reflect a desire for the peaceful resolution of the dispute. In addition, there is a Commonwealth Watchdog Committee on Belize which includes Canada and the United Kingdom and serves as a deterrent to any invasion by Guatemala.

Insurgency

Unlike any other Caribbean state, Belize suffers from the problems of insurgents operating out of Belizean territory into neighbouring countries. This development is seen by some as raising questions about the development of peaceful relations between Belize and Guatemala, and the nature of possible future security guarantees to Belize by third nations.

Refugees

Unlike its Caribbean counterparts Belize suffers from a significant refugee problem with rural workers fleeing from El Salvador, Guatemala and elsewhere, seeking sanctuary inside Belize. This generates both domestic political strains on the economy and difficulties in Belize's relations with its close neighbours.

Dominica

Political Factors

The Dominican opposition is fragmented into a series of small political parties with shifting alignments. Certain parties have shown no qualms in the past about forging alliances with countries or representatives of countries such as South Africa or Libya. These factors tend to make political change within Dominica potentially volatile.

Coups and Instability

In 1979 the newly elected Prime Minister Eugenia Charles inherited a situation of political and economic instability. The previous administration of Mr Patrick John had been unable to deal with the economic problems generated primarily by a series of hurricanes, and Mr John had also been involved in a number of dubious and abortive business deals including the routeing of South African oil through Dominica and the sale of a part of the island to a Texan business man for the building of a tourist and gambling resort.

Since her election, Miss Charles has survived a number of coup attempts, both internally generated and externally involving mercenaries and reputedly linked to gambling and drug interests. In early 1981 Mr John and a number of key army personnel were arrested on charges of attempting to overthrow Miss Charles' government, and the island's small defence force was disbanded. Because of the parlous state of the island's economy, the unrest is likely to continue.

French-Speaking Caribbean

Political Factors

Although parts of metropolitan France, the *Départements d'outre Mer* (DOMs) of Martinique, Guadeloupe and French Guiana all have political problems which could lead to instability.

Independence Movements

Each of the three *Départements* have small indigenous independence movements with factions, especially in Guadeloupe, prepared to take direct action through a programme of bombings and other small scale guerrilla activities in both metropolitan France and the countries themselves. While the support for direct action is poor, the independence movements enjoy a measure of electoral support. In addition, an indigenous Communist Party related directly to that in France enjoys some support.

Bases

The presence of the Ariane European Space Programme's rocket base at Korou in French Guiana makes the French DOMs in the Caribbean of vital strategic importance to France. The base can only easily be serviced through Martinique and Guadeloupe and as a result any significant political change in the two islands is regarded as a potential security threat to France's global foreign and defence policies. In addition, France maintains a substantial military and air capability in Martinique and Guadeloupe as well as communications facilities. In French Guiana there is additionally a jungle warfare training facility.

Dominica

Because of its strategic location midway between Martinique and Guadeloupe, political developments in Dominica have always been closely monitored by France. On occasions France has provided intelligence and both overt and covert military support to the Dominica Government to combat threats and subversion. At least one political party in Dominica maintains close links with the element of the Martinique/Guadeloupe independence movement that has been involved in guerrilla activities in the DOMs and France. Contact is maintained by small schooners and it has been suggested that on occasions attacks have been facilitated by the provision of arms and equipment by this method.

Cross Border Activities

Surinamese exile groups based in French Guiana have attempted on more than one occasion to organise a counter coup against the Suriname ruling military council using mercenaries and apparently with tacit French support. In addition, it has been reported that a Radio Free Suriname is broadcasting from French territory into Suriname.

Grenada

Political Factors

The events of October 1983 make normal, future, political change in Grenada, within a Westminster-style model, subject to unusual pressures. While elections in 1984 took place with background security provided by American and Caribbean forces, this will not be the case in the future. Although the centrist New National Party won the election taking all but one seat, its long-term political cohesion is not certain. Other parties considered likely to play future political roles are the right-wing Grenada United Labour Party (GULP), led by Sir Eric Gairy, a re-orientated socialist Maurice Bishop Patriotic Movement, and the re-emerging hard line Marxist–Leninist New Jewel Movement (NJM). Of these, the NJM and GULP have a history of direct action, and future centrist Grenada governments may be hard pressed to maintain internal security given the concern that there may be a residue of a high level of arms in the country amongst supporters of the Bishop government.

The United States is unlikely to forget the events in Grenada and will continue to wish to influence the country's moderate democratic parties. In addition, for both Cuba and the Soviet Union the 1983 events in Grenada were a major setback and both countries will undoubtedly try to maintain relationships with parties or groupings in Grenada.

Politicised Youth

Unlike any other English-speaking Caribbean country, the island's youth from 1979 to 1983 were exposed to some intense political education. These, together with the now disbanded Peoples Revolutionary Army, represent an unassessable potential for dramatic and possibly, in some cases, violent political change.

Police Force

During the 1979–83 period the island's police force was effectively down-graded to fulfilling basic duties. The police force has been re-trained and strengthened and the United Kingdom is providing training for a 500-strong police force. In addition, the United States is providing para-military training and, in view of this and the background against which the force has been re-established, it is possible that there may be a political perspective to the force.

Guyana

Political Factors

Political change in Guyana is likely to involve significant upheavals after President Burnham has passed from the scene. Guyana has a history of racial division and often violent political confrontation. While alignments have been made between political parties at various times, all parties represent left of centre views. Change in Guyana in the past and in the foreseeable future is of concern to the United States, Venezuela, Brazil, Britain, the Soviet Union and Cuba. Matters are made more complex by the military and para-military groups within the country having a political role and patronage from the individuals within the government they support. As a result, all scenarios for future political change in Guyana appear likely to involve a period of significant instability.

Border Disputes

Guyana faces claims on five-eighths of its territory from Venezuela. In addition, Suriname lays claim to part of the Eastern area. Although at times there have been border incursions, Venezuela has made no attempt to exert overt military pressure in its claim. Instead, both Venezuela and Guyana have decided to try to resolve their claim through the United Nations. However, while the claim remains open, hostilities could occur.

External Relations

Guyana's external relations are unusually complicated as it has sought first to develop a non-aligned posture and more recently has tried to deepen relations with Eastern Europe and Cuba. At various times the United States has placed pressure on the government through international financial institutions to change its policy. Regional relations are also complex as Guyana has experienced many differences of opinion on major issues with its Caribbean neighbours and also opposed the military intervention in Grenada.

Netherlands Antilles

The kingdom of the Netherlands Antilles is a wide-spread federation containing one condominium with France, the secessionist island, Bonaire, and the islands of Curaçao and Aruba, which are heavily dependent on Shell Oil's refinery plant for their economic survival. The islands in the group wish to move to independence eventually but have differing time-scales for so doing. Future instability may stem from a decision by Shell to close their refineries. There is also the dormant claim to Aruba, Bonaire and Curaçao by Venezuela.

St Kitts/Nevis

Political Factors

Unlike other micro-states, St Kitts/Nevis has a federal constitution giving substantial power and constitutional rights to the Nevis parliament. The Federal government consists of a coalition between the Nevis Reformation Party (originally a secessionist group) and the St Kitts Peoples Action Movement. The constitution was drawn up at the time of independence by the two parties and is opposed by the St Kitts opposition Labour Party. Should the Labour Party achieve a majority in St Kitts, there is a high possibility that Nevis will secede despite its close proximity to St Kitts and its small population.

Defence Force

St Kitts has a small defence force which was in the past politically aligned to the opposition Labour Party. This created problems for the PAM/NRP coalition and subsequently members of the force were dismissed and it was disbanded.

St Lucia

Political Factors

Although elected in 1982 with a secure majority, the St Lucia Labour Party split into two factions with each determined to take control of government. Eventually the divisions between the two factions led to the Party and the government collapse and its division into separate entities. If St Lucia is to maintain its model of parliamentary change after every two terms, it remains to be seen what type of opposition may emerge.

Third Nation Involvement

In August 1983, Prime Minister Compton claimed that Libya was intending to provide terrorist training to St Lucia and other Eastern Caribbean nationals. This was possibly with the intent of generating an instability that would draw in the United States and would then bring about insecurity on the United States' southern flank. The claim related to scholarships granted by Libya to supporters of the opposition party led by George Odlum. Attempts had been made in the past by Mr Odlum, when Foreign Minister in the Labour Party government of Alan Louisy, to politicise the police force by transferring senior officers and attempting to train in Grenada a small politically motivated group. These attempts were largely resisted but raised questions about the possible political manipulation of the force.

St Vincent

Political Factors

The announced intention of the new administration of James Mitchell is to establish a system of proportional representation. If Mr Mitchell does decide to break with the Westminster model this will probably lead to smaller left of centre parties eventually being involved in government, generating possible questions about the long-term cohesion of future governments.

Local Rebellion

In 1981 a small group of rastafarians on Union Island rebelled against the government and attempted to seize local power. The uprising was put down jointly by the St Vincent police force and the Barbados defence force.

Regional Security

St Vincent's new Prime Minister, James Mitchell, has said that he has no wish to participate in the proposed Regional Security Service as he believes it is an unnecessary expenditure. He has also indicated that he remains concerned that an element of the police force may still be loyal to the previous administration.

Suriname

Political Factors

Since the 1980 military coup, there have been at least five attempted coups, both externally and internally generated. The civilian government which was established by the ruling Military Council has gone through several changes of personnel and of Prime Minister. Real power is held by the Military Council which itself has been riven with serious internal dissension over the years. Without a return to an acceptable form of constitutional and elected government, domestic non-violent disension is likely to continue.

Opposition

Netherlands-based Suriname dissidents openly plan for the downfall of the army regime. Attempts in the past have included armed forays through neighbouring French Guiana. The Suriname government has said that mercenaries have also been involved. Further coup attempts are likely.

Domestic opposition reached a peak in 1982 when a nationwide strike seriously threatened the security of the government. Part of the response to this was the execution of 15 opposition leaders in December 1982. Despite this, in 1984 there were also major strikes resulting in the serious deterioration of an already extremely fragile economy. Internally, there has been no significant counter-revolutionary activity by political groups. Counter coups have tended to involve elements of the Suriname army.

International Relations

Suriname has a long-standing border dispute with Guyana but this is not likely to reach a threat threshold. Although the Bouterse regime recently forcibly evicted some 1,000 Guyanese illegal migrant workers, this is unlikely significantly to affect relations between the two states.

Until 1983, the post-coup government emphasised links with Cuba and Grenada, but after the Grenada intervention the regime, motivated by fears of coercive pressure from the United States, asked Cuba to withdraw its ambassador. (Relations with Cuba have since been restored.) The government also took steps to improve its relations with the Netherlands. In the past Suriname's political and economic links with its neighbours have been insignificant and its marginal location suggests that it will be left very much to its own devices as events there do not significantly affect its neighbours or involve great power interests.

British Dependencies

Although Britain remains responsible for the defence of her remaining Caribbean dependencies – Anguilla, Cayman Islands, British Virgin Islands, Montserrat, Turks & Caicos – there remain a number of potential weaknesses which could be exploited.

British Virgin Islands

The Organisation of Eastern Caribbean States (OECS) recently agreed to grant the British Virgin Islands associate member status and it is widely expected that it will participate in the joint security provision of the treaty. A special duty unit has been established within the police to operate in incidents involving hostages or organised criminal groups. Internally, the only real threats to order have arisen in recent years when a British Governor refused to sign documents confirming the death penalty on a convicted murderer. Although ignored externally, the event generated sufficient concern for Britain to consider taking limited direct action.

Montserrat

Despite having a constitution similar to the other dependencies, the Montserrat government has behaved with a greater degree of independence. Its Chief Minister, John Osborne, while paying lip service to the need for independence, appears to have accepted that local pressure is for the retention of dependency status. Despite this, Montserrat is not only a member of the OECS but also its Chairman in 1985 and it has acceded to the OECS Memorandum of Understanding on security. Indeed, at one stage, Chief Minister Osborne was mandated to put together proposals for the establishment of a coastguard for the Leeward Islands. The contradictions of Montserrat's position were most apparent when the Chief Minister, in consultation with the United States, decided to send a detachment of police to Grenada with OECS interventionist forces, only to be informed by Britain, through its Governor, that they must be recalled. Internally, Montserrat has a developed system of political parties often in alliance with trade unions. An electoral accommodation is said to exist between the governing party and a left-wing trade-union based party which has close political connections with the Communist Party of Cuba and like-minded regional parties.

Turks & Caicos Islands

In the late 1970s, the Turks & Caicos Islands became one of the major trans-shipment points for narcotics originating from Central and Latin America and destined for the United States. Despite efforts by the British authorities and co-ordinated action with the US Drug

Enforcement Agency and the Bahamian coastguard, the traffic through the islands remains substantial. Income from organized crime has distorted elements of the local economy and there are growing indications of the use of hard drugs in the islands. As a result of action involving British and American Government agencies, the island's chief minister and other ministers have been charged in the United States with allegedly assisting those involved in narcotics trafficking. They have subsequently resigned, provoking a constitutional crisis of sorts for the British Government of the islands.

Towards a Regional Security Service

Up to the 1979 Grenada revolution, awareness of vulnerability to domestic and external threats and general security weaknesses in the Eastern Caribbean was minimal. Antigua maintained a police force and a small poorly-trained and badly-equipped defence force; Barbados had a well-organised police and defence force, although poorly equipped; the Bahamas maintained a police force and a poorly equipped defence force; Dominica, St Vincent and St Kitts/ Nevis had to rely solely on poorly-organised police forces; Belize, while maintaining a police and defence force, largely relied on the British military presence; Guyana, for both external and internal reasons, was in the process of developing its defence force. Only Grenada, after 1979, was highly conscious of its security as it feared either direct or indirect United States attack or an attempt at a counter-coup by the deposed Eric Gairy.

Although there had been talk of a coastguard for the micro-states, the 1979 Grenada revolution galvanised the other Eastern Caribbean governments into action. In particular, discussions centred on establishing, with British, American and Canadian support, a common coastguard with a residual defence capacity. Talks proceeded, but were in part hampered by ideological differences with Grenada. In the interim, Barbados and St Vincent went ahead with the purchase of necessary equipment and the establishment of a command structure.

In 1981 the Organisation of Eastern Caribbean States came into being and a final agreement was reached on a joint memorandum of understanding on security. The memorandum provides for multilateral security co-operation between Antigua, Barbados, Dominica, St Lucia and St Vincent. It also covers funding, political responsibility, training, planning, jurisdiction, command and procurement.

Although the memorandum, which formed the basis of the Grenada intervention, marked a new awareness of the problems facing the area, it also raised new questions, which can be summarised as:

(a) How and on whose terms would the treaty be put into effect?

(b) How could any security mechanism have a command structure that could make swift decisions but be politically accountable to all governments?

(c)) How could such a command structure develop the intelligence necessary for accurate decision-making?

(d) Who would fund the equipment, training and transport requirements of such a force?

(e) Could a consensus ever exist among the signatory states as to the nature of a security threat?

Reacting further to growing concern about the lack of security, in 1982, Commonwealth Caribbean governments began considering the establishment of some form of security and defence treaty which would operate on a region-wide basis. Such a treaty was envisaged as providing for support in the event of any external threat. Although no public mention was made of the matter, discussions on the establishment of a Treaty for Mutual Assistance took place at a number of regional meetings.

The matter was first formally discussed during the CARICOM Heads of Government meeting held in Ocho Rios, Jamaica in November 1982. Although the discussions were not mentioned in the final communiqué of the conference, a decision was taken at that time to establish a working group within CARICOM to produce papers for further discussion on possible treaty options. Such moves stemmed from a locally felt and, in part, externally encouraged awareness that the Caribbean was one of the only areas in the world without either defence treaties with major powers or any form of agreement on mutual defence.

The region's interest centred on three possible options:

(a) Possible accession to the Inter-American Treaty of Reciprocal Assistance, known as the Rio Treaty. This Treaty ties most

Latin American nations to the United States and provides for all signatory nations to treat any nation that attacks a signatory country as being at war with all Treaty nations.
(b) The establishment of a Rio-type treaty involving only Caribbean states. This option would be so designed as to exclude non-Caribbean nations and the United States.
(c) Other treaty options involving non-agression pacts with potentially hostile nations.

Consideration was also given to variations and combinations of the three options.

There was a growing feeling that the Rio Treaty option was unacceptable, although favoured by nations with close ties to the United States. Critics argued that it would enable the United States to intervene militarily in the region if it so wished. They also said that the Rio Treaty would in effect mean that CARICOM nations could potentially find themselves supporting nations that had territorial disputes with other CARICOM countries. Critics of the regional Rio Treaty approach argued that the area has neither the military wherewithal to react to any threat nor the political homogeneity to make military agreements possible.

Other suggestions appeared to favour the idea of non-aggression pacts being signed with the United States and Cuba and any other nations in the area considered to represent a threat to security. Consideration was also given to the idea of establishing the Caribbean as a Zone of Peace. CARICOM Foreign Ministers set up a study on this matter but no further action seems to have been taken.

A Growth in Military Capability

The October events in Grenada and their aftermath rendered elements of the discussion above academic. Within three months of the intervention, the United States had embarked upon a major programme of military assistance to Caribbean nations that participated in the events of October 1983. The assistance was aimed at ensuring that there would be no repetition of the experience of Grenada in the Eastern Caribbean.

The programme, which is still under way, involves the provision of military equipment and training. It is being funded, in part, out of the US$15 million in security assistance being provided to Grenada and the Caribbean Peacekeeping Force on the island. United States advisers are currently undertaking military programmes with newly established para-military wings of East Caribbean police forces aimed at establishing special service units. Police training in Grenada and elsewhere is being undertaken by Britain as part of a continuing assistance programme as well as a special £0.75 million package for the island.

About 150 United States military police will remain in Grenada until the island's police force is trained up to a sufficient level. Drawn into five platoons, these forces are intended to be able to move swiftly within Grenada to ensure that any possible guerrilla threat can be easily contained. The troops are supported by Land Rovers mounted with machine-guns, six helicopters and about 300 other personnel providing logistical, psychological, medical and intelligence support. The United States stay-behind group assumes the continuing presence of two Jamaican special service units of approximately 175 men each, who are trained and equipped to United States combat standards. It is expected that these will leave Grenada in mid-1985. In addition, the United States has placed four coastguard vessels – three patrol boats and a tender – in St George's to respond to any external threat in the immediate region.

Supporting the United States and Jamaican troops until mid-1985 are some 650 men from the police forces of Barbados, Dominica, St Lucia and St Vincent and the defence forces of Antigua and Barbados. While such police forces assist the local police force and the United States military patrols, Britain is undertaking extensive police training of the island's 280-man police force, which is eventually likely to be expanded. In addition to providing training to the force in both Grenada and at the regional police college in Barbados, other equipment as well as technical support is being given.

Elsewhere in the region, OECS states have all taken delivery of equipment. This includes: M16 rifles; sub-machine-guns; rocket launchers; small arms; telecommunications systems; radio receivers and transmitters; vehicles; uniforms; and rations. Referring to the capability that such equipment will provide to para-military police units in the region, Dominica's Prime Minister, Eugenia Charles, has made it clear that such equipment is to ensure that countries will now be able to withstand any internal or external attack. In addition all OECS nations have had military advisers attached to police forces to provide special training in para-military techniques. OECS nations have additionally been provided with coastguard patrol boats.

A Regional Security Service in 1985?

Beyond this immediate assistance, detailed discussions took place in 1984 on the establishment of a Regional Security Service (RSS) for the Commonwealth Caribbean which, it was proposed, should initially bring together the large and small countries of the region.

Central to early considerations was a request to the United States government from some Caribbean heads of state for substantial new military assistance for the establishment of a 1,000-man plus regional defence force. (Guyana, the Bahamas and Trinidad were not party to this request.) The matter was raised in Bridgetown in early February 1984 in discussions between Caribbean nations and the United States Secretary of State, George Shultz, and stemmed in part from a meeting held at the end of January 1984 in St George's to consider Grenada's security. However, while the United States made it clear that it was anxious to ensure that adequate provision was made for regional security assistance, there was a growing reticence in Washington about the cost and implications of further militarising the Eastern Caribbean.

At the February meeting, Caribbean leaders solicited American help in training and equipping a Regional Defence Force which would be headquartered in Barbados – probably at the decommissioned United States base at St. Lucy – and put under the overall command of Brigadier Rudyard Lewis, the Sandhurst-trained Chief of the Barbados Defence Force. Mr Shultz promised training, but expressed a preference for building up individual defence forces and para-military police forces on each island rather than dealing with the region collectively. This was seen in some quarters as representative of a feeling in Washington that there was a need to shift away from dealing with the English-speaking Caribbean as a collective group, to dealing with nations on a bilateral basis. However, Barbados' late Prime Minister Tom Adams expressed the view that it would be more practical and economically more sensible to have a single Caribbean Defence Force.

By late 1984, the concept of a unified RSS had run into both political and financial difficulties. Barbados still favoured the abandonment of individual defence forces and para-military sections of police forces and their replacement by a single Caribbean Defence Force, under a unified command based on three islands. Officials suggested that such a joint defence force would be economically more feasible and militarily safer, since it could, if necessary, protect some of the small governments from their own armies or police forces. For an effective RSS, they argued, the region would need: transport, helicopters for rapid deployment as well as some kind of short takeoff and landing transport aircraft; helicopter gunships; armour to provide the muscle for the force, and a high level of combat training so they could hold territory while more substantial assistance was obtained from abroad, presumably from the United States.

To be viable, it would also have to establish a regionally integrated intelligence service with links to friendly agencies. However, increasing doubts as to such a plan were expressed by Dominica, St Lucia and St Vincent and perhaps more importantly by the United States and Britain who were being expected to fund the proposals. Without the financial support of the Bahamas, Guyana and Trinidad, the dependence on the United Kingdom and the United States for funding was even greater. Concern about loyalty, the command structure and the political trigger mechanisms to mobilise the RSS were at the centre of a growing feeling of disquiet and by late 1984 clarification was being requested by funding agencies.

Since then, further meetings have taken place and an outline agreement has been reached for an RSS based on individual special support units in each nation, undertaking joint exercises from time to time. Western funding for equipment and training will come from Britain, the United States and Canada, but it is unclear how the RSS's daily activities will be funded.

Grenada: A Special Case

Grenada, however, remains a special case. At a January 1984 meeting of OECS leaders, officials from Jamaica, Barbados and senior representatives of the United States administration and military in Grenada discussed the overall security situation in the island. In the light of a stated desire by the United States to withdraw its 280 troops still on Grenada at the earliest possible date, consideration was given to inviting additional Commonwealth participation, in particular, from Canada and Trinidad.

It was also agreed that a small military mission will remain attached to the United States Embassy in Grenada to maintain liaison both with the remainder of the Caribbean Peacekeeping Force (CPF) and the future Regional Defence Force. It is expected that the CPF in Grenada will be finally wound up in mid-1985, by which time the newly-trained and equipped Grenada Police Force will be ready to assume all remaining security duties.

It has also been agreed that aspects of the collective security mechanism of the OECS treaty will be revised so as to make action taken in future unchallengeable in international law, as far as this is possible.

The Future

Despite present difficulties and disagreements, there are indications that a Caribbean Regional Security Service (RSS) based on Special Support Groups and involving the East Caribbean micro-states and Barbados, and possibly the dependencies of the British Virgin Islands and Monserrat will come into being. It remains unclear, however, how much the RSS will cost; whether forces will be organised in two or more geographical centres or on an island-by-island basis; how the command structure will be politically responsive, and, most importantly, who is to pay for joint exercises.

Allied to this is the danger that such a service may be rendered inoperative in the longer term by personality politics in individual states, questions about the future political loyalty of individual Special Service Units, and legitimate political change leading newly elected governments to decline to participate in previously agreed security arrangements. All of these issues raise questions about the long-term cohesion of such a service.

In addition, little account seems to have been taken of the range of threats detailed earlier and how such a force could respond. Equally, reaction to problems in non-participating nations, or in fellow CARICOM nations with border disputes, has not been accounted for. It also remains to be seen whether CARICOM Heads of Government have a strong enough common purpose to agree to broaden the RSS proposals.

In conclusion, it is worth noting that some military experts from outside the region believe that, ultimately, Caribbean nations will not be able to pursue the courses of action envisaged. Rather, they suggest that they will end up with small scale individual Special Support Groups operating domestically and with bilateral treaties with nearby developed nations with similar political philosophies who could provide military support in the event of a crisis.

Annex C: The Pacific

The states and territories of the Pacific Basin fall into two distinct groups: the continental rim of mainly prosperous and influential states whch border on the Pacific; and the scattered groups of small island communities with few resources in the South and Central Pacific. The latter are our primary concern since most of the micro-states are situated in this area.

It is worth noting, however, that the states bordering on the Pacific include not only the two superpowers, but also China, Japan, Korea, the ASEAN states, Australia, New Zealand, Canada and the eastern seaboard states of Latin America. Antarctica lies beyond the southernmost rim of the Pacific Basin. It has recently been estimated that by the end of the century 60 per cent of the world's consumers will live around the Pacific rim and half of the world's super-cities will be situated there.[1] These 'outer rim' Pacific states or territories are relevant to this study to the extent that they either pose a threat to individual micro-states, or contribute directly to their security and well-being.

Historical Background

Historians believe that the main island groups of the Central and South Pacific were populated over many centuries by waves of migration from East and South-East Asia.[2] European explorers did not arrive on the scene until the sixteenth century; first the Spanish and Portuguese, followed by the Dutch, the British and the French. From then on, the islands of the Pacific became pawns in international rivalries. By the beginning of the twentieth century, most of the archipelagos of the Central and South Pacific had come under some form of Western 'protection' and control. The British (having successfully colonised Australia and New Zealand) had also

173

assumed control over Fiji, the Gilbert and Ellice Islands, the Solomon Islands and Tonga. The United States took over Guam from the Spanish after the Spanish–American War of 1898. They had been awarded Eastern (American) Samoa under the Three Powers Convention of 1899 although they only formally took over the territory in 1926. The Germans (who arrived late in the scramble for the Pacific) set up a protectorate of the Marshall Islands in the 1880s, and subsequently bought Spain's remaining Micronesian possessions. They also acquired Nauru, New Guinea and Western Samoa.

The islands of the South Pacific were comparatively unaffected by the fighting in the First World War. After the defeat of Germany, however, its Pacific territories changed hands, becoming Mandated Territories of the League of Nations, administered by one or other of the victorious Allies.[3] During the Second World War, on the other hand, the South Pacific was a major theatre of war. The Japanese attack on Pearl Harbour was launched from bases in the Japanese mandated Pacific Islands Territory and thereafter these islands, as well as many other small islands in the Pacific, suffered heavy civilian casualties, and sometimes almost total destruction of their resources, as their homelands became the battlefields for Western and Japanese combatants in an all-out war.

Since the Second World War, the wind of change has blown through the small island dependencies of the Pacific. The former British territories of Fiji, the Gilbert and Ellice Islands (now Kiribati and Tuvalu), the Solomon Islands and Tonga have all become independent members, or Associate members, of the Commonwealth. All but Tonga are also members of the United Nations. The Anglo-French condominium of the New Hebrides opted for independence as Vanuatu and has become a member of the Commonwealth and the United Nations. Of the former UN Trust Territories, Nauru, the world's smallest state, opted for independence and Associate membership of the Commonwealth (but not of the UN); New Guinea, administered by Australia, opted to merge with the adjoining Australian dependent territory of Papua as the independent State of Papua New Guinea [4] and is a member of both the United Nations and the Commonwealth; Western Samoa (administered by New Zealand) opted for independence and has become a member of the United Nations and of the Commonwealth.

The only remaining Trust Territory is the former League of

Nations mandated Territory of the Pacific Islands administered by Japan until it was captured by the United States in the Second World War and subsequently made a UN Strategic Trust Territory under American administration. This Territory has reached the final stages of self-determination. Referendums held so far under UN observation indicate that it will almost certainly split into four States after termination of the Trusteeship Agreement (it cannot do so before). The Northern Mariana Islands have already approved a Covenant to establish a 'Commonwealth' in political union with the United States. The other three entities (the Marshall Islands, the Federated States of Micronesia and Palau) are all likely to opt for some form of Free Association with the United States, under which the latter would retain certain responsibilities for defence and development. Referendums on Agreements of Free Association are in the process of taking place. If approved, these will then be subject to approval by the three relevant political bodies in the Trust Territory and by the US Congress. (All four entities have already elected constitutional governments.)

The remaining French dependencies, French Polynesia, New Caledonia and Wallis and Futuna, have the status of Overseas Territories of France. American Samoa and Guam are 'unincorporated territories' of the United States. The Cook Islands and Niue are self-governing in Free Association with New Zealand and Associate members of the Commonwealth. Tokelau, with an estimated population of 1,620 remains a non-self-governing territory administered by New Zealand.[5]

The Problems of Survival in the Post-Colonial Era

The colonial era in the Pacific has thus virtually drawn to a close and the European powers, with the exception of France, no longer have dependent territories involving them directly in the affairs of the South Pacific. In place of the earlier colonial empires a number of small island states have emerged which are incapable either of defending themselves from military threats on the smallest scale, or of protecting their fisheries and other marine resources from poachers. What is the nature of the threat facing these small Pacific states. Where can they turn for aid in safeguarding their newly won independence, protecting their resources and ensuring minimum living standards for their people?

Protection or Threat? The Outer Rim States and the Security of the South Pacific

The United States
The world's two most powerful navies, the American and the Soviet, operate in the Pacific. The United States has historically been concerned with the security of the Pacific, its trade route to China and Japan, since the early part of the nineteenth century. President Theodore Roosevelt, one of the first American leaders to recognise the potential importance of the Pacific, observed that 'Western history began with a Mediterranean era, passed through an Atlantic era, and is now moving into a Pacific era'.[6] During the Second World War the main United States' theatre of war, and the one in which they sustained the heaviest casualties, was in the Pacific. The chief naval battles between the Americans and the Japanese were fought for small and hitherto little known islands in the Pacific which had few resources, but which served as strategic stepping stones for the contestants in their struggle for supremacy.

The defeat of Japan in 1945 left the United States as the dominant power in both the East and West Pacific. The United States occupied Japan and the Ryuku Island chain on behalf of the victorious allies until the conclusion of the Peace Treaty of San Francisco (September 1951) which restored sovereignty to Japan. However, the United States retained its strategic base in the East Pacific since its bilateral Security Treaty with Japan, concluded on 8 September 1951, granted the United States land, sea and air bases 'in and around Japan',[7] both to defend Japan from external attack 'and to contribute to the maintenance of international peace and security in the Far East' (article I). Japan also undertook to deny similar rights to any third party without the prior consent of the United States (article IV).

During the Second World War, United States forces had also captured and occupied the Pacific Islands formerly under Japanese mandate. In 1946 these were designated a United Nations Strategic Trust Territory under American administration.

In both the Korean War and the War in Vietnam, United States forces made use of their island bases in the Pacific. The American C-in-C Pacific is based in Honolulu, Hawaii, in the North West Pacific. The United States has other island bases and staging posts in the Pacific including Guam (Naval and Air Bases), the Marshall islands (a missile range), the Northern Marianas, American Samoa and Johnston Island. It also has three important bases in Australia, and port facilities are also available to United States warships in Australia and New Zealand [8] under the terms of the ANZUS Treaty and in Fiji under a recently concluded agreement.

The Pacific is now the United States' most important market. For the last five years United States trade with East Asia and the Pacific is reported to have been greater than with any other region of the world. In 1984 it accounted for 31 per cent of total United States trade. It is also expanding rapidly. In 1983, for example, American trade with the Pacific increased by 8 per cent whereas total American world trade rose only by 0.5 per cent. As Mr Shultz commented, 'Economically, as well as politically and strategically, the Pacific is vital to America's future.'[9]

The Soviet Union

Although historically the Russian, and later the Soviet, navy, confined its Pacific sphere of operations to a fairly restricted area of the North Pacific, this is no longer the case. There has been a significant expansion of Soviet maritime power in the last five years. The Report of a US–Japanese Advisory Commission released in Washington and Tokyo on 17 September 1984 stated that:

> The Soviet military buildup is especially significant in naval forces. The Soviet Pacific fleet has become the single largest unit in combatants with at least 125 submarines, about 30 of which are ballistic-missile equipped. The fleet's combat readiness has also been augmented by the presence of one or two Kiev-class aircraft carriers at any one time.[10]

The number of Soviet bases in the Pacific region has also increased. In addition to its bases in Siberia, the acquisition of naval and air bases in Cam Ranh Bay and Da Nang (both in Vietnam) has extended the Soviet sphere of operations in the Pacific. According to one press report,[11] a new Soviet base is under construction on Can San Island in the South China Seas and an army corps headquarters has been built in the Kuril Islands (ceded to the Soviet Union by Japan at the end of the Second World War). Soviet naval exercises in the Pacific are becoming more frequent. Vessels of the Soviet fleet now carry out regular patrols throughout the North Pacific. They also operate, though less frequently, in the South Pacific and have occasionally been detected in the Tasman Sea. So far, however, the

Soviet Union has failed to secure a permanent base for its fleet in the South Pacific.

The activities of the Soviet navy in the South Pacific are a source of concern among small states in the region, prompting at least one to take counter measures. The Prime Minister of Fiji, Sir Kamisese Muta, paid a visit to Washington at the end of 1984. He subsequently announced that he had negotiated an important aid agreement with the United States and that in return the Fijian Government had agreed to allow American nuclear armed warships to use the port facilities of Suva. In explaining this decision the Prime Minister said:

> We know that the Soviet ships are already in the Pacific – don't let us fool ourselves. But we have a responsibility for the security of this country and its people, and we have to do what we can. We hope that by allowing American warships into our ports we may deter the Russians from increasing their influence in the area.[12]

Japan

The post-war Pacific role of Japan has been equivocal. Economically, it is the second most powerful state in the Pacific, but, militarily and to some extent politically, it has been inhibited by its past from taking a more active part in the defence of the Pacific.

Historically, Japan played an important strategic role in the Pacific, particularly from the end of the nineteenth century onwards. The spectacular Japanese victory of Tsushima in May 1905 during the Russo–Japanese War heralded the emergence of a formidable new maritime power in the Pacific. This was also a period of Japanese colonial expansion southwards and into the Pacific. Japan colonised Taiwan (1895) and Korea (1910), and, after the First World War, succeeded to the former German colonies in Micronesia under a League of Nations Mandate. These last in particular provided key naval and air bases for the Imperial Japanese Forces in the Central South Pacific. Japanese military power reached its apogee in the period immediately following their attack on Pearl Harbour in December 1941 when for a short time Japan became the dominant power in the Pacific, extending its direct political control as far south as Papua New Guinea and also occupying the Solomon Islands.

The defeat of Japan in 1945 left the Japanese without military power or overseas possessions and Japanese nationals, including large numbers of Japanese settlers in the South Pacific, were repatriated. The Japanese constitution (adopted after the Second World War) renounced war and the use of force. Although this constitution was imposed on Japan at the time by the victorious Allies, it also reflected Japanese revulsion against the militarism which had left the country in ruins. The San Francisco Peace Treaty (1951) modified this prohibition only to the extent of recognising Japan's inherent right 'of individual or collective self-defence' and its right to enter into collective security arrangements. Japan therefore still only maintains 'self-defence forces' and its defence spending is restricted by its constitution to a maximum of 1 per cent of GNP.

The Treaty was based on the concept that Japan's role would be limited to defence, with assistance from the United States, and that the latter would be responsible for Pacific regional security. This unequal division of the defence burden no longer reflects Japan's political influence and economic strength and has become increasingly irksome to succeeding American Governments which have recently been pressing the Japanese to make a greater contribution to the defence of the Pacific.[13] However, there remains considerable opposition in Japan to any expansion of the Japanese military role beyond its own self-defence requirements.

This concern, as the Japanese themselves recognise, is shared by countries in the Asian–Pacific region which were former victims of Japanese militarism. Japanese Governments have therefore been at pains to issue reassurances. In May 1983, for example, Prime Minister Nakasone, speaking in Kuala Lumpur shortly after taking office, explained that Japan's own security was based on the maintenance of its arrangements with the United States, supplemented by the minimum self-defence capability allowed under its constitution. It had no aspirations to become a military power threatening neighbouring countries.[14] A joint report to President Reagan and Prime Minister Nakasone by a US–Japanese advisory commission published in September 1984, recognised that Japan needed the American military assistance provided under the Mutual Security Agreement to supplement its own self-defence arrangements because it could not provide the additional forces required 'except at very high cost and at levels of military preparedness politically unacceptable to the Japanese people and Japan's neighbours'.[15] However, although Japan's military role in the Pacific today is restricted to its own defence, the Japanese are increasingly active in other spheres which indirectly contribute to the stability of the micro-states in the South

Pacific. Indeed Japanese leaders often argue that the most appropriate contribution which Japan can make to the security of the
Pacific is through its economic aid and technical assistance
programmes, since these promote the stability and the well-being of
developing countries in the region.

At present Japan's bilateral aid (some 65 per cent of its total
Overseas Development Assistance) goes primarily to the more
developed countries of the Pacific Basin: Indonesia, South Korea,
Thailand, China, and the Philippines.[16] The micro-states of the
region receive very little either in absolute terms or in comparison
with aid from others. For example, in 1983 Japan provided less than 2
per cent of Vanuatu's aid and only about 17 per cent of the aid
received by Fiji. In addition, Japanese loans are extended on
relatively hard terms, with the grant element well below the average
of OECD members. The proportion of untied aid, however, is above
average (63 per cent against an average of 43 per cent).

Japan once again has important trade links with countries in the
South Pacific, including the micro-states, and there is also significant
Japanese investment in the area. Japanese businessmen and
Japanese tourists are visiting the Pacific in increasing numbers. In
1982, for instance, it was reported that more than three-quarters of the
tourists to the Northern Marianas came from Japan and that there
were eleven weekly flights linking Saipan and Tokyo.[17]

With their considerable experience of the economic problems of
the region, Japan could provide valuable additional aid, investment
and technical assistance in many fields to the micro-states of the
Pacific. If well-directed to meet the genuine needs of the population,
such aid could indeed contribute to the stability of the Pacific region,
as well as to the prosperity of the small territories concerned.

The Japanese are also pursuing a more active political role in the
South Pacific. In January 1985 Mr Nakasone undertook a tour of the
South Pacific which included visits to Fiji and Papua New Guinea
(the first official visit by a Japanese Prime Minister to either country).
The main objective of the tour, according to the Japanese Foreign
Ministry, was 'to establish stronger ties for the twenty-first century
between Japan and these countries by further deepening mutual
understanding through a frank exchange of views with the respective
leaders'.[18] Successive Japanese statesmen since the 1960s have also
floated ideas for some form of Pacific Community. However, the
response from other Pacific states has so far been tepid and the
Japanese are not at present pressing these proposals, recognising the

risk of provoking reminders of the wartime Japanese Co-prosperity Sphere.

Australia and New Zealand
The category of an 'outer rim' state is in many ways no longer applicable to Australia or New Zealand. Although their populations are predominantly of European stock and many still retain political and cultural ties with Britain, first the Pacific War and then British entry into the European community brought home to both countries the geographical facts of life and encouraged them to seek closer links with the countries of the Pacific Basin, including their neighbours in the South Pacific, who share many of their concerns (notably on nuclear issues), and whose security and stability are vital to their own security. That the micro-states themselves accept Australia and New Zealand as full members of the South Pacific club is clear from the fact that they were invited to become members of the South Pacific Forum (the political body set up on the initiative of the South Pacific micro-states themselves), whereas Britain, France and the United States, which are fellow members of the non-political South Pacific Commission, were not invited. Both countries play an active and constructive part in these two regional bodies.

Both Australia and New Zealand provide development aid, technical assistance and defence co-operation to countries in the South Pacific. In the case of Australia, 38 per cent of its 1984–5 Development Aid Programme and 46 per cent of its Defence Co-Operation Aid Programme for the same year went to territories in the South West Pacific, including Papua New Guinea which, as a former Australian dependency, received the lion's share. Almost all New Zealand's aid is concentrated on the South Pacific.[19] It also maintains mobile forces 'to provide on request, military assistance, technical aid, surveillance of outside activities, search and rescue, and disaster relief services in the South Pacific'. In addition limited military training is offered in New Zealand to South Pacific countries.[20]

The Underpinnings of Security

The recently independent states of the Pacific have virtually no defence capability of their own. Their limited resources would not in any case enable them to provide more than token defence forces from their own budgets. Fiji and Tonga have regular military forces trained with British help, but these are on a small scale. Fiji has a small infantry force which has distinguished itself in UN Peace-keeping operations in the Lebanon (UNIFIL) and in the Multi-national Force and Observers in the Sinai. It also has patrol craft and a comparatively strong police force. Tonga has a small military defence force and two patrol craft in addition to its police force.

Vanuatu is believed to have a para-military force in addition to its police force. There is a small American defence force in American Samoa. French forces are based in French Polynesia and New Caledonia, both dependent territories. Co-operation in defence matters is primarily on a bilateral basis between the ANZUS states, Britain and France, and individual micro-states in the Pacific. The exception was Papua New Guinea which helped to put down the Santo uprising in Vanuatu at the time of the latter's access to independence.

In a regional context the two most important existing provisions for the maintenance of international peace and security in the Pacific are the ANZUS Treaty and the American–Japanese Treaty of Mutual Security.

ANZUS

The ANZUS Treaty was signed in September 1951 between the United States, Australia and New Zealand to co-ordinate their collective defence in the Pacific. The parties to the Treaty undertake to 'consult together whenever, in the opinion of any of them, the territorial integrity, political independence or security of any of the parties is threatened in the Pacific' (article III). Each party is bound to act to meet the common danger according to its constitutional processes, since each party recognizes that an attack on any of the parties would be dangerous to its own peace and safety (article IV). An armed attack in the terms of the Treaty includes 'an armed attack on the metropolitan territory of any of the parties, or on the island territories under its jurisdiction in the Pacific, or on its armed forces, public vessels or aircraft in the Pacific' (article V). 'Pending the development of a more comprehensive system of regional security in the Pacific area and the development by the United Nations of more effective means to maintain international peace and security', the ANZUS Council (established under the Treaty) 'is authorized to maintain a consultative relationship with States, Regional organ-isations, Associations of states, or other authorities in the Pacific area' in a position to further the purposes of the Treaty and 'to contribute to the security of that area' (article VIII).²¹ Although article V only specifically covers the dependent island territories of the parties to the Treaty, the signatories can also be expected to take a serious view of an attack on an independent micro-state in the area since the general thrust of the Treaty is the preservation of peace in the Pacific. Their attitude has indeed been made clear in a number of public statements. In the Communiqué issued by the ANZUS Council in July 1983, for instance, 'the Council members noted that the security of the Pacific island states is closely related to that of the ANZUS partners'. It also noted that 'defence co-operation programmes of the ANZUS partners are continuing to make a practical contribution to regional security'.

The three ANZUS powers conduct joint exercises, and exchange technical information and strategic intelligence. Defence co-operation and training programmes are arranged on a bilateral basis with other countries in the region, including the micro-states in the South Pacific. Besides military aid, the ANZUS powers provide on request technical aid, surveillance of outside activities, search and rescue and disaster relief services in the South Pacific. The government of New Zealand recently announced plans for a South Pacific 'trouble shooting battalion'.²²

There is, however, one security problem which is of concern to the ANZUS signatories: the nuclear issue. In the final communiqué issued by the ANZUS council in July 1983 (following a meeting in Washington to review the Treaty for the first time) its members noted the 'very deep concern over the nuclear issue in the South Pacific' but at the same time

> stressed the importance of upholding the principles of freedom of navigation and overflight as provided in international law. They also noted the importance to the alliance and the region of security considerations, including access by Allied aircraft and ships to airfields and ports in accordance with the sovereign rights of states to receive such visits.²³

At the beginning of 1985, there were two incidents which highlighted the problem. In one incident, the Australian government of Mr Hawke expressed its reluctance to allow American aircraft monitoring MX intercontinental ballistic missile tests to refuel and fly from Australia, although the arrangements had been agreed with the previous Australian government. The Americans diffused this crisis by making alternative arrangements following a meeting between Mr Shultz and Mr Hawke in Washington.[24] More serious, perhaps, was the refusal by the New Zealand government to grant port clearance to the American warship, *Buchanan*, because of Washington's refusal to confirm whether or not the ship was armed with nuclear weapons. However, despite the subsequent furore, the Prime Minister of New Zealand, Mr Lange, emphasised that his country'is and intends to remain, a committed member of ANZUS'.[25] None the less, as a result of the New Zealand action, the United States cancelled the 1985 ANZUS defence exercise and reportedly ceased providing New Zealand with intelligence. The ANZUS Council meeting, planned to take place in Canberra in July, was also cancelled.[26]

Sources of Stress

The Nuclear Question
The attitudes of Australia and New Zealand on the nuclear issue differ little from those of many of the governments in the South Pacific. The strong views held on this question are relevant to this study to the extent that these may sour otherwise friendly relations, affect existing regional and bilateral security provisions, and inhibit agreement on new arrangements, for fear of nuclear complications.

Islands in the South Pacific region have been used by Western nuclear powers as bases, or testing grounds, ever since American aircraft based on the Northern Mariana Islands carried out the atomic attack on Japan in August, 1945. The deep-seated fears of the islanders on all nuclear issues are thus understandable, particularly in view of the earlier gross and tragic misjudgement by the experts as to both the long-term medical effects of exposure to radiation (including the slowness of symptoms to develop) and the duration of contamination of the environment, including marine resources and food crops. The nuclear tests carried out in the Bikini and Enewetak Atolls (Marshall Islands) between 1946 and 1958 left the Islands desolate and dangerously contaminated. The people of Enewetak were only able to return in 1980 and then only to part of the Atoll. Bikini Atoll is not now expected to be safe for habitation for another fifty to sixty years.[27]

Other nuclear tests took place in Johnston Island and Christmas Island (both in uninhabited areas of the Pacific). Between 1957 and

1959 the United Kingdom tested seven H-bombs and three A-bombs on Christmas Island. In 1962 the island was loaned to the United States, which was reported to have detonated 'not less than 25 bombs, of which at least 3 were H-bombs in the 10 megaton range' before the 1963 Partial Test Ban came into force.[28] The French set up testing ranges in the Pacific at Fangatanfa and Moruroa in the Tuamotuan atolls in French Polynesia in the early 1960s when the independence of Algeria precluded further use of the Sahara, their earlier testing site.

The only nuclear tests which are still taking place in the South Pacific are French underground tests at Moruroa Atoll. In 1983 in response to repeated expressions of concern and calls for the termination of all nuclear testing in the South Pacific region by both the South Pacific Forum and individual member governments, the French government invited member governments of the South Pacific forum to send a scientific mission to visit the test site. The detailed joint report by the Australian–New Zealand–Papua New Guinean Scientific Mission which visited Moruroa Atoll was published on 9 July 1984. The Mission found no evidence of immediate health hazards attributable to the nuclear test programme,[29] but some evidence of damage to the structural integrity of the Atoll. The Heads of Member Governments participating in the South Pacific Forum considered regional nuclear issues at their meeting in Tuvalu in August 1984. The Communiqué issued at the conclusion of the meeting referred to the Scientific Mission's findings and noted that although these:

> allayed to some degree the concern that had been expressed about the short-term effects of the French nuclear tests, they provided no reassurance about long-term consequences nor in any sense diminished Forum opposition to testing in any environment. They accordingly reiterated their strong opposition to continued nuclear testing in the South Pacific region by France or any other country.[30]

Visits by nuclear armed ships or requests for bases which might store nuclear weapons are also causes for concern for some of the micro-states of the South Pacific. For example, the people of Palau have up till now been unwilling to amend their constitution to make it compatible with the otherwise advantageous proposed Compact of Free Association with the United States, by removing the nuclear-free provisions, although the latter is pressing them to do so. It is significant that the Heads of Government at the South Pacific Forum in August 1984 unanimously decided to set up a working party of officials to draft a Nuclear Free Zone Treaty for consideration at the next Forum Meeting in 1985. The draft is to be based on principles set out in an Australian working paper which include the following:

> that South Pacific countries should be free to live in peace and independence and to run their own affairs in accordance with the wishes and traditions of their people

and that:

> there should be no use, testing or stationing of nuclear explosive devices in the South Pacific; no South Pacific country would develop or manufacture, or receive from others, or acquire or test any nuclear explosive device; nuclear activities of South Pacific countries should be in accordance with applicable international principles and treaties, notably the NPT and take into account regional arrangements; and that South Pacific countries retain their unqualified sovereign rights to decide for themselves, consistent with their support for these objectives, their security arrangements, and such questions as the access to their ports and airfields by vessels and aircraft of other countries.[31]

Mr Hawke, the Australian Prime Minister, said that it would be left to each country to decide whether to accept visits by nuclear powered ships. New Zealand has already announced that it would ban such visits.

The dumping of nuclear waste material in the Pacific by countries with Pacific coastlines is another issue of great concern to the micro-states of the Pacific because of the possible contamination of fish, a staple food as well as an important economic resource. Fears were aroused by Japanese proposals in 1982 to dump low-level nuclear waste in the Pacific which, Japan argued, was not prohibited under the London Dumping Convention. In view of the hostile reaction of the South Pacific states, Japan has since stressed that its sea disposal programme would be carried out only with the understanding of the countries and territories concerned. This has not so far been forthcoming and the South Pacific Forum at its August 1984 meeting agreed to examine a proposal by Nauru to seek to strengthen the London Dumping Convention.

Fears on nuclear issues are less widely held in some states than in others. Fiji, for example, has seen merit in offering facilities to American warships. But anti-nuclear sentiments are sufficiently prevalent to suggest that these issues should be handled sensitively and treated with respect, particularly in view of the historical record of nuclear testing.

Internal Instability

With the exception of Vanuatu and New Caledonia, the micro-states in the Pacific have achieved independence without the bloodshed and bitterness which have accompanied the process of decolonisation in some other parts of the world. The transfer of power has been carried out smoothly and moderate governments have emerged. Some territories have opted to remain dependent. Most have remained on excellent terms with the former metropolitan power.

In most of the South Pacific states and territories, particularly in the Outer Islands, traditional values and customs persist and the traditional leaders continue to exert considerable influence and power. Many of them have run for office and thus also play a full part in non-traditional politics. Some of the new democratic constitutions adopted include special provisions to protect customary law and traditional practices. This melding of democratic and traditional values appears to have a stabilising effect, easing the transition to constitutional government.

The South Pacific is not without political problems, however, which are either already causing instability, or could do so in the future. The French territory of New Caledonia is a case in point. It is a country where there has been considerable French investment and which has one of the largest nickel deposits in the world, as well as chrome manganese and iron ore. But New Caledonia is less fortunate in the composition of its population. It has the classical 'settler' problem which has complicated the decolonisation process in other parts of the world (notably Algeria and Rhodesia). Significantly, many former French settlers in Algeria went to New Caledonia after Algerian independence and now own some two-thirds of the land. Out of a total population of 140,000 the indigenous Melanesians (Kanaks) account for roughly 43 per cent, the French settlers, 36 per cent, and the Asians and Polynesians (brought in originally to work in the mines and plantations) 21 per cent. The last two groups have tended to combine to resist Kanak pressure for independence and agrarian reform. They also have powerful groups of supporters in Metropolitan France among those who oppose President Mitterrand. Reports in 1984 that a small group of Kanaks had received military training in Libya and that party activists had also been in Algeria reinforced the fears of the settlers.[32] The Kanaks, on their side, have been encouraged to increase their political demands by the advent of independence in neighbouring islands, and by the election of a French Socialist to the Presidency in France.

The situation became more polarised following elections in November 1984 to a new Territorial Assembly, which were boycotted by the Kanak Socialist Liberation Front. Violence broke out between Kanaks and French settlers and a special envoy, M. Edgar Pisani, was sent by the French Government to try to negotiate a settlement. His proposals envisaged the holding of a referendum in July 1985 to decide on the future status of the territory. If the proposals were then approved, New Caledonia would become independent on 1 January 1986 and eligible for membership of the United Nations. France would however retain control of defence and internal security under a Treaty of Association, and French citizens who decided to take up New Caledonian citizenship would be accorded a special status as 'privileged residents'.

The proposals were rejected by the settlers, large numbers of whom rioted in Noumea, the capital. Thereafter the state of unrest was so serious that a thousand police reinforcements were sent out from France, a curfew was imposed and a State of Emergency proclaimed. This last step had been taken only once before in the history of the Fifth Republic – in Algeria in 1961. On 19 January 1985 President Mitterrand paid a twelve-hour visit to New Caledonia in an attempt to resuscitate the Pisani proposals and to restore confidence to both sides. On his return to Paris he announced that France intended to retain its strategic position in the region. It was further reported from Noumea that France would be building an important air and naval base for French strategic operations in the South Pacific. Although it was stressed that the base was not intended for use in policing the territory, it was suggested that its presence would reassure the settlers and attract foreign investment.[33] President Mitterrand's bold initiative appears to have restored some hope of resumed negotiations but the situation is highly volatile and likely to remain so.

In Fiji, where the Indian population slightly outnumbers the Fijians, the potential exists for disturbances on racial lines which would destroy the existing fragile *modus vivendi* between the two races. Although the present leaders of both communities appear to recognise the dangers of such a development and are anxious to avoid it, there is reputed to be growing hostility between the two communities at grass-roots level. The lack of serious trouble between the communities at and since independence is possibly due to the fact that only native Fijians are allowed to own land.

Vanuatu, the former Anglo–French Condominium of the New Hebrides, is arguably the least stable of the independent South Pacific micro-states. Its leaders are certainly amongst the most radical. The opening of diplomatic relations with Cuba caused concern at the time and the Opposition accused the Prime Minister of dragging the country towards communism.

Regional Links

The transition from dependency to independence has been eased by the setting up of a number of regional organisations. These are important not only for the services they provide, but also because they forge new links between individual Pacific States and between individual leaders which often did not exist before independence.[34] Such links could be particularly valuable in times of crisis.

The first regional organisation, the South Pacific Commission, was set up in 1947. Its activities are of a non-political character, it provides training and assistance in economic, social and cultural fields. Each territory has its own programme of development activities. The participating governments are: Australia, Cook Island, Fiji, France, Nauru, New Zealand, Niue, Papua New Guinea, Solomon Islands, Tuvalu, United Kingdom, United States, Western Samoa. Countries and territories also entitled to be represented at the South Pacific Conference are as follows: American Samoa, Federated States of Micronesia, French Polynesia, Guam, Kiribati, Marshall Islands, New Caledonia, Northern Mariana Islands, Palau, Pitcairn Islands, Tokelau, Tonga, Vanuatu, Wallis and Futuna Islands. The total regular budget of the Commission for 1983 was 497,313,600 francs CFP, derived from proportional contributions by member governments. Projects funded from external sources (for example, UNDP, UNEP, UNFPA and individual governments) cost 194,410,000 francs CFP in 1982. A South Pacific Conference is held annually, attended by delegates from countries and territories within the Commission's area of action.

The regional political body is the South Pacific Forum, which was set up in 1971 on the initiative of the South Pacific States themselves. It has no written constitution or formal rules. It is a gathering of eleven Heads of Government of independent and self-governing States in the South Pacific Region; i.e. unlike the Commission, the United States, United Kingdom and France are not included.[35] It meets anually, or when issues require urgent attention. Before the formal meetings start, the Heads of Government meet for a day without officials to try and establish a consensus on key issues. The former Prime Minister of New Zealand, Mr Muldoon, described its role as follows: 'Over the years we have built up confidence in our part of the region. We know each other well. We are bound together by geography, democratic traditions and common experience'.

In 1973 the South Pacific Forum set up an economic bureau, the South Pacific Bureau for Economic Co-operation (SPEC), to promote and facilitate co-operation and consultations between members on economic matters. One of its chief achievements has been to establish a subsidized regional shipping line, the Pacific Forum. This is important both for the promotion of inter-island trade and development, and for security reasons, since it ensures regular links between all the island communities. (Attempts to rationalise air services have so far not succeeded.) The Governments of Australia and New Zealand each contribute one-third of the annual budget of SPEC, the remaining third is shared equally between the other member Governments. The South Pacific regional organisations also maintain links with ASEAN and the European Community; the latter contributed to the Pacific Forum line through the European Investment Bank.

The Law of the Sea is another issue on which the Pacific Forum has been active. It has established a Forum Fisheries Agency to assist small member countries to deal effectively with the foreign governments and companies whose sophisticated distant water fishing boats deplete the marine resources within their Exclusive Economic Zones. Although the land areas of these Pacific Island States and territories are small, they are also widely dispersed, so that their Economic Zones are often extensive and beyond their present capacity to patrol.[36] The scattered character of the Pacific archipelagos is also, of course, a security problem. It would be all too easy for secret landings to take place in outer islands for subversive purposes, including the smuggling of arms and drugs. Many of the South Pacific States would like to develop their capacity to police their own zones, and this would be a fruitful field for greater Western co-operation. All these regional activities help to promote political and economic stability in the South Pacific and to forge closer links between the component states which should make them less vulnerable from the security point of view.

Economic Factors and Security

In our opening chapter we stressed the role of economic factors in promoting political instability. The micro-states of the Pacific share many common problems: they have very small land areas, very limited natural resources and rapidly growing populations. Without substantial external aid, they lack the means, the infrastructure and the technical expertise to maintain, even in modified form, the standards and services (including elementary health and educational services) which their people learned to expect under Western rule and the influence of Western ideas. It is no longer possible, in a world of modern communications, to put the clock back and revert to the way of life of their ancestors before the advent of the Europeans. For the foreseeable future, therefore, the only way in which these small Pacific States will be able to provide for their minimum needs will be to secure outside sources of financing and technical assistance. Economic self-sufficiency could only be achieved by reducing already spartan living standards to a degree which would be unacceptable to the population and likely to promote political instability.[37]

The UN and its Specialised Agencies are an important source of technical assistance in the South Pacific. The UNDP has offices in Fiji and Western Samoa. The Commonwealth also provides various technical assistance programmes to its members in response to requests. In addition both the Commonwealth and the South Pacific Forum have taken various steps to help the micro-states of the Pacific to tackle their economic problems.

The micro-states of the Pacific are also the recipients of bilateral aid and technical assistance, on a modest scale, chiefly from countries with historic links with the Pacific (the United Kingdom and France) and from the developed states of the Pacific Basin mentioned earlier in this chapter. Britain and France, for instance, are the chief providers of aid to their former dependent territories in the South Pacific.

General comments on the economic problems of micro-states and recommendations on the types of aid and technical assistance most urgently required appear elsewhere in this study. However, since it is sometimes misleading to generalise and since there are notable differences in development and culture between, for instance, the micro-states of the Caribbean and those of the Pacific, some comments and proposals in the context of the specific needs of the island states of the South Pacific follow.

Lack of funds, a shortage of trained personnel, inadequate infrastructure and remoteness from world markets are amongst the main constraints on development in the area. Aid for infrastructural projects and for education and technical training are both priorities. It is not possible to attract foreign capital, or develop small industries, without adequate communications and reasonably reliable power supplies together with the engineers, electricians, and maintenance workers to service them. In Chapter 6 we recommend that all aid projects should include provision for on-the-job training of local staff to replace any expatriate staff. Such provisions should also be included in the case of projects undertaken by foreign commercial firms. (Some already do this.) In most micro-states the development of agriculture and livestock is important, particularly where food is imported, to achieve greater self-sufficiency.

The South Pacific is an important fishing area and the 200-mile EEZs provide the micro-states in the area with new opportunities for expanding their fishing industries (as well as considerable difficulties in patrolling these sometimes vast areas). Fiji, for instance, has tripled its catch since 1977. In Truk, in the Trust Territory of the Pacific Islands, the establishment of a comprehensive fisheries complex, including a 100-metre ton cold storage facility, and vocational training was reported by the 1982 UN Visiting Mission to have raised the catch significantly.[38] However, since infrastructure, technology and trained manpower is increasingly required, this too would be a valuable choice for aid projects in the South Pacific.

Education, particularly higher education, teacher training and vocational training is an area where aid is particularly needed. In assigning such aid, recognition should be given to the high cost of sending students overseas for training and the consequent need to develop more local and regional educational and technical training centres in the longer term and to provide student grants in the interim period.

Tourism is a growing industry in some parts of the Pacific, understandably in view of its exceptional scenic beauty, unspoilt beaches and interesting culture. But development is at present limited by the lack of amenities (hotels, roads, water and electricity supply) in many islands and the remoteness of the area from world population centres, which makes the cost of travel at present unacceptably high for mass tourism. This is probably just as well since tourism can have adverse social consequences if expanded too rapidly. It should be carefully planned in order not to overwhelm small and fragile economies, and to conflict with local customs and traditions. There would appear to be particular scope for the development of specialised aspects of tourism, such as deep-sea diving and other marine sports.

Notes

1. *The Sunday Times*, 6 January 1985.
2. The islands fall into three main geographical groups: Polynesia, Melanesia and Micronesia. *Polynesia* includes Western Samoa, American Samoa, Tonga, the Cook Islands, Niue, Tokelau, Wallis and Futuna, Tuvalu, and French Polynesia. The total population is around 300,000. *Melanesia* includes Papua New Guinea, the Solomon Islands, Vanuatu, New Caledonia and most of Fiji. The total population is over 4,000,000. *Micronesia* includes Nauru, Kiribati, the United Nations Trust Territory of Pacific Islands and Guam. The total population is approximately 306,000.
3. The Marshall Islands, the Marianas and the Caroline Islands (already administered as one territory by the Germans) became the Pacific Islands Territory under Japanese administration. Nauru became a joint mandate of Britain, Australia and New Zealand, administered by Australia which also administered New Guinea. Western Samoa was administered by New Zealand. All were administered on behalf of the League, although this became a dead letter in the case of Japan.
4. Papua New Guinea with a population of over 2 million is not a micro-state within this study's definition, although it has similar problems and belongs to the same regional associations.
5. The Cook Islands, Niue and Tokelau were all former British dependencies handed over to New Zealand.
6. George Shultz, United States Secretary of State, in an address to the United States Committee for Pacific Economic Co-operation on 21 February 1985.
7. Article III of the Peace Treaty allowed the United States to retain full jurisdiction over various small islands formerly under Japanese sovereignty including the Ryukyu chain. The United States continued to administer part of the latter, including Okinawa, until 1972.

8. Since the advent to power of Mr Lange's Labour Government, however, New Zealand has placed a ban on visits by ships equipped with nuclear arms.
9. Shultz, *op. cit.*
10. Report of a US–Japanese Advisory Commission to President Reagan and Prime Minister Nakasone set up in 1983 to consider, *inter alia,* how the United States and Japan could better fulfil their long term responsibilities for the maintenance of world peace.
11. *Sunday Times,* 6 January 1985.
12. Report in the *Sunday Times,* 30 December 1984.
13. In response to such pressure Japan has now undertaken to defend its sea lanes from Tokyo and Osaka for 1,000 miles.
14. See Kinju Atarashi, 'Japan's Economic Cooperation Policy Towards the ASEAN Countries', *International Affairs,* Vol. 61, No. 1, Winter 1984/5, p. 120.
15. The Commission was charged with considering how the United States and Japan could better fulfil their long-term responsibilities for world peace and a healthy international economy. The Report was released in Tokyo and Washington on 17 September 1984.
16. These figures are taken from various publications of the OECD Development Assistance Committee, particularly its *1984 Review of Development Cooperation.*
17. *Report of the UN Visiting Mission to the Trust Territory of the Pacific Islands, 1982.* Trusteeship Council, Official Records Fiftieth Session (May–June 1983), T/1850, New York: UN 1983, p. 61.
18. *Report of the UN Visiting Mission, op. cit.,* p. 61.
19. OECD DAC statistics.
20. New Zealand Official Yearbook 1983, p. 293.
21. *Documents on International Affairs, 1951,* Oxford University Press for the Royal Institute of International Affairs.
22. *Commonwealth,* Vol. 26, No. 5, April 1984.
23. *ANZUS Council Communiqué,* New Zealand Foreign Affairs Review, Vol. 33, No. 3., July–September 1983.
24. Joint Statement by Mr Shultz and Mr Hawke issued in Washington on 6 February 1985.
25. Press statement by Mr Lange on 1 February 1985.
26. *The Times,* 5 March 1985.
27. *Report of the UN Visiting Mission to the Trust Territory of the Pacific Islands* in 1982, *op. cit.*
28. Bengt Danielsson, 'Under a Cloud of Secrecy: The French Nuclear Tests in the Southeastern Pacific', *AMBIO,* Vol. XIII, Number 5–6, 1984, p. 336.
29. The Mission had, *inter alia,* studied current radiation levels at Moruroa, radiation doses to the population of French Polynesia and cancer statistics.

30. Text of Communiqué issued on 28 August 1984 at the conclusion of the meeting of the South Pacific Forum.
31. Text of communiqué issued on 28 August 1984 at the conclusion of the meeting of the SPC.
32. *International Herald Tribune*, 10 December 1984.
33. *Guardian*, 23 January 1985.
34. This was true not only in the case of European colonies which tended to be orientated towards the Metropolitan Power but also in US-administered territories including the Trust Territory of the Pacific Islands.
35. The Membership of the Forum is: Australia, Cook Islands, Fiji, Kiribati, Federated States of Micronesia (observer), Nauru, New Zealand, Niue, Papua New Guinea, Solomon Islands, Tonga, Tuvalu, Vanuatu and Western Samoa.
36. The Trust Territory of Pacific Islands, for example, includes more than 2,100 islands scattered over an area of some 7.8 million square kms. in the Western Pacific. These islands, about a hundred of which are inhabited, have a combined land area of approximately 1,850 sq. kms.
37. The exception is Nauru. Thanks to its phosphate, the Government is able to provide a comprehensive welfare system and, *inter alia*, run an international air-line. Although the deposits are expected to be exhausted by 1995, various provisions have meanwhile been made for the future which should help to safeguard the islanders' prosperity in the short term at least.
38. *Report of the UN Visiting Mission to the Trust Territory of the Pacific Islands, 1982*, op. cit., para. 391.

List of States with a Population of Less than One Million

A. Independent States

Africa and the Indian Ocean

Botswana (830,000)
Brunei (213,000)
Cape Verde (306,000)
Comoros (385,000)
Djibouti (350,000)
Equatorial Guinea (325,000)
Gambia (592,000)
Guinea-Bissau (777,000)
Maldives (143,000)
Mauritius (924,000)
São Tomé & Príncipe (83,000)
Seychelles (62,000)
Swaziland (570,000)

Central America and the Caribbean

Antigua & Barbuda (72,000)
Bahamas (234,000)
Barbados (258,000)
Belize (152,000)
Dominica (83,000)
Grenada (110,000)
St Kitts-Nevis (48,000)
St Lucia (113,000)
St Vincent (118,000)

South America

Guyana (824,000)
Suriname (375,000)

Europe

Andorra (32,000)
Cyprus (625,000)
Iceland (240,000)
Liechtenstein (26,000)
Luxembourg (364,000)
Malta (317,000)
Monaco (25,000)
San Marino (19,000)

Middle East

Bahrain (350,000)
Oman (220,000)
Qatar (245,000)

Pacific

Fiji (619,000)
Kiribati (59,000)
Nauru (7,000)
Solomon Islands (215,000)
Tonga (90,000)
Tuvalu (7,500)
Western Samoa (157,000)
Vanuatu (99,000)

B. States, Islands or Territories which are not Independent or which are in Association with another State

Africa and the Indian Ocean

Ascension (1,000, UK)
Azores (292,000, Portugal)
Ceuta & Melilla (132,000, Spain)
Madeira (266,000, Portugal)
Mayotte (50,000, France)
Namibia (1m.)
Reunion (485,000, France)
St Helena (5,250, UK)
Tristan da Cunha (300, UK)

America and the Caribbean

Anguilla (6,500, UK)
Bermuda (55,000, UK)
Cayman Islands (17,000, UK)
Guadeloupe (325,000, France)
Martinique (308,000, France)
Montserrat (12,000, UK)
Netherlands Antilles (256,000)
Turks & Caicos (7,000, UK)
St Pierre & Miquelon (5,250, France)
Virgin Islands (11,500, UK)
Virgin Islands (75,000, US)

South America

Falkland Islands (1,800, UK)
French Guiana (64,000)

Europe

Gibraltar (30,000, UK)
Greenland (50,000, Denmark)
Faroes (13,500, Denmark)

Asia

Macau (248,000, Portugal)

Pacific

American Samoa (290,000)
Cook Islands (18,000, NZ)
French Polynesia (137,000)
Guam (105,000, US)
New Caledonia (134,000, France)
Niue (4,000, NZ)
Pitcairn Islands (63, UK)
Tokelau Islands (1,575, NZ)
Trust Territory Pacific Islands (Micronesian Island Groups, less Guam) (133,000, UN Strategic Trust Territory administered by the US)
Wallis & Futuna (9,000, France)

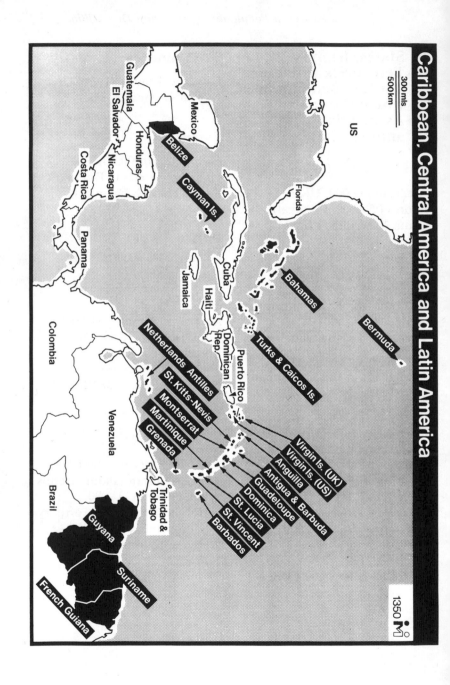

Caribbean, Central America and Latin America

300 mls
500 km

US

Mexico
Guatemala
El Salvador
Honduras
Nicaragua
Costa Rica
Panama
Colombia
Venezuela
Brazil

Belize
Cayman Is
Florida
Cuba
Jamaica
Haiti
Dominican Rep.
Bahamas
Bermuda
Turks & Caicos Is.
Puerto Rico

Netherlands Antilles
St. Kitts-Nevis
Montserrat
Martinique
Grenada

Virgin Is. (UK)
Virgin Is. (US)
Anguilla
Antigua & Barbuda
Guadeloupe
Dominica
St. Lucia
St. Vincent
Barbados

Trinidad & Tobago

Guyana
Suriname
French Guiana

1350

North Pole

Alaska

USSR

US

Japan

China

Pacific Ocean

Hawaiian Is.

Macau

1355 Mi

Philippines

Brunei

Trust Territory,
Pacific Islands

Guam

Kiribati

Distance of Fiji from:
Australia, 1625 mls (2600 km)
Japan,   4500 ·· (7200 ··)
US,   6000 ·· (9600 ··)

Papua
New Guinea

Tuvalu   Tokelau

French Polynesia

Indonesia

Nauru

Western Samoa

Solomon Is.

American Samoa

Wallis &
Futuna

Vanuatu

Niue

Pitcairn

Australia

Fiji

Tonga   Cook Is.

New Caledonia

New
Zealand

Indian Ocean

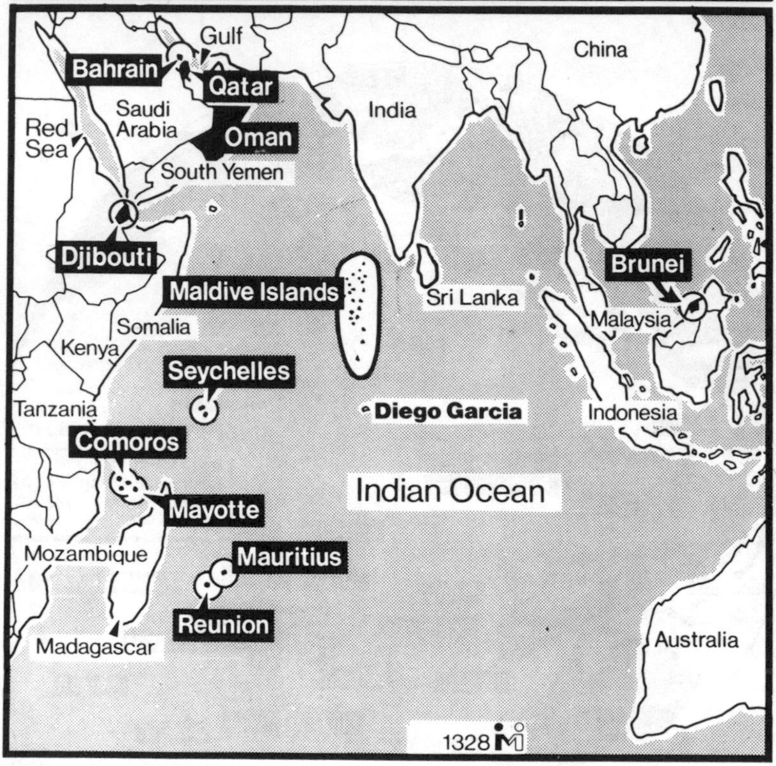

Gulf

China

Bahrain

Qatar

India

Saudi
Arabia

Red
Sea

Oman

South Yemen

Djibouti

Maldive Islands

Sri Lanka

Brunei

Malaysia

Somalia

Kenya

Seychelles

Tanzania

Comoros

Diego Garcia

Indonesia

Mayotte

Indian Ocean

Mozambique

Mauritius

Reunion

Madagascar

Australia

1328 Ⓜ

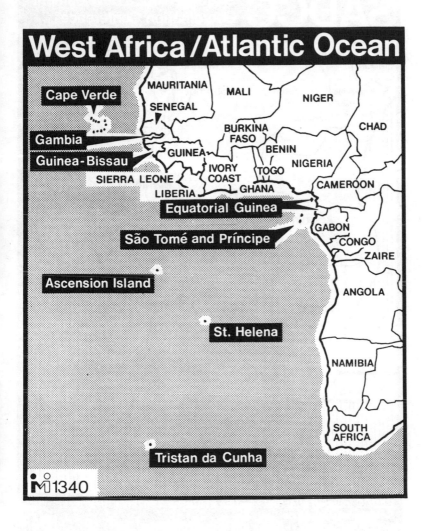

West Africa/Atlantic Ocean

Cape Verde

Gambia

Guinea-Bissau

Equatorial Guinea

São Tomé and Príncipe

Ascension Island

St. Helena

Tristan da Cunha

MAURITANIA

SENEGAL

MALI

NIGER

BURKINA FASO

CHAD

GUINEA

BENIN

SIERRA LEONE

IVORY COAST

TOGO

NIGERIA

LIBERIA

GHANA

CAMEROON

GABON

CONGO

ZAIRE

ANGOLA

NAMIBIA

SOUTH AFRICA

1340

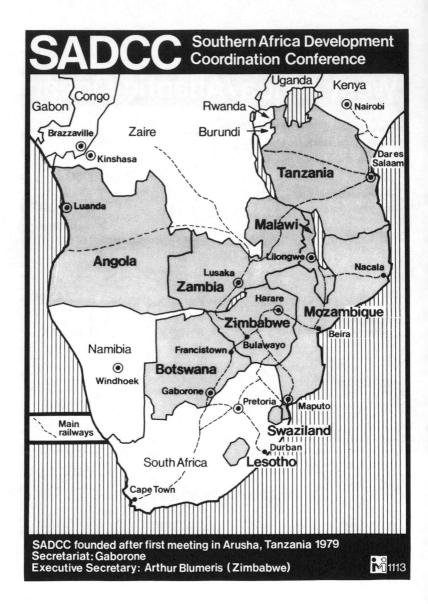

SADCC Southern Africa Development Coordination Conference

Congo
Gabon
Brazzaville
⊙ Kinshasa
Zaire
Uganda
Rwanda
Burundi
Kenya
⊙ Nairobi
Tanzania
Dar es Salaam

⊙ Luanda
Angola
Malawi
Lilongwe ⊙
Nacala

Lusaka ⊙
Zambia
Harare ⊙
Mozambique

Zimbabwe
Beira

Namibia
Francistown
Bulawayo
⊙ Windhoek
Botswana
Gaborone ⊙
Pretoria ⊙
Maputo

Main railways
Swaziland
Durban
South Africa
Lesotho

Cape Town

SADCC founded after first meeting in Arusha, Tanzania 1979
Secretariat: Gaborone
Executive Secretary: Arthur Blumeris (Zimbabwe)

1113

Index